Walking with Angels

Walking with Angels
JOURNEY TO SANTIAGO

L. S. Stanley

Copyright © 2019-L. S. Stanley
Apart from any fair dealing for the purpose of private study, research, criticism or review, as permitted under the Copyright Act, no part may be reproduced by any process without permission from the author. Every effort to comply with copyright requirements has been made by seeking permission and acknowledging owners of source material used in the text.

Disclaimer:

i) This book is a collection of memories. Information gathered has come from a wide variety of sources. The personal stories and memories by individuals recorded here are their version of events and have been both provided and reproduced in good faith with no disrespect or defamation intended. Every effort has been made to ensure the researched information is correct. No liability for incorrect information or factual errors will be accepted by the author.

ii) The views and opinions expressed in this work are solely those of the author. Some names may have been changed to protect privacy however they reflect real people and events.

A catalogue record for this book is available from the National Library of Australia

A catalogue record for this book is available from the National Library of Australia

ISBN: 978-0-975011-84-3 (Paperback)
ISBN: 978-0-975011-85-0 (Hardback)
ISBN: 978-0-975011-86-7 (Ebook)

Publisher:
Lizard Publishing
www.lizardpublishing.biz
info@lizardpublishing.biz

Cover and interior layout:
Pickawoowoo Publishing Group www.pickawoowoo.com

Printing and distribution:
Lightning Source (USA, UK, AUS, EUR).

My profound thanks to my darling husband for putting up with me through this journey and to our gorgeous daughters and their spouses for being there for me and for each other whenever needed. I love you all.

Contents

Preface · ix

Day One–France · 1
Granddad · 5
Astral Traveling · 8
Seeking Answers · 17
Marcus–My Guiding Angel · 23
Western Australia—Four Years Earlier · · · · · · · · · · · · · · · · 26
Day Two–Spain · 36
Laughter–The Best Medicine · 40
Renewed Bravado · 52
Larry-Confronting Change · 57
My Spirit Guides · 62
Finding Healing Where You Seek It · · · · · · · · · · · · · · · · · · · 74
The "Mad Hatter" Frenchman · 82
Catching My Own Jumbo Jet · 95
A Long-Term Goal Beyond Recovery · · · · · · · · · · · · · · · · 112
The Promise · 124
Traumatised by Louis · 127
The Staring Italian · 134
Friendships on the Camino · 138
The "Humpfing" Woman · 144
Spiritual Energy of the Camino · 148

Clarity · 154
Bunk Thief · 158
Con Men and Searing Heat · 168
Camino "Walking Sisters" · 178
Crossing The Mountain · 187
Honour Your Own Needs · 200
Conquering the Final Range · · · · · · · · · · · · · · · · · · · 209
The Final 100kms · 224
My Spiritual Journey · 230
Lessons Learnt on the Camino · · · · · · · · · · · · · · · · · 235

      Epilogue · 241

Preface

'I WALKED THE CAMINO,' I told my acupuncturist. The **Camino de Santiago de Compostela** (Way of St James) in Spain. A rugged testing journey of the body mind and spirit. *Yes, I'd broken my back. Yes, I'd lost hope. Yes, I'd almost died.* But … I walked the Camino. Walked it to a new life. And this is my story …

CHAPTER 1

Day One–France

Day One–16 August 2006 (St Jean Pied de Port, France)
IT WAS COLD AND DARK as I stepped out of the refuge. The sharp clang of my trek poles on the ancient cobblestones seemed to noisily advertise my solitary departure from the refuge. The dark shadows on the lonely lane caused a knot of fear to tighten in my belly. Fearful of the dismal loneliness, I strode off too quickly at a pace I couldn't maintain to begin the steep mountain ascent. Before long the sun's warm rays crept over the valleys and mountains, then quickly rushed across the velvet hills of the French farmland below.

Within minutes the steep ascent has my chest heaving and struggling for breath, I am forced to pause often. An earthy aroma permeates the Pyrenean landscape where distant white farm houses are scattered like discarded toys on a vivid green blanket of undulating pastures. Wisps of smoke drift upwards from their red roofs. The faint sound of tinkling cow bells floats softly on the mountain air as the well-worn pilgrim trail winds precariously between craggy rocks and the Camino snakes its way up the mountain.

Climbing high, a welcome gentle breeze kisses my flushed cheeks, inviting me to pause and enjoy the vista of the peaceful farmland below. The fear in my gut of what might lie in wait on the lonely eight hundred kilometres ahead eases.

By late morning a light rain begins to fall and the wind picks up a little. I pull on a plastic poncho and continue up the mountain. Minutes later the wind whips itself to a fury as a fierce storm hurtles over the mountain. Light rain becomes a deluge. The temperature drops and the raindrops freeze. Icy needles sting my face and hands as the howling wind pushes and pulls, trying to knock me off my feet.

Shocked by its suddenness and frightened by its fury, I toil against it. The wind takes hold of my flimsy poncho, ripping it to shreds. It wrenches one of my two scallop shells–the symbol of St James that identifies pilgrims on the Camino–from my backpack, and flings it down the rock face. The shell tumbles down the mountainside and out of sight. *I want that shell.* I brought it with me from Australia. I struggle to see through the stinging ice. Fighting the wind's fury to stay on my feet, I have no choice but to let the shell go. The blackened sky unloads its icy reservoir onto the mountainside. Soaked to the skin, my hiking boots slosh full of water.

The rocky mountainside offers me no refuge. Blinded by pelting ice I stumble determinedly up the track. The gale intensifies, trying to drive me back down the mountain. I recall the words of the Camino registrar–back in St Jean Pied de Port: 'A blizzard can blow in over the Pyrenees in an instant, and if it does, you should turn back. Storms are very dangerous here.'

I must be at least half way to Roncesvalles; I've gone too far to turn back now. I'll have to keep going. Keep my head down, put one foot in front of the other. Keep going.

The temperature plummets. Numb with cold, I can no longer feel my feet and hands.

If it snows, I'm not prepared. Am I walking to my death? Am I being foolish to continue?

Fear turns to panic.

Take control. Don't panic. If I'm to survive I've got to control fear, to focus on getting through this. Ignore the ice and focus on staying upright. Keep moving forward.

My backpack, now much heavier with the weight of drenching rain, increases the burden. Chilled hips scream under the stress of cold and weight. A pain shoots down my leg, then through both knees.

I can't stop now. No shelter. Keep going.

Marcus! I cry out to my guiding force. *What should I do?*

No answer came. *Where is he when I need him? I'm not giving in, I'm not! Gotta continue. Can't lose this battle. Won't lose this battle. Keep going. Don't stop!*

Leaning into the tempest, I trudge on. An hour further and hunger pains gnaw. It's midday. A plastic bag, holding an apple and a ham baguette, swings tied to my belt, but frozen fingers cannot get a grip to untie it.

Damn! I can't get at it. Forget it. Just keep walking. The useless bag dangles as I stumble on. *Gotta get through this—Gotta get to Roncesvalles—Gotta get there before dark. If I'm stranded on this mountain at night it could mean death from hypothermia, I've got no choice, I must continue.*

Slipping and sliding in the mud, I push on. Hours pass. Intently focused on pushing through the pain I'm unaware the terrain has changed. Now heading downhill, I've crossed the summit into Spanish territory.

The ice turns back to rain and although it doesn't let up, a thick forest now gives some protection from the wind. I slip and slide on the forest's steep muddy floor and fall repeatedly. The strain of trekking through the storm is taking its toll. Exhaustion drains my reserves. The grueling battle to continue has gone beyond physical. It's now a mental battle.

I can do this—I can do this—I can do this. I push my battered body. The pain and cold are excruciating and make progress infinitesimal. Half dragging, half pushing, I inch my way down the other side of the mountain.

Muddy. Slippery. Downhill. Be careful. Ahrg! Searing pain tears through my knee. *Can't walk—I must walk. Don't cry.*

The little voice inside me wants to quit; wants the easy option. The little voice wants an easy life, wishes I'd stayed at home; doesn't want to take chances or risks. The voice of fear inside me wants an ordered life within its comfort zones; wants an established routine, a regular nine-to-five lifestyle.

Determination forces its way up through the myriad of negative thoughts my fear is churning out.

Don't give in. Think! Must be something I can do! There's always an answer. I look around again for Marcus. He's still nowhere to be seen.

Lean on the trekking poles. Let them take the weight from your knee. Use them to lower yourself down the mountain. Using the poles for support I drag myself through the slippery mud of the steep forest descent.

Must keep going. Gone too far now. Can't go back. Keep moving. Gotta get through this.

The storm blows away my cries of pain. The rain sluices away my tears. Focusing on the task at hand, I drive one leg forward after the other down the slope. The trekking pole I'm gripping skids across the slippery rock. I fall sideways, crashing through bushes and a collapsing overhang. Landing heavily, a stabbing pain tears through a badly-angled foot as fine bones fracture on impact.

Half buried in mud from the fallen ledge, my strength ebbs away. Facing death that night on the icy peak, I surrender. The mountain has won.

CHAPTER 2

Granddad

FLOATING TOWARDS THE OBLIVION OF eternal sleep, images tumble randomly through my mind: the brightly coloured bunting along the streets of St Jean Pied de Port this morning, waving farewell; Larry's anxious face as he drove me to Perth airport a few days ago; family calling to say goodbye before I left; images from my childhood drifting by.

My beloved departed grandfather's face, smiling at me. It was not long after my tenth birthday when he came to my bedside one night at 2.10 am and gently shook me.

'Linda,' Granddad had whispered softly. 'Linda.' I woke and seeing him standing beside me, sat up in my bed.

'Hello, Granddad.'

'Linda, I've come to say goodbye.'

'Where are you going, Granddad?' He'd never come to our house that I could recall. Mum always took me to visit him and Granny at their home. I didn't wonder why he was waking me in the middle of the night nor how he'd got there.

'It's time,' he replied. 'I've got to go now.'

'Where are you going, Granddad?'

'I've got to go now. Goodbye, Linda,' was all he would say. He began to float upwards towards a dazzling place up near the corner of my bedroom ceiling.

'Don't go, Granddad. I don't want you to go.' His farewell seemed so final. I didn't know where he was going, but wherever it was, I didn't want him to go there. I jumped up and tried to catch hold of him; tried to stop him from going. I couldn't get hold of him. I leaped towards him and grabbed again, but he slipped through my fingers.

'Granddad, Granddad ... don't go!' I yelled; stretching and jumping, trying in vain to grab hold of him—to stop him from leaving.

'Granddad! Don't go! Granddad!' My calls became screams as he disappeared out of sight. I was standing on my bed; sobbing, screaming and reaching up into the air, as mum rushed into my room and flicked on the light.

'Granddad's gone.' I sobbed, as mum took me into her arms to console me.

'You've just had a bad dream,' she said. 'Now lie back down and go to sleep. It was just a bad dream. It's alright. Now go to sleep.'

Mum's brow creased in a deep frown as she tucked me back into bed. Flicking off the light she closed the door as she left. Darkness. Almost silence. Distressed and confused by my 'bad dream' that had seemed so real, the heavy blackness made it hard to breathe.

My heart pounded in my ears. Then I heard another sound. Listening intently, I focused on the strange unfamiliar sound. My mother was crying. In the confusing gloom I listened to her muffled sobbing. Her agonised weeping filled me with guilt.

Now my bad dream is making mummy cry. Why is my dream making her cry?

An hour and a half later, the ringing of the front door bell ripped through the darkness. I knew Mum was still awake. As I crept towards the front door Mum appeared ahead of me. On tiptoes, afraid she would be cross if she saw me out of bed, I followed her. She opened the door to our family doctor who lived two doors away.

'I'm sorry to disturb you at this hour,' he began. 'but I thought you'd want to know ...'

'It's my father, isn't it?' Mum cut in. Then without waiting for a response, continued.

'He's gone, hasn't he?'

'Yes ... yes, he has.' The doctor's eyes widened in surprise.

'Tell me,' Mum asked. 'Was it at ten minutes past two? Did he go at ten past two?'

The doctor's brow furrowed. He tilted his head to one side, puzzled.

'Yes,' he paused. 'He did. How did ...?' he began, but was cut short as Mum turned to make sure she was alone with the doctor. She saw me standing behind her.

'Go back to bed, Linda,' she ordered, her eyes red and puffy.

'Where's Granddad gone?' I asked, anxiety welling up inside me.

'Go back to bed,' Mum commanded.

My belly churned. I knew that, somehow, I'd caused something bad to happen. I went back to bed and lay straining to hear the conversation I'd been expelled from. All I heard were murmurs.

Where's Granddad gone? Why did the doctor come to tell Mum about it? How does the doctor know Granddad's gone somewhere? Why won't Mummy tell me where Granddad's gone?

Later that day mum explained that Granddad had gone to heaven.

CHAPTER 3

Astral Traveling

BLACKNESS BECKONS, CONSCIOUSNESS SWIRLS IN the muddy semi-grave on the Spanish crag; the courtship of surrender makes an appealing beau. As I drift toward oblivion, memories dance before me.

I recall being a child and not knowing I was seeing dead people; spirits, who came to visit. They were simply visitors. It did puzzle me that others didn't seem to see them too. They were like secret visits that existed only between my visitors and me. I would often know who was about to arrive and what they'd be wearing or what they'd say.

'Your mum's coming, you have to go home now,' I told a girlfriend once as we sat playing with dolls in my backyard.

'No, she's not, she's gone into town. I've got another hour yet, and then my brother will come and get me,' Heather replied.

Her mother walked around the corner of our house a moment later and seeing us sitting on the lawn, called out to Heather, telling her she had to go home right away. The rest of the mother's sentence was lost behind Heather's terrified screams as she leapt up, ran and threw herself into the arms of her bewildered mother. Heather's rounded eyes were full of fear as they stared back at me.

I learnt to be cautious about what I said after that, to anyone. I learned to observe and listen, and speak little.

Bed times were times of dread. Sleep meant tumbling through space. Arms and legs spread star-shaped I hurtled until I landed somewhere. It was the tumbling I feared; it made me dizzy and nauseous. I went to bed willing myself not to go plummeting through space; apprehensive about where I'd end up, but it happened anyway.

My mother was a practical, resourceful woman. At nineteen she emigrated alone from Newcastle, England, leaving behind a lover, after a tiff. At twenty-three, when she married my father, Mum refused to pay rent. 'I'd rather live in a tent than pay rent,' she said. And they did. It was 1932 and they lived in a tent until Mum saved enough money for a down-payment on a block of land. She planted fruit trees and vegetables on the block. They dug a well for water and Mum saved up until they could buy building materials. Dad built their house himself. Mum looked for the logic in everything and was not afraid to do things differently if she thought of a better option. I was their seventh child and by the time I was born she'd learnt a lot about being thrifty and making ends meet. She bought me boys' pyjamas to wear.

'They are stronger and better made than girls' pyjamas,' she told me. She always bought them a size or two too big, so they would last a few extra years.

'You'll grow into them,' was her response whenever I complained.

That was a major problem for me with my nocturnal travels. Girls at school always had pretty frilly feminine clothes. I wore boys' pyjamas. New–they were enormous; a few years old–they were tatty; and they were boys', with a fly. It was humiliating. Desperate to be the same as the other girls, the fear of being seen on my nocturnal travels, wearing my boys' pyjamas, knotted my belly into a ball every night. Although I knew that people didn't seem to be able to see me on my travels, I still feared they might, and travelling in boys' pyjamas was an embarrassment.

When I was ten, about six months after my grandfather's death, a school friend, Sandra, invited me and the rest of the girls in our class, to her birthday party the following weekend. All week the party was the topic of excited chatter. Saturday arrived. Wearing my best party dress, I gathered up the birthday gift and at five o'clock, waved goodbye to Mum and Dad.

'You be home before nine o'clock,' Dad warned.

Excited at the thought of the party and feeling like a princess in a party dress my sister had made me, I skipped all the way to Sandra's house. The pitch of energised squeals amplified a little more each time a car arrived to set down another enthusiastic party-goer. Sandra's mum and siblings organised games of Pass the Parcel, Pin the Tail on the Donkey, the Three-Legged Race and the Egg and Spoon Race. Although a top athlete at school, I was painfully shy and totally without confidence. I hated to stand out and playing games like these embarrassed me. I hung back whenever possible and felt conspicuously foolish when I dropped the egg in the Egg and Spoon Race.

'Time for dinner now,' Sandra's mum called.

Hot, sweaty, and bubbling with merriment, we all ran to the table. It was spread with slices of fairy-bread, tiny homemade pastry rolls with sausage meat inside, little red cocktail sausages swimming in tomato sauce, tiny triangle-shaped sandwiches filled with sweet curried egg, sliced meat or cheese. Sponge cupcakes were covered in white or pink icing with 'hundreds and thousands' sprinkled on top; others had two thin slivers of cake placed on their end in the icing, so they looked like butterflies sitting on the top of the cakes. Cubes of ice melting quickly in the warm night air clinked together in jugs of orange or green cordial.

When the savoury treats had been devoured, Sandra's big sister carefully carried a chocolate birthday cake to the supper table. Lathered with thick brown icing, the cake was crowned with ten flickering candles. As the cake bearer approached, the lights were turned off; it was the cue to start singing "Happy Birthday". The cake was ceremoniously placed in the centre of the supper table. Sandra took a deep breath and blew out the candles to a cry of 'make a wish' from her father, who had just arrived home from work. When the cake had been cut, shared out and devoured, we were sent off to play.

The party was still at full pace when Dad arrived at twenty past nine.

'The girls have not long finished supper, I'll drive Linda home when I take the other children home around ten o'clock,' Sandra's mum offered.

'I told her to be home by nine!' Dad was angry.

'The children are still playing. Linda can stay and play a little longer …' began Sandra's mother.

'No! She's coming home now! Linda! Home! Now!' Dad gesticulated towards the road. Embarrassed by the attention he was drawing, I hung my head–disgraced. I knew better than to argue; that would result in a beating and even more humiliation.

'Thank you for inviting me to the party.' I offered a frightened whisper to Sandra's mother.

'Just a moment, I'll get your lolly bag.' She rushed into the house and reappeared a moment later with a bag of lollies, which she shoved into my hand.

'Bye, Sandra,' I proffered softly, as Dad pushed me ahead of him toward the path home.

'Go on, get home to bed,' he ordered. 'You should have been home by now. I've a good mind not to let you go to any more parties if you can't do as you're told.'

'Please don't be hard on her,' Sandra's mother called. 'It wasn't her fault. The girls were all having such fun that time got away from them.' Her voice trailed off as Dad marched me out of the gate and down the road.

'Go on! Get home!'

Bill was an angry man. The chip on his shoulder needled his temper. Orphaned as a child–and one of a large family–he and his siblings had been split up and put into foster homes. Bill's foster family were catholic. Bill was Anglican. Bill's adopted family treated him as their whipping boy and servant. He was intelligent, with an almost photographic memory, but was forced to leave school and go out to work at fourteen. He grew up hating catholic people, the church and religion in general. He became an atheist. He resented people he considered less intelligent than himself who'd had the opportunity to get an education and get good jobs. He was clever with his hands and could build things, but things had not gone his way. He was a munitions technician and after the war ended was laid off at fifty-two with seven kids to feed. This one in front of him now was the seventh. He was too old to be bothered with another kid. At sixty-two he should have been starting to think about retirement. Instead he had this one still at home - this mouth to feed - to educate. The world had not been fair to him and the chip on his shoulder was weighty.

Fearing a whipping, I broke into a run, racing as fast as I could. If I could get into my pyjamas and into bed before Dad reached home, I might escape a thrashing. Dad was in a rage when he reached the house. Hiding under the blankets, I listened, terrified, as he ranted about me to Mum, before storming into my room. Wide-eyed, I peeped out to face his wrath. He yelled and threatened, then left. I was lucky that time.

Alone in the safe, reassuring solitude of my bedroom I gave thanks to the presence I sensed was watching over me and snuggled down under the blankets.

Please, God, don't let me start spinning tonight? In a few minutes I was asleep; spinning sickeningly, tumbling through space.

When the spinning stopped I was back at the party. I peeped around the hedge. Annette was jumping on the trampoline. The squeals from the other girls told me they were around the other side of the house. Annette had a dreamy look on her face. She was jumping higher and higher. Too high. She bounced right off head first onto the concrete pathway. I ran to her. There was blood on the concrete.

'Annette, Annette!' I called. There was no answer. Blood was spreading in a pool around her head. I ran to the others.

'Annette's hurt,' I called to Sandra's mum. 'She's fallen off the trampoline! Come quickly!' Nobody heard me. The girls kept playing and Sandra's mum stood smiling - watching them. I ran back to help Annette; as I did one of the girls stopped playing and frowned. She wandered toward the trampoline area and saw Annette lying on the concrete, saw the blood. Screaming, she ran back to tell the others. Sandra's mum came running, saw Annette, and ran back to the house. She called an ambulance and Annette was rushed to hospital.

The next day, the school was abuzz about Annette being found unconscious on the concrete path. Nobody knew how the accident had happened. I told Sandra that Annette had been jumping on the trampoline, jumped too high, bounced right off and landed head first on the concrete. That evening after school, Sandra's mother came to visit.

'Thank you, Linda, for telling us what happened to Annette. She's woken up now and confirmed what you said,' Sandra's mother told Mum and me.

Squirming, I was uncomfortable with the attention.

'Linda, there's just one thing I'd like to ask,' Sandra's mum continued. 'How did you know what happened to Annette?'

'I was watching. She bounced too high, and bounced right off the trampoline and landed head first on the ground.' Sandra's mother nodded as I continued. 'There was blood and she wouldn't wake up.'

'Thank you for telling me, Linda, I really appreciate it. You've been very helpful.' Sandra's mother paused a moment before continuing in a gentle tone. 'There's just one thing … the accident happened at around ten o'clock.' I nodded. Sandra's mother paused before going on slowly. 'Linda, you went home at twenty past nine. How did you see it happen, darling?'

Fear churned my belly. I'd been caught out. I hung my head in silence, I didn't know what to say. I didn't know how I saw it. I didn't know what the spinning and travelling was. I knew I'd done something wrong; if Mum told Dad that I'd gone back to the party I'd get a beating. What could I say?

'Linda, you're not in trouble,' Sandra's mother said softly. 'I'm not growling at you. I'm very grateful that you told us what happened. I just want to know how you saw the accident.'

'I don't know.' It was almost inaudible. I stood looking at the ground. There was silence for a moment before Mum spoke.

'It's all right. Go and play now.' Mum dismissed me and took Sandra's mother into another room. I raced outside and hid in a box behind the shed. If I stayed in my hiding place long enough Sandra's mother would leave and Mum might forget about the conversation and everything would be back to normal. It wasn't mentioned again.

From that time on I tried even harder to stop the "travels", but I couldn't.

Years later in my teen years, curiosity surfaced. Why was I weird? Why did things happen to me and not to my friends? What was it about? Why was it that Granddad came to me to say goodbye, and not to my Mum? Why did I feel there was someone guiding me? Who was it? What was the purpose of the travels? What was I supposed to do with it all?

I became a daily visitor to our local library and began to read every book on psychology and the paranormal that I could get my hands on. I learnt there were other "weird" people in the world; that was a relief. Buddhists call the travels, "astral travelling". Buddhist monks can astral travel at will. Intrigued, I wanted to know how to take control of it.

At eighteen I married Al, the boy next door. Al wanted a family, a home life. I wanted to be loved. After we were married I found Al couldn't cope with anything paranormal. Things had to be founded in science for Al; clearly explained and fully defined. He was uncomfortable with me even talking about spirits and telepathy.

We'd been married a couple of months when a nightmare began to plague me. In the dream, I saw someone driving a big black car. I couldn't see the driver's face; couldn't even tell if the driver was male or female. There was a baby in a bassinette on the back seat. Then there was a crash, the driver hit another car. Nobody was hurt in the accident, but a few days later the driver of the car died. The dream tormented me; I'd wake screaming and trembling as the driver died. Al would wrap his arms around me and hold me until I stopped shaking.

'That nightmare again?' he'd ask.

Then after three weeks the dreams stopped.

Two days later, Al, my cousin, her boyfriend and I, went to a fair ground to meet up with a friend of ours, Rachel. Rachel was our up-line in a range of products that I was selling in my spare time. Rachel had asked us to meet her at the fair where she was going to be manning a booth selling the products. We arrived at the fairground in high spirits and after a walk around, found the booth. Rachel wasn't there. Another lady was manning the booth.

'Where's Rachel?' I asked.

'Who are you?'

'We're friends of Rachel. We've got a meeting with Rachel here tonight.'

'Don't you know? Rachel's dead.'

'What? No! That's not possible. I was speaking to Rachel at the beginning of the week. We've got an appointment with her tonight. I think we must be talking about a different person.'

I was in awe of Rachel. She was full of life, a vibrant young outgoing person with so much ambition she couldn't possibly be dead. There had to be a mistake. It was someone else this lady was talking about. We were at the wrong booth.

'Rachel Sterling?' the woman stated, rather than asked.

'Yes,' a hoarse response floated from somewhere.

Numbness set in at the realisation that this woman was talking about our friend. Heaviness pressed on my chest; it prevented me from inhaling fully. 'What happened?'

'Rachel committed suicide. Stuck her head in a gas oven. Killed herself.'

'No! She wouldn't do that. She's such a happy person, so bubbly. She couldn't commit suicide.' I was shaking my head. This person had it all wrong.

'Rachel had been very stressed for months, over doing well in her new business.' The woman began to explain. 'She was under a lot of pressure. Her family had very high expectations. They didn't approve of her branching out into her own business. Then early this week she was driving her fiancé's car. Smashed it. Her sister's baby was on the back seat. No-one was injured and the baby was okay. But Rachel felt so guilty over what happened. Her fiancé flew into a rage. He was very angry about the damage to his new big black car. She just couldn't handle all the guilt. She felt she'd let everyone down. It was too much for her. Two days ago, she went home to her flat and gassed herself.'

Shocked at the news—no longer in the mood for a fun fair—we made our way back to the car. In the car on the way home we discussed Rachel's story. Then, a movie of my nightmare played in front of my eyes, but this time the face of the driver turned around and looked at me. It was Rachel.

'Haar!' I gasped. 'It was Rachel! The dream. The big black car. The baby. The driver that died. I couldn't see the face before. It just turned around. I saw the face. It was Rachel!'

'Why didn't they show me before? I might have been able to stop her. Why did they show me now? What am I supposed to do with this? Why do they do this?' Sobbing and distraught, I was babbling. Al tried to calm me down and at the same time explain to my cousin and her boyfriend about the nightmare. Al was confused. He didn't believe in extra sensory perception. It was all nonsense; in fact, it frightened him. He didn't understand what happened that night.

'Never mind, love. Even when they lock you up in an asylum I'll still come and visit you every day.' He was trying to soothe me.

Al thinks I'm insane. He could have me committed. All he must do is tell authorities that I hear voices, talk to ghosts, and have visions. Most people will think just like Al.

I couldn't take that risk. That night, the reality of perceptions dawned; it wasn't safe to mention my dreams, astral travels or conversations with spirits, ever again. From that night forward I shut Al out of a large and important part of my life.

Pulling the curtain to close the window to the "other side" I focused on ignoring what I saw and heard from the spirit world. It didn't work. Nor did my marriage; five years later Al and I separated.

CHAPTER 4

Seeking Answers

MANY YEARS PASSED. THEN I met Ethan. One day I mentioned to Ethan that I wanted to put a bore down to get water. Ethan had a friend who was a water-diviner, as my grandfather had been. I lived on what had been my grandfather's property. On that property, Granddad had divined and dug a well for water many years before. The well had provided my grandparents with water for many years, but recently it had dried up. Now Ethan's friend agreed to divine a new location to put a bore down.

'The underground stream probably changed course over the years,' he told me and some of my friends who'd gathered to watch the diviner at work.

It was a hot day. The sun beat down as we all watched the water-diviner pace out where the stream now flowed. When the diviner finished, he told us where the new hole should be drilled. Then he offered his divining rods to us.

'Here, have a go.' He handed his rods over to my friends and showed them what to do. They all paced up and down, as instructed, and focused on the thought of water. One by one they failed to achieve any response from the divining rods, and laughed it off.

'Here, Linda.' He held the rods out for me to try. 'Your turn.'

'No, I don't need to. I believe in it. I saw my grandfather do it when I was little. I don't need a turn, thanks.'

'*Go on.* Don't be a spoil sport. We all did it.' My friends chorused their disapproval at my reluctance. '*Go on. Have a go! Don't be a piker.* What's wrong? You afraid or something?'

'Oh, all right.' I took the rods and listened to the diviner's instructions.

'Think of water as you walk,' Ethan's friend told me.

I started to walk holding the rods in my palms. I walked a short distance, then stopped and tried to hand the rods back.

'See, it doesn't work for me.'

'Oh, fair go, give it a decent distance. Go on, walk a bit further.'

I reluctantly lifted the rods again and began to walk, this time focusing my mind on water. The rods began to turn in my hands. I thought they were slipping from the sweatiness of my palms. I slid my little fingers under the rods to support them and intently focused my mind. It seemed I'd only walked a short distance, when Ethan's friend ran to me and grabbed my shoulders. He shook me out of the trance-like state I was slipping into.

'Why did you do that?' he said, with agitation.

'Do what?' I asked, as I roused myself from the dreamlike state.

He took the rods back and turned my palms face up. They were bleeding. My friends and I gasped as we saw the cuts the rods had made in my palms.

'Why did you try to stop them turning? I saw you put your fingers under the rods to stop them turning.' He was distressed.

'I thought they were slipping from the sweat on my hands. I was trying to stop them slipping.'

'That was not sweat causing them to slip; it was the underground stream pulling the rods down. I've never seen it work that strongly before. If it works like that for water, you could do it for gold—or diamonds—or anything.'

I shook my head, staring with disbelief at my bloodied palms.

'You said your grandfather divined for water?'

I nodded—still in shock—and then began to relate what I'd seen him do.

'My grandfather divined water for the local people. I remember him showing my brother something once, when I was very little. He took us over to that well there. There was a rod across the top of the well, with a bucket tied to the rod, and he used that bucket to draw water from the well. On that rod, he also had a sort-of pendulum hanging from a piece of string.

My brother asked about the divining and Granddad showed him. He held his hand a few inches above the piece of string that the pendulum hung from–not touching the string or the pendulum–but the pendulum began to swing in a circle; slowly at first, *then faster and faster*, until he took his hand away again.'

'Hmm. I've heard of things like this, but I've never seen it myself,' the diviner answered. 'Take off your gold ring and give it to me. I'm going to bury it somewhere on this block. Ethan, you take Linda around the corner of the shed so she can't see where I hide it. Then, Linda, I want you to focus on gold and use these rods to find the ring.'

'No way! You'll lose it. There's five acres here. There's no way I'll find it. No! You'll lose it.'

'We'll know exactly where the ring is, it won't get lost. Besides, I think you'll find it,' the diviner replied.

'Go on!' my friends urged. *'Give it a go.* We'll watch where the ring is. It won't get lost.'

I argued–but outnumbered and outvoted–I reluctantly agreed, mumbling about it being a waste of time as Ethan led me around the corner of the shed and out of sight. Once the ring had been hidden, my friends came to fetch me. At the sight of the whole group appearing around the corner, I shrieked.

'It will be lost now, you won't know where it is! We'll never find it now!'

'You'll find it,' the diviner handed me the rods. 'Now go and search.'

I took the rods and focused on my gold ring as I walked. The rods seemed to talk to me. *Turn this way, now go that way.* I listened and followed as the rods turned. Two minutes later, out in the middle of the paddock, the rods crossed in front of my chest.

'What I am I supposed to do now?' I asked, and then looked up at the watching group. Two had their mouths agape. All looked stunned.

'Scratch between your toes,' the diviner croaked, hardly believing what he'd just witnessed. I bent over, scratched the soil between my two big toes and uncovered the ring. Dumbfounded, I retrieved my ring, stood up and placed it back on my finger.

'I've read about this sort of thing,' the diviner told the group. 'But this is the first time I've seen it.'

That day marked the beginning of a renewed quest for understanding. Ethan was open-minded about clairvoyance and the paranormal. He encouraged me to talk about my dreams and visions. He even sensed when a spirit was speaking to me and he'd ask me to explain what I was hearing or seeing. Ethan wanted to understand what was happening in my world.

'You should open up to it, learn how to use it,' he told me. 'You're not weird, you're special. You have a gift, and with it an inherent responsibility to use it.'

'I've spent so many years trying to shut it out; I don't know how to use it.'

Ethan brought books on clairvoyance from the library for me. Sometimes he would read them too, and then discuss ways I could practise to develop skills. With Ethan's encouragement, I commenced a journey to understand clairvoyance and clairaudience, and to try to take control of it.

My friends who had witnessed the water divining also scoured libraries for books on divining for me. Each new piece of information was like a clue to a puzzle. It felt like we were building a map, looking for a Pirate's secret treasure. We were adventurers, journeying together on a voyage into the unknown.

Divining, we learnt, is an ancient skill. Cave art in Africa that's estimated to be eight thousand years old shows tribesmen watching a man with a forked stick dowsing for water. The bible mentions Moses and Aaron using a rod to find water. In the Middle Ages dowsers in Europe used it to find coal deposits. In Napoleonic times, it was the main method used to locate tin, lead and other minerals necessary for war.

Books on divining led us to dowsing–another type of divining–one that relies either on connecting to energy fields or the Universal Consciousness, to detect what is being sought. Albert Einstein said, 'That a dowsing rod is a simple instrument which shows the reaction of the human nervous system to certain factors which are unknown to us at this time.'

We spent weeks devouring books on dowsing and divining. Those weeks were then followed by months of experimentation. I regretted the years I'd wasted trying to shut out the non-rational and difficult-to-explain. Now, with encouragement and assistance, I felt I could begin to make sense of the unexplained.

Brainwaves of dowsers searching for underground water, tin, lead, or other metals, were; according to the books, like brainwaves during meditation: cycling in a much lower frequency than during normal function. With Ethan's help, I explored the side of my life that had been shut down for so long.

Before long though, the true side of Ethan's character began to reveal itself: he had difficulty with the truth. His lies to me began to catch up with him; truth seemed to elude him. He told so many lies that it often seemed he couldn't differentiate between truth and untruth. Then one day the bailiff knocked on the door with a summons for Ethan. The first of many visits. Ethan had a trail of personal debt that horrified me but didn't seem to concern him at all. I contacted his creditors and arranged to pay them all off–a little at a time.

One Friday, while Ethan was at my place, his friend arrived, with murder in his eyes. He told me Ethan had slept with his wife.

'I've come to kill him.'

'Ethan's not worth it,' I told him. 'He seduces all of his friends' wives. He's simply not worth going to prison for.'

One day, in a black rage, Ethan put a loaded rifle to my head after an argument. That was the end of our friendship.

A year later, seeking deeper answers on how the mind and brain waves interact with energy fields to locate the unknown, I commenced a psychology degree. It failed to provide the answers I sought and after two years of study I left the course. Then I took up Transcendental Meditation. I practised it daily; searching for another key to the puzzle. I began using dowsing, asking yes or no questions, to seek guidance.

Sometime later, I learned that kinesiology practitioners used muscle testing to get yes or no answers, so I took a course in Kinesiology. That led me to Reiki, and Reiki led me to Theta Healing. Theta Healing focuses on lowering the energy frequency of the brain to a point much lower than normal meditation, in order to connect with God, the Source, the Universal Consciousness. Theta, I felt, took me closer to the answers I sought and Theta meditation then became a daily practice.

Through meditation, I found it was possible to take control of astral traveling. To see how far I could "travel" I decided on a "test" visit to a new friend, Larry. Larry lived in England. I'd never been to England and I'd only met Larry a couple of times. Traveling to the other side of the planet was the biggest challenge I could think of.

I relaxed my body, slowed my breathing, and meditated; dropping my brain waves. When I was in a deep "Theta" state, I focused on Larry.

An instant later, I was in front of him. Larry was talking to a group of farmers in a muddy field. He and the farmers were wearing thick coats. The sky was grey. As he spoke his breath looked like steam. It was summer in Perth. Suddenly landing in an alien winter landscape startled me.

This isn't right! I'm invading his privacy. I'm a peeping Tom. I can't do this. An instant later I was back home. *I won't do that again. It was like spying on him.*

Two weeks later a letter arrived from Larry. He wrote, 'The strangest thing happened the other day. I was working in a field, teaching potato farmers, and suddenly you appeared in front of me. You looked so real I could have reached out and touched you.'

Several months passed before I mustered enough courage to admit to him what I'd done. From then on Larry labeled me "Spock". He wrote that he would sit in a romantic restaurant dining alone and think to himself, *Beam yourself over, Spock.* Larry and I married a few years later.

CHAPTER 5

Marcus–My Guiding Angel

Roncesvalles–Spain
'LINDA! LINDA!' SOMEONE'S CALLING, BUT the blackness is comforting.

'Linda!' The voice calls again.

I open my eyes and look up into a face of love; Marcus is shaking me gently. Eyelids too heavy, close again.

'Linda. Your destiny awaits you, it's time to get up.' Marcus' long robes billow around him as he patiently coaxes me.

'Can't,' I mumble.

Invisible arms lift me. I'm upright and wobbly. Someone is supporting me. Marcus, smiling and beckoning, nods towards my trekking poles lying on the ground.

'Take up the poles,' he urges softly.

I bend over to pick them up.

'Ahrg!' A stabbing pain shoots through my back. Leaning on the poles I slowly straighten up.

'It's time to go now, Linda. Look inside yourself. Seek the place deep within that is the core of your strength. Acknowledge it. Allow it to rise up and lead you.' His smile radiates tenderness.

I have no choice. I must push on. My trek has only just begun. Adjusting the weight of my backpack–and gulping back tears of pain–I slide my hands through the loops of the trekking poles. The searing agony in my foot almost matches the ache in my hips. I wipe away tears. They're mud. Shuddering sobs sniffed back, I ease my weight onto the poles. Invisible arms steady me as I struggle to get my balance. *Too sore. Too tired.* Feeling sorry for myself, I want to quit. I look into Marcus' eyes, pleading for help. His face radiates compassion, but his reassuring smile shows me quitting is not an option. I have to continue.

Where will I get the strength? I'm spent. I look up at the path from which I've fallen. The rain seems to mock my weakness.

Somewhere, buried deep in my gut, is a source of strength. I dig deep and mentally take hold of it. I beam down on it with my mind and focus my thoughts on getting through this; I know I can't give in, not yet.

Agony slashes up from my injured foot. I shift my weight to the other leg. It's only slightly easier; I've wrenched that knee too. Using the poles as levers, I pull my body up the collapsed embankment and back onto the trail. A few inches at a time, I snail my way down the mountain trail. It's nightfall when I limp: soaking, cold, grey-faced and filthy, into the hotel at Roncesvalles.

'*Avez vous une chambre?*' Do you have a room, I ask the Spanish bartender; in my high school French.

'*Non! Complet! Full!*'

'*Ou est une chambre?*' Where will I find a room?

'*Refugio!*' The Refuge.

His unsympathetic demeanor is more than I can take. I want a hot shower, food, a warm bed, and sympathy. I'm oblivious to the fact that I'm not using his language. Choking back tears of pain, fatigue, and despair, I continue:

'*Ou est le Refugio?*' Where is the refuge?

He points without looking up, then goes back to polishing the beer glass in his hand. A trail of dripping water follows me as I retrace my footsteps on his dusty litter-covered floor, to drag myself out into the rain once more.

'Come in quickly. Come in. Have you been out in that storm?' A volunteer at the refuge takes hold of my backpack as I stumble through the door.

'You're injured. You need a long warm shower to get some warmth into your body, into your bones and muscles. Once you've warmed up we can look at your injuries.'

I can't speak. Don't need to. She leads me through the dormitory, down the steps to the showers, and turns on the hot water tap.

'Get yourself under that. We'll put your clothes through the washer and dryer. We can sign you in and do the paperwork later.' She leaves me to peel off my sodden clothes and step under the steaming shower. Soothing water flows over my aching body, sluicing the anxiety down the drain. Relief and self-pity tumble randomly over and through me; I'm safe. I want to cry, but have no strength for tears.

The lady is a Dutch volunteer, one of a group of four who are overseeing the refuge at Roncesvalles. Each one has walked the Camino. They know what it's like. My lady, Marissa, is an angel of understanding; her empathy's a rich balm on my shattered spirit as she signs me into the refuge.

'Linda Stanley, Australian,' I hand over my *credential*, the pilgrim passport that entitles pilgrims access to the refuges. Marissa dresses my wounds and blistered toes, massages my torn and screaming muscles and gives me some mild pain-killing tablets.

'Salsa while you walk,' she advises. 'Swing your hips from side-to-side. If you swing your hips as you walk it helps a woman to bear the weight of the pack. Learn to Salsa as you walk.'

But will I be able to continue tomorrow? Will the pain ease and allow me to go on? Or have I missed my jumbo jet?

On the bunk, inside my sleeping bag; fatigued, sore, and full of despair, I undo the lunch bag that had swung from my belt during the afternoon, and munch on the baguette. Curled up, warm at last, I run through the day and muse on what had brought me to Roncesvalles and this point in my life.

I recall the day, four years earlier, when my life abruptly changed; the day this journey really began.

CHAPTER 6

Western Australia—
Four Years Earlier

13 July 2002 (Piesse Brook)
IT WAS AN OVERCAST WINTER'S Saturday afternoon at home, when my journey actually started. We lived in the Darling Ranges east of Perth, opposite the Kalamunda National Park. When I say we; I mean my husband Larry, myself, and our children. It looked promising for rain. After two years of drought we hoped that blessed raindrops would fall.

Our builder was working to finish off a verandah extension in time for my birthday party in eighteen days. Our verandah perched over a granite outcrop with a sweeping view of the valley and the forest below. The builder had finished putting the battens on the verandah's gabled roof that Friday.

'I'll put the corrugated iron roof sheets on the battens on Monday. If you want, you could paint the battens over the weekend,' he suggested once he'd finished for the day. 'It will be easier for you to paint them before the iron goes on. I'll leave you the trestle and drop sheets to use if you want.'

It was early Saturday afternoon when Larry, Serena—our fourteen year-old daughter, and I, began painting the battens. The three of us in a row on the trestle teased and joked with each other, laughing at our own silliness until I finished off painting my bit in between the two of them. Climbing down from the trestle I surveyed our handiwork; happy with the progress we were making and enjoying the afternoon of family bonding. Gazing out across the valley it was a view that always filled me with a deep sense of peace. A flock of raucous black cockatoos looped overhead before settling in tall Marri trees to feed. Two eagles circled high on a warm updraft. A family of Splendid Blue Wrens splashed in the birdbath nearby. Inhaling the cool fresh scent of pending rain, I gave silent thanks for this valley I loved.

Unable to stand idly admiring the scenery while others worked, I shook myself out of my reverie and looked around to see what else I could do while I waited for Larry and Serena to finish their sections and move the trestle over. A ladder was leaning on the far side of the verandah.

Ah! I can use the ladder to do some painting while I'm waiting.

I picked up the ladder, placed it in position, dipped my paintbrush into the paint tin, clamoured up to the top of the ladder, and started painting. I was at full stretch painting the highest section of the gable roof when the sky began to slide away.

This can't be happening. Yes, it is!

The ladder was sliding out; I was falling backwards, heading to go over the edge of the verandah onto the granite boulders metres below. There was nothing to grab hold of; I could do nothing to stop my fall.

If I go over the edge of the verandah, I'm dead!

Thoughts raced through my brain at such a speed, it seemed the fall was happening in slow motion.

If hitting the verandah edge doesn't kill me, the granite boulders below will finish me off. I must stop myself from going over the edge. My only chance of survival is to land on the verandah.

In a desperate bid to save my life I twisted my body as I fell, flinging myself sideways. I heard a crunching thud as my body crashed onto the verandah. Excruciating pain exploded in my back. Someone somewhere was screaming; a ghastly agonised sound.

It's me!

The scream was erupting from the depths of my gut. My brain was acting independently from my body: running through the logic of my situation, analysing my dilemma.

Don't move! Lie still. Something's wrong with your back. Tell them not to move you. Tell them to call an ambulance.

But my body couldn't respond to the order. It couldn't stop screaming. Larry leapt off the trestle to my side. Serena froze on the trestle. She too was screaming.

'Serena! You can get down now,' Larry ordered.

Serena jumped down; *frantic.*

'I'm so sorry! I'm so sorry!' Larry gasped to me.

'Call a neighbour,' he yelled at Serena.

A neighbour! Why on earth do you want to call a neighbour? Call an ambulance! But my body couldn't speak my thoughts. It was still screaming.

Agony stabbed with every breath. *Oh, my ribs are broken too.*

Pain was shooting in all directions. I wanted to tell Larry and Serena what to do, but I couldn't. Larry wanted another adult there to help; Serena was only fourteen. Serena disappeared inside the house and reappeared a few minutes later.

'There's no answer from the neighbours, so I've called an ambulance.' Then, seeing that her father had gone into shock, she took control.

'Don't touch her! Don't move her!' she shouted. Serena disappeared inside the house and re-appeared with a pillow and a blanket. She carefully placed the pillow under my lopsided head and covered me with the blanket. A gentle shower of rain began to fall. Serena raced back into the house and returned with another pillow. Cautiously she slid the pillow under my left knee.

'Now, as I support mum's leg, you slide the ladder out slowly,' she instructed Larry. He did as Serena asked.

'Don't move her,' Serena shouted again. 'I'm going down to the road to wave the ambulance up here when they arrive.' Toshi, our Maltese dog, licked my face. Serena shut him inside the house and sprinted down the long driveway to the road below. It was 3.30 pm.

Six minutes later the ambulance arrived. My breathing had become labored and rasping. I was struggling to take in air and drifted in and out of semi-consciousness.

'How would you rate your pain on a scale of one to ten?' the ambulance officer asked.

Well, I'm alive. I'm not nearly dead, so it can't be a ten, or even a nine, but it feels very bad, so it must be an eight. My brain was fogging.

'Eight,' I rasped.

'Eight?' he sounded startled as he popped a pain killer under my tongue. With his partner, they eased me onto a stretcher.

Later, in the emergency department of Murdoch Hospital, still on the stretcher, my torment was so great I looked up into Larry's eyes in a plea for help. I wanted him–*needed him*–to somehow take some of the pain away, to fix everything. But instead, what I saw was worry, fear, shock and despair. I knew I had to find the strength for both of us. I had to reassure Larry that I'd be alright.

It was time to be proactive; I had to call on Spirit for help. With my mind a swirling pandemonium, there was no way I could quieten it sufficiently to be able to hear a response from Spirit, but at least I could ask. Closing my eyes, forcing my breath to slow and my mind to become as still as possible, I visualised white light coming down from above. Mentally wrapping myself in the light, I concentrated on it, asking for peace and calm to flow through my body so I could think logically. I needed to analyse my situation. Forcing the pain away from the core of my attention, I pushed it to the periphery and centred my mind so I could analyse my situation and prioritise possible injuries.

What is the Priority One worst-case scenario? Spinal cord damage.

I wriggled my toes, moved my feet, and twiddled my fingers.

Well I can move everything, so there's no spinal cord damage.

I relayed my assessment to Larry. His expression didn't change; he still looked terrified.

So, what is Priority Two? The pain in my back is excruciating, so perhaps I have broken some ribs in my back.

I gently probed each rib, first down one side all the way to my pelvis, then down the other.

No pain there, so I can't have broken any ribs.

I reported this to Larry. It didn't cheer him up; his face remained pale and full of fear.

So, I can move my toes and fingers and my spine is fine. I haven't any broken ribs; I must have merely jarred my back in the fall.

I thought about my summation for a moment.

But if I've jarred my back, why can't I breathe properly? I pondered a moment longer. *I must be winded.*

'I've been figuring it all out,' I informed Larry. 'I've just jarred my back and I'm winded. They'll probably either send me home tonight, or keep me in overnight for observation and send me home tomorrow. So, everything's going to be fine.'

Larry wasn't convinced; the fear and worry in his eyes didn't lessen. The doctors arrived and wheeled me away for an x-ray. I'd almost convinced myself that the x-rays would show no injury.

It seemed an eternity before a doctor, his white coat swirling around him, burst into the room. Waving the radiologist's report in the air, his brow creased in worry, he rushed towards me. The look of concern on his face tangled my gut into a knot of dread.

'It's not good news, I'm afraid.' He was shaking his head. Then seeing me wriggle my feet, he shouted. 'Would you PLEASE stop moving your legs!'

He held the x-ray up to the light and began explaining what the images meant. Even to my untrained eye it was obvious the size and shape of the vertebra he was pointing to was sickeningly abnormal. My brain went numb.

'… it appears there may be bone fragments in the spinal canal, so we will need to do a CT scan to determine the exact location of any fragments of bone.' He paused to let his words sink in before continuing. 'If there are bone fragments in the spinal canal, there is a risk of damage to the spinal cord.' He paused again. 'If there are bone fragments in the spinal canal, we'll have to operate to remove them.'

His finger traced the outline of fractures in another vertebra, I was struggling to focus on his words as he explained that those fractures were lesser problems. Terror had gripped my mind.

I don't want anyone operating on my spine! I believe in natural healing: minimum interference. Operations interfere with natural healing processes. But ... if it means paralysis without an operation ... I'll have no choice.

I felt trapped. My brain was racing out of control. I tried to calm myself; to think rationally. I couldn't. Pressure between my temples sent pain shooting through my brain; nausea welled up. Neither Larry nor I spoke. I searched his eyes for reassurance that didn't exist.

Wave after wave of terror crashed over me. I'd seen images on television of patients being wheeled into tunnels for scans. The vision of being wheeled into a long tunnel to have a CT scan filled me with dread; my whole body was shaking in terror. The nurse came and wheeled me away.

She's going to put me in a tunnel to have a CT scan. I want to bolt off the bed and run.

'Please keep your eyes closed until I tell you to open them again,' the nurse instructed as she rolled the bed toward the CT scan area. Petrified of being inside a claustrophobic tunnel, I squeezed my eyes tightly shut. There was absolutely no way I would open them inside the tunnel. My heart was racing, my palms and forehead clammy. I was so panic-stricken at the thought of going into a tunnel I had to clench my jaw to stop myself from screaming.

The scan only took a few minutes. 'OK, that's it. All done.'

I opened my eyes, only to find I hadn't been in a tunnel at all. It was more like an archway with a strip scanner in it. The whole archway would not have been more than about 40cm wide. Relief washed through me, flushing away the anxiety and leaving in its wake a feeling of deep foolishness. My imagination had created intense unnecessary dread in my mind.

The nurse wheeled me back to a distressed Larry and starving Serena, to await the results. The scanned images had been sent electronically to a radiologist who was working from home. It was almost 11.00 pm.

'I think the radiologist must have gone out for the evening,' I joked to Larry. He didn't think it was funny at all.

When the results came back, the CT scan showed there were no bone fragments in the spinal canal, however, a burst vertebra was pushing against the spinal cord. A neurosurgeon needed to determine if an MRI scan was necessary to investigate whether any soft tissue damage had been done to the spinal cord. A neurosurgeon was booked for the next morning.

Celeste, our eldest daughter, arrived in the emergency ward. She'd brought food for the family. Serena ate ravenously, but Larry struggled to get even a mouthful down. Once hunger had been appeased, Serena and Larry each gave Celeste their version of the day's events along with the current updates from the doctors.

'It's late, and you all look so tired,' I began, once Celeste had heard everyone's stories. 'I appreciate you coming in to be with me but there's nothing more you can do tonight. You may as well go home and get some sleep.'

I hugged and kissed each of them before they filed out of the hospital. I was finally admitted into a ward at 1.30 am. Morphine carried me into a troubled patchy sleep.

Doctors instructed me to lie flat on my back and not move. A vice-like clamp of searing pain gripped my head—so extreme I spewed up repeatedly. Vomiting from a prone position distressed and humiliated me; the migraine magnified my agony a hundred-fold. Nurses tended me throughout the night. They placed an alarm buzzer in my hand with instructions to call each time I was about to throw-up.

The night was a blur of pain, alarms, vomiting, torch-light heralding nurses, spew pans under my chin, wet cloths wiping my face, tears and cries of agony. *It hurt to cry. It hurt to move. It hurt not to move.* I wanted relief from the torment, but got none.

Sunday 14 July 2002

Light at the window indicated the first seemingly endless night had passed. Morning, brought no relief from the cycle of distress. The neurosurgeon arrived with my MRI results. I had, he explained: exploded my twelfth thoracic vertebra, double-fractured the fifth lumbar, damaged discs in my neck, and torn a tendon in my shoulder; but did not appear to have damaged the spinal cord. I would, he advised, need a metal back brace to support my spine and keep it straight until it healed.

'Will I walk again?' I struggled with the words.

'That is not our concern at the moment.' The doctor smiled.

What is there to smile about? I thought.

'Your migraines and vomiting are the immediate problem now. You've had a nasty bump to the head. You may have suffered some damage to your brain. We need to carry out some more tests.' He smiled again, turned, and outlined instructions to the nurses beside him.

My insides began to wretch again.

'Nurse!'

Too late. Vomit sprayed all over the plastic sheet the nurses had spread over my bed. With a look of disgust, the neurosurgeon stepped into the corridor to finish giving his instructions to the senior nurse, while another nurse cleaned up the mess. Morphine had dulled the pain and my senses, but it had not stopped the migraines or the vomiting.

Larry and Serena came to visit. Serena sat silently on a chair beside my bed while Larry stood stroking my burning forehead. I described my night to them and relayed what the doctor had said about possible brain damage. When I'd finished, Larry began to fill me in on events at home and when the rest of the family would be coming to visit.

An instant later, I was not mentally present.

'Larry, would you climb down that ladder at the end of the pier and test the water temperature for me please? I want to take a swim.' I pointed to the end of my bed.

Serena's eyes widened and her jaw dropped as she stared at me.

'Please, Larry? Would you go down the ladder and see if the water is warm enough for a swim?'

Colour drained from Larry's face.

'Where do you think we are?' he asked, puzzled.

'In Birmingham,' I declared, wondering why he would ask such a question, 'on the pier.'

'Do you know where Birmingham is?' Larry asked slowly, deeply uneasy with the turn the conversation had taken.

'Of course, I do!' I replied with an edge of frustration in my voice. 'It's in England.'

'Do you know where in England?' he persisted gently.

At that moment I flipped back from the hallucination and mentally returned to the hospital ward.

'Oh! … It's okay, Larry … I'm back now.'

'Do you know where in England?' He repeated, not understanding what had just happened nor that my hallucination was now over.

'In the Midlands. But it's okay. I am back now.'

'And do you think there is any water or a pier in Birmingham?' Larry was still trying to figure out what was going on.

'No, there's no water. I tripped out, Larry, but I am back now.'

Larry was devastated; it was far too much for him to deal with. He and Serena left soon after that discourse.

Two days later Larry flew to South Africa to work for two weeks. Larry is an agricultural teacher who runs workshops for farmers.

He could have made some sort of effort to try and be with me now when I need him most. I bet he didn't even try. He just wants to escape from the problems! Everyone's abandoned me.

I was scared, sick, in pain and feeling sorry for myself. I wanted someone to hold my hand and tell me that everything was going to be okay. Instead I lay alone and frightened in days of delirium.

Doctors came and went. Tests. Nurses. Pain. Vomiting. Injections. Visitors. Everything merged together.

My friend Baxter rang to wish me well and to tell me his wife Trudy had just suffered a stroke. 'I won't be able to come and help out in the national park, Linda.' Baxter had been a keen volunteer with the conservation group

I'd set up. 'I need to be with Trudy now. She and the children need me. They are my priority now. *Sorry, Linda!* I've taken leave of absence from work to take care of Trudy and the children. I know you'll understand.'

'Thanks for phoning, Baxter. Please give Trudy my love. I hope she gets well soon.' As I hung up the phone my mood plummeted.

Baxter's taking time out to care for Trudy and his family and Larry's got on a plane and run away from me. He doesn't really care about me at all. If he did he'd stay when I need him most. He always runs away when I need him. Will he leave me for good?

Vomiting became almost constant and although brain scans revealed no brain damage, the scorching pain in my head grew increasingly intolerable. Doctors decided the vomiting must be a reaction to morphine and prescribed *Maxalon* with the morphine to stop the vomiting. With the *Maxalon*, the vomiting eased and life became a degree less distressing.

CHAPTER 7

Day Two–Spain

Day Two–17 August 2006 (Roncesvalles, Spain)
CURLED UP IN MY BUNK in the refuge at Roncesvalles, I munch my baguette, as I recollect the months and years of pain and struggle after my fall. The accident, the recovery, and the promise I made myself during that time to backpack across Europe–was after all–the reason I was here in Spain. I reflect on those events, then pull the sleeping bag up over my head, bury my face in my pillow, and with body aching and worrying if I can continue tomorrow; I cry myself to sleep.

In the morning, a surreal harmony of chanting monks float through the refuge. For a moment before total wakefulness, I think I mustn't have survived my ordeal on the mountain the previous day, I think I must be in heaven. Then I move and feel the stiffness and pain and know I'm still alive. The Dutch volunteers play the chanting every morning to wake pilgrims. Peeling back the sleeping bag I tenderly ease myself out of its covers. On inspection, I see that my foot and several toes are turning purple. Later, barely able to walk, I arrange another night's accommodation in the village to rest and nurse my wounds.

Should I go on? Can I go on? For now, I need to give my wounds some time to heal.

By the third morning I can still only hobble, but decide I must try to continue. I saw a sign on the refuge wall offering a bag-carrying service to the next *albergue* or *refugio*, both terms are used interchangeably and mean refuge. Without the weight of the backpack, I think I might be able to hobble to the *albergue*. I ask one of the volunteers in the refuge to phone the number and arrange the service for me. With a bag-carrier, called Carlos, organised, I sit out front of a nearby restaurant and wait for him to arrive.

Other pilgrims make their way in a steady stream out of the refuge and down the mountainside. I learn that most pilgrims don't start at St Jean Pied de Port in France as I'd done; most start on the Spanish side of the Pyrenees at Roncesvalles.

No wonder they all look so fresh and chirpy.

Sixty percent of the pilgrims are Spanish, twenty percent are French and the rest of the world make up the remaining twenty percent. The mixed languages of the chatter confirm those percentages as the pilgrims head off for the start of their Camino adventure.

Time ticks past. The sun rises higher in the sky. Still I wait. I begin to wonder if Carlos the bag-carrier will ever appear. The pilgrims have gone and the village is almost deserted and still I sit, alone and conspicuous, on the stone wall.

An Ernest Hemingway look-alike appears and says something to me in French. I shake my head to indicate I don't comprehend.

'Do you speak English?' he tries another language.

I nod.

'Is there a public phone booth around here?'

'Sorry, I'm a stranger here too.' Much, much later, I would wonder why he asked me that question.

He hoists himself up on to the wall next to me and strikes up a conversation. He walked the Camino a few years ago, and since then travels through Spain and France in his motor home in summer, walking sections of the Camino.

'I walked from Roncevalles to the French border yesterday,' he continues.

I nod, not really in a chatty mood.

'What are you doing sitting on the wall? The other pilgrims have already gone. Are you lost?' he asks.

'I'm waiting for a bag-carrier to arrive to take my backpack to Zubiri. I got caught in a storm yesterday. My hips, knees and feet are too sore. I can't carry the pack.'

He smiles knowingly.

'I'm afraid my back may not last the journey to Santiago de Compostella. I want to take it gently now to make sure my back will hold out. I have a bad back, but I must reach Santiago de Compostella,' I explain to the stranger.

'Do you speak Spanish?' he asks.

'No.'

'Hmm,' he pauses pensively. 'You'll probably be okay. But let me warn you this next section is also a killer. It's a very steep descent down the mountain. If you've a bad back and knee, then I recommend you get a lift to Pamplona and rest for a few days. Then from Pamplona the terrain is much more manageable. I wouldn't try and walk this next stretch if I were you.'

At that moment, a van pulls up and a chap gets out. I assume it's my bag-carrying service arriving late. I ask the driver if he is Carlos and he seems to confirm he is. Hemingway speaks to Carlos in what sounds like fluent Spanish. He asks him if he'll take me to Pamplona. He agrees to, although he looks slightly puzzled. The two men chat for several minutes. It turns out that Carlos is not Carlos, my bag-carrier, but indeed a taxi driver who's just driven a passenger from Pamplona. He dropped the passenger in the village centre at Roncesvalles and stopped next to me because he wanted a cup of coffee in the café before returning to Pamplona.

As Carlos, my bag-carrier hasn't turned up, Hemingway negotiates for the taxi driver to take me back to Pamplona at half price, considering he would've gone back empty anyway. The deal is made.

'The driver wants a coffee first before he returns to Pamplona. Why don't you buy him a coffee?'

Further discussions in Spanish between Hemingway and the taxi driver reveal that the taxi driver knows Carlos the bag-carrier. The taxi driver calls Carlos on his mobile and cancels my booking. Hemingway tells me that the taxi driver doubted that Carlos had intended to come at all. The taxi driver relays via Hemingway that if I'd called him, then the fare would have cost fifty-five euro, but as he's come up to Roncesvalles with a paying passenger, he'll happily take me back for thirty.

As Hemingway walks away, leaving me with the taxi driver, I think Hemingway must be an angel sent to help me. I would later change that opinion, completely.

The taxi driver says something about a coffee and points to the restaurant, indicating for me to join him. We go inside. I offer to buy him the coffee but he refuses and instead insists on buying me a drink. I order tea and nod my thanks to the smiling taxi driver. His friendliness relaxes me and although he speaks no English and I no Spanish, it doesn't matter. I buy a bread roll with cheese to take with me for breakfast then we climb into the van and drive off.

It's a warm, blue-sky day; all signs of yesterday's storm have vanished. The air is fresh and moist and the landscape crisp and green. Lack of a common language makes conversation a challenge but an enjoyable one. Hand gestures and searching for understanding of certain words keeps us amused and laughing for most of the journey. Only when we've exhausted all possible comprehendible topics, do we fall into a happy silence. Time passes quickly and we are soon in Pamplona. The driver drops me in the city and I make my way to the *refugio*.

As night falls I see that I'm sharing a room with a very large Spanish family; from a grandmother in her early eighties to a small boy of about eight years old. They appear to be on a summer holiday. I'm puzzled how they can all be walking the Camino. It's a challenge for me; I wonder how the old lady and the small boy can possibly manage it.

In fact, the refuge seems to be full of Spanish holiday makers; they don't appear to be pilgrims at all. I later learn that August is the month that Spaniards take their holidays and they use refuges as a source of cheap accommodation, which is totally against refuge rules.

The high-spirited family shrieks and shouts until late into the night, playing cards on the top bunk. I'm glad I kept the eye mask and ear plugs from the plane. I put them on, turn over, pull the sleeping bag over my head and try to block out the din. As I strain to shut out the noise, my thoughts return once more to the *long healing road* that brought me to this point in time, the journey that led me to Spain.

CHAPTER 8

Laughter–The Best Medicine

AFTER ANOTHER TEN DAYS IN hospital I was fitted with a steel brace that wrapped around my torso to hold my spine straight. Then I was sent home with instructions to stay flat on my back in bed.

Once home, I was delighted to find a futon bed had been set up for me in the front living room and a phone extension installed next to the bed. My girls had thought it through well. Putting me in the front living room meant I wasn't isolated from daily life. In fact, I could see activity happening in three directions: through to the dining room in one direction; out the window towards the office in another direction; and through the window to the driveway–to see who was coming to the front of the house, in the other direction. The firm futon mattress provided good support. A potbelly fire radiated warmth and an ambience of comfort. The living room was a space people could access from outside through sliding doors at the front of the room, so visitors could come and go with ease. A sign on the front door directed visitors to the sliding doors on the now completed front verandah.

From my bed, I could see through the window to the cottage next door where my daughter Amy and her partner Eddy lived. I could watch Amy and Eddy going to work in our office each morning. Through one door I could see Serena walking around the house. Every morning, Eddy came in to light the fire in the potbelly, to keep me warm, and every morning Serena brought my breakfast. Larry was still away working in South Africa.

I'd always been stubbornly independent. Now unable to get out of bed, I couldn't bathe myself, or go to the toilet unaided; I was entirely dependent on others for all my daily needs. I felt utterly useless. I was enormously grateful to my family for the thoughtfulness and care they gave me but at the same time I hated being a burden on them. I had to learn not only to accept help, but worse still, I had to learn to ask for it. It was difficult.

Lying flat on my back made eating a challenge, plus it affected my digestion; it gave me very loud sporadic hiccups. On my first day home, Celeste came to visit. Wracked with pain, and tired of being on my back, I wanted desperately to turn onto my side.

'Celeste, I really need to roll onto my side. Would you please put one hand on my shoulder and one on my hip, and on the count of three, roll me onto my side?'

Celeste was afraid she would hurt me and was unwilling to do as I asked. 'I will roll with you on the count of three. I need to change position. *Please Celeste?*' I begged.

Reluctant and hesitant, Celeste nervously agreed. She put one hand on my hip and the other on my shoulder, as I directed, and at the count of three, rolled me onto my side.

'Thanks, Celeste, that feels so much better.' It was an enormous relief to change position. Celeste was concerned she might have injured me by the rollover, and was afraid she'd done the wrong thing.

'Now come and sit down next to me.' I smiled to her and patted the bed near my belly, inviting her to sit, so we could chat. Celeste slowly began to lower her bottom towards the bed. Just as her posterior made tentative contact with my bedcover, a loud hiccup exploded from my gut. It startled Celeste; she leapt upwards in fright, hurling herself toward the ceiling, arms and legs spread-eagled in a star-jump. She thought she'd hurt me, that I'd cried out in pain.

She jumped so high it looked like she was going to touch the ceiling. I shrieked with laughter at the sight of my star-jumping daughter. In between my gasping laughter, I tried to tell her that I'd only hiccupped. But the look of horror on Celeste's face sent me into more squeals of hysterical laughter. Tears rolled down my cheeks. Celeste was confused; she couldn't understand what I was trying to say and thought my tears and shrieks were from pain. She was convinced she'd damaged me.

The laughter dropped my pain levels from excruciating to nothing; no pain at all. Celeste's star jumping was a blessing and the first learning experience on my journey of recovery.

'Celeste, you've just done me a huge favour,' I began, once I had wiped the tears of laughter from my eyes and sufficiently composed myself to be able to speak. 'The pain has gone. The laughter's taken away all the pain.'

'Serena!' Serena came running.

'Serena, the pain has gone. Celeste made me laugh, and the pain went away.'

Both daughters looked at each other, baffled.

'Laughter really is the best medicine,' I told them, still wiping the tears from my cheeks. 'It takes away the pain.'

'Great …' Serena responded, understanding dawning slowly. 'We'll have to get you funny videos to watch.'

Celeste was too traumatised to understand what I was getting at; it was two weeks before she came back to visit again.

I was very grateful to her for that first lesson in the importance of laughter for pain relief. From that day forward, Serena insisted in bringing as much humour as possible into the house. We hoped it might not only reduce my pain but possibly speed up my healing too. Amy, Serena, and Eddy kept me supplied with bundles of funny videos and anything else they could think of that might make me laugh.

Drinking from a prone position is also a challenge. We found placing a glass in the crook of my armpit and sipping from a bendable straw was the only way I could drink. Serena went shopping and returned with a selection of whacky re-usable plastic straws; one was shaped like a comic crocodile, another like a cartoon duck; all ridiculous enough to make me laugh.

Looking for the amusing side of everything became an obsession; no negativity was permitted to be uttered in my presence. Focusing on the funny side of events and situations helped the girls and I maintain a positive outlook and reduced my pain levels dramatically. We laughed and joked our way through every day of recovery, whenever possible.

On the morning of my third day home, Serena came into the living room and climbed into bed beside me.

'I feel sick, Mummy,' she said. 'I've got a headache and a tummy ache.'

I hugged her to me against my metal brace. I suspected she was worried about going to school and leaving me alone. I didn't want her to miss school but knew I would not win any debate over it that morning. Her headache and tummy ache were probably quite real, but I guessed, were induced by worry over me.

Serena had taken on the role of tending to my needs. She gave me my breakfast each morning and helped me with my washing and toilet needs. After school, she cooked the evening meal, helped me wash myself and assisted me to the toilet. That meant lifting me out of bed, helping me to the bathroom and lowering me onto the toilet seat.

The first visit to the toilet after coming home from hospital was another learning experience. Toilet seats are designed far too low; the seat should be higher. When you cannot bend your back, squatting unaided is impossible. Serena walked me to the toilet, lowered me onto the seat, and left the room. When I finished, not being unable to bend in my metal brace, meant my arms weren't long enough to reach my bottom.

Oh horrors! No! I can't ask for help to wipe myself! That's just too demeaning!

I sat trying to think what to do. Serena was waiting outside the door to help me back to bed. Several minutes passed.

'You okay, Mum?' She called through the door.

'No,' was my embarrassed response.

'What's wrong?' She flung the door open.

'I can't reach to wipe myself.'

Serena stared at me. As she comprehended the situation, her eyes rolled heaven-ward.

'Oh Jeez … No way!'

'I can't reach, love.' I felt totally humiliated.

Then I saw the funny side of my dilemma.

'I've wiped your bottom plenty of times,' I reminded her with a grin.

'But you're my mother!' She grimaced.

'But I can't reach.' Then we were both laughing.

'Wait a minute.' Serena disappeared.

She reappeared a few moments later with a pair of kitchen tongs and a wad of rolled up toilet paper in their grip.

'Here, use these.' With a smirk she shoved the tongs in my hand and waited a moment while I tried to wipe myself with them.

They didn't curve where I needed them to. We struggled to contain our laughter as I grappled with the tongs again, before I lost my grip and dropped the wad of paper.

'Won't bend. Still can't reach,' I giggled at the ridiculous situation.

'Hmm.' Serena took the tongs back and looked at me quizzically.

'Just a sec.' She dashed off again.

She reappeared with a dish washing brush in her hand. It had a slight bend in it and a sponge on the end.

'Try this.' With a grin she thrust the dish brush into my hand. It worked, sort of. Good enough for now.

'What happens when I have to do a number two?' I tried to conceal an embarrassed grin.

Serena was on the ball.

'Didn't the doctor say that when you are lying in bed you don't have to do a number two very often?'

'Hmm … you're right, he did. Let's hope he was right.' We were both chuckling as she helped me to my feet and then dressed me.

Two weeks later, a withdrawn and reclusive Larry returned from working in South Africa. He was still having trouble dealing with the trauma and the dramatic change to our lives. My hallucinations in hospital had tipped him beyond his ability to cope. Prior to the accident, Larry always used to eat his lunch in front of the television while watching the "World at Noon" news on television. Keeping up with current global affairs was, he said, essential for his work.

He'd hardly spoken to me since he'd come home. I was looking forward to him joining me at midday in the living room to watch the news on television. I thought he'd take a few minutes after the news had finished to sit and chat. At noon, Larry came to the house from our office next door, prepared his lunch, and disappeared. He didn't come to watch the news. He took his lunch back to the office to eat it there. He'd never done that before. Deeply disappointed that he hadn't joined me, I wondered why he'd changed his routine.

That evening he brought my dinner and left again to eat his evening meal in the dining room with Serena. I'd hoped we'd all eat together in the living room but Larry was avoiding spending time with me. I felt as though a sharp knife was carving away at me, leaving a dark gloomy blanket of depression.

The doctor said I needed some positive emotional events to lift my spirits. He suggested holding a belated birthday party to cheer me up.

My family rallied around and took over organising the party. For the big gathering they hired a BBQ roaster and my sister became chef for the day. The day was apparently full of drama, but I was kept unaware. The gas ran out while cooking the roasts and the meal was late but my guests chatted and socialised and didn't seem to mind the late lunch.

Another sister brought along a walking frame. 'Here, you can use this to help you get around.'

Once I had been lifted out of bed and put into an upright position I could wheel myself around to mingle with guests. It was excruciatingly painful and exhausting, but as it was my special day I refused to allow the pain to prevent me from enjoying myself. I certainly did not want to be an invalid at my own party. The companionship warmed my heart, but it was too much. It wasn't long, before suffering and fatigued, I had to be put back to bed with some strong painkillers. It was worth it though; the camaraderie lifted my spirits and banished some of my loneliness.

There was a great deal of discussion among medical friends at the party about my neurosurgeon; they all knew of him and his reputation. The strongest and most forthright comment came from a theatre nurse who was a close friend of Amy.

'*He's a butcher!* She should get another neurosurgeon,' the nurse told Amy, who passed the message on to me.

My neighbour, a medical specialist, left the party feeling troubled by the treatment I'd been given by the neurosurgeon. The following day he sent a note suggesting I get a second opinion from a neurosurgeon he recommended. I'd not been comfortable with my neurosurgeon's comments or treatment, and my friends' concerns reinforced my doubts. I thanked my neighbour for his recommendation and decided I would change doctors.

The following day we hired a shower chair so I could sit while being showered and a toilet frame to go over the toilet, to raise it a little. A Silver Chain nurse was booked to come and bathe me and a cleaner to clean the house.

I'd not yet arranged a new neurosurgeon when a letter arrived from my current one, advising it was time for my four week check-up. I was astounded that a patient with a spinal injury was expected to get in a car and travel twenty kilometres to Murdoch for a four week check-up. I could not bend over; how would I get in a car? Anxiety manifested; the thought of making the trip left me dizzy. I distrusted the neurosurgeon and feared he may cause me further damage. I was hesitant to go, but I knew it would take several weeks, once I had a referral from my General Practitioner– Doctor Derovi–before I could get in to see another neurosurgeon. I wanted to ensure my recovery was on track, so decided I would make the appointment and arrange for a new neurosurgeon after this visit.

Larry was away again. I needed to arrange for someone else to take me to see the doctor. Another neighbour, Art, offered to take me.

On the morning of the appointment Art carried me to the car. My dog, Toshi, had known Art all his life and he loved him. Yet that morning as Art carried me to the car, Toshi, barking and growling, gripped hold of his ankle and wouldn't let go. Art carefully placed me in the car then took the Maltese aside. Firmly but gently he explained to Toshi that he'd take care of me and would bring me back soon.

'I'm so sorry about Toshi,' I began, as Art started the car.

'It's ok,' he cut in. 'Toshi's only protecting you. Don't worry about it.' Art was a horse whisperer; he understood animals.

As we arrived at the hospital, where the neurosurgeon's practice was situated, anxiety induced dizziness and nausea made me swoon.

'Are you okay? Do you need to sit down?' Art grabbed hold of and steadied me.

'I need this to be over.'

Inside the practice, the neurosurgeon told me to take the steel brace off and bend over. Faint with fright at the request; blackness loomed. I grabbed the chair back to steady myself.

He's the specialist, Linda. He knows what he's doing. Don't panic.

I didn't believe what I was telling myself. I had no faith in this man, but very gingerly, afraid I might do some damage, I did as he asked.

That's it! I most definitely need a new neurosurgeon. I won't be coming back to see this man again.

Weeks turned into months. My fragile hold on positivity began to diminish, though I wasn't aware my mood was in decline. The previous night Larry flew to work in South Africa again. In the morning, before taking my painkillers, so my thoughts were clear, I meditated and asked Marcus for answers. Marcus had been my spirit guide for many years. He was always there in the background, waiting to show me the way–when I was prepared to listen. He let me make mistakes when it was necessary for me to learn a lesson. Marcus had taught me that sometimes when bad things happen, the alternative could have been far worse. He taught me to always see the opportunities in everything and to learn from every life-step I take.

'Why has this happened to me? What lesson do I need to learn from this?'

'Before the accident, Linda, you kept running through your mind, saying to yourself, *I'm fed up. I've had enough*,' Marcus began.

That's true, I had been feeling that way. I felt my marriage was very one-person focused; that my life revolved around Larry and Larry's life revolved around his work. I wanted my life to have more balance between work, personal needs, and family. Life was always so fast-paced that there never seemed to be enough time to talk things through with Larry. He was only home for a few days at a time and those moments were too precious to bring up problems. At least that was the way it had seemed in the past. I felt like a mouse on a treadmill–running, running, running–but not getting anywhere. My subconscious self-talk had been, *I've had enough!*

'It was not my intention to end it all,' I responded. 'I was tired of the way things were going. I felt burnt out, drained, emotionally empty. I needed to change the way my life had been functioning. That was all.'

'By thinking a thought over and over, you focus your mental energy on that thought and send a powerful message to the Universe. You told the Universe you *had had enough!* When you focus mental energy on something, the Universe responds.'

'I didn't mean to send a message.'

'Nevertheless, that message was sent, Linda. You were creating the energy with your thoughts and drawing those thoughts to yourself. The Universe answered you. Your words and thoughts create your reality. Be careful what you think!'

I sat silently for a few minutes and contemplated all the negative emotions and negative thoughts that churned uncontrollably through my mind.

'I am always the one telling the kids to think positively, and yet I was the one who'd let my own thinking become so negative.'

'How you live your life, and what you get out of life, is always your own choice,' Marcus continued. 'You attract what you give your energy to, what you give your thoughts to, what you speak about. You're constantly creating your own destiny. It's all your choice. The decisions, the choices you make, conscious or subconscious, are all constructing your life journey. Whatever situation you find yourself in is a direct result of choices you make in life. Staying and accepting, changing, or leaving, whatever you decide to do, it's your choice. You can ask God, or the Universe—for guidance and help—*but the final choice, the final decision, the final action, is up to you.* You sent the message to the Universe, that you *had had enough!* and the Universe responded by giving you the option of choice. You could choose to stay, or you could choose to go.'

Marcus replayed that moment of choice: I saw the day of the accident again. I saw the moment when the ladder began to slip. I was falling. I saw that I would hit the verandah edge, saw that I would tumble over the edge of the verandah. I saw that I would crash head-first onto the granite boulders below; saw the crunching of my spine; my neck crumbling and my skull smashing. I saw my death.

I saw that I had been given a choice. I heard, in that instant, the Universe speaking to me.

Do you accept this, Linda? Is this what you want? You said you'd had enough. The choice is yours.

I recalled that moment of choice.

If I hit the edge of the verandah, I'm dead! That thought had raced through my brain. *If the verandah edge doesn't kill me, the granite boulders will.*

No, I choose to live.

It happened so fast, I wasn't conscious of being offered a choice at the time. I twisted my body around as I fell and flung myself sideways towards the verandah, rather than fall over the edge. I landed on the verandah. I'd chosen to live.

Marcus closed the replay of events I'd been watching.

Over the following weeks and months the Universe gave me another choice: I could accept disability and simply give up, or I could choose to overcome it. I'd have to struggle, to work very hard to regain physical strength and ability. It wasn't the easy road. Giving up would've been easier. But if I was to return to some sort of normality, I'd have to fight against the odds. I chose to fight.

'You see, Linda, everything does happen for a reason. Sometimes that reason is because you attract to yourself what you give your energy to, what you think about, or through the words you use every day. The choice of how you live your life is yours. Choose your thoughts carefully. Choose your words carefully. You move towards what you think about and what you talk about. Give energy to what you want to receive.

Don't think or talk about what you don't want in your life. By giving energy to what you don't want you are giving that negativity the power to grow and expand, to come into existence. By thinking about it, you attract it into your life.

Focus your thoughts and words and mental energy on what you most want to receive. Then you will attract it. Live in choice, Linda.'

Marcus's words reverberated in my thoughts.

What choices do I have right now? I need to heal my body so I can one day lead a normal life again. Once I am back to normal, then I can think about other life choices. What will a "normal" life be for me?

I considered for a moment, then my thoughts returned to the present.

Larry still avoids me as much as he possibly can. If I should ever become disabled or wheelchair-bound, will he stay with me, or will he leave me? Does he really love me at all? Surely, he'd make more effort to be around me and give more emotional support if he did.

That night Serena snuggled into bed beside me. We watched comedy videos until it was time for sleep. A stronger and closer bond had developed between us since the accident. It amused me to watch Serena enjoying the opportunity to be boss and dictate to me what was going to happen. At the same time, she seemed to know instinctively when I was feeling low. She'd wrap her arms around me and hold me, freely imparting love, warmth and understanding. Her empathy meant a lot more to me than the young girl could possibly understand. It gave me something to hold on to when there seemed to be nothing else left.

The following night was Sunday. Eddy and Amy brought dinner over to share with Serena and me. With the potbelly fire warming the room and plates on our laps, Amy and Serena snuggled on the bed beside me, and with Eddy nearby, we did something that before the accident had always been banned; we ate dinner watching television. We watched comedy videos until late into the night and my soul felt nurtured.

Prior to the accident, I drove Serena to school each morning and each afternoon I drove her home. Now she had to walk. She complained loudly over the steep three-kilometer climb up the hill in the mornings, but didn't mind the downhill walk home in the afternoon. Our neighbours drove past every morning to take their children to school, so I rang around and asked them for help. On the Monday, they began a roster system to pick Serena up in the morning as they passed and drop her at the top of the hill. From there it's not so far for her to walk to school.

Wednesday was my scheduled appointment with the recommended new neurosurgeon. Art carried me into the car and drove me to the doctor. This neurosurgeon was very thorough, explaining everything he did and why. Immediately I felt confidence that I never felt before.

'I think you need a fusion operation on your spine, Linda,' he said. Cold prickles of fear ran down my back at the suggestion. 'I am going to refer you to a lumbar fusion specialist to seek his opinion. He'll make the decision on whether he thinks it's necessary.

I can see that you are traumatised by the accident. You should speak to your GP about going on antidepressants,' he added, before dictating his letter to the lumbar fusion specialist.

What a cheek! I'm not traumatised. I don't need antidepressants.

CHAPTER 9

Renewed Bravado

Bilbao (Spain)
THE THICK FOAM MATTRESS IN the *refugio* in Pamplona offers no support for my aching back–I'm in agony when I wake.

Oh dear! I can't carry a backpack. I can barely walk.

Refugio rules state that only one night's accommodation is provided for genuine pilgrims. *If I plan to stay another night in Pamplona I must find alternative accommodation.*

I check out of the refuge, limp to a hotel in the city centre and book a bed for a second night. Check-in time is 12 noon. *It is only 7.30 am, I've got a few hours to fill before I can get into the room. I can't walk around the city; my feet and back are tormenting me. I'll be a tourist. I'll take a bus to Bilbao to see the Guggenheim Museum. Sitting in a bus I can rest my feet and back and do some sight-seeing at the same time. A walk around a museum will be an easy way to fill in time until I can check into the hotel.*

I deposit my backpack at the hotel reception and go to the bus terminal. The ticket counter at the bus terminal is shut. I sit and wait for it to open. A young German chap sits next to me. On his backpack, a scallop shell–the symbol of St James–identifies him as a fellow pilgrim.

'Are you on your way to Santiago de Compostella?' I ask, curious what he's doing at a bus terminal.

'I walked from Pamplona to Compostella two years ago. This time I walked from Le Puy in France to Pamplona. I've finished now and am on my way to Bilbao to catch a flight back to Berlin. The track from Le Puy is one of many trails across Europe that join the Camino.'

We chat about the Camino while waiting for the bus and I give him a very brief version of my story.

My Spiritual Guide sent me to walk the Camino but there have been so many blocks to my journey. Now I have a multitude of ailments preventing me from going on, making me wonder if I'm being told *not* to do it, *not* to walk the Camino.

'The Camino doesn't want you to fail. It's just testing you. The first week is always the hardest because your muscles are adjusting to the rigours of the walk. After that, when you've got into the rhythm of the Camino, it becomes easier.'

Encouraged by his words, I'm about to ask him something, when a trio of French pilgrims arrive at the terminal. One of the trio points to me.

'Ah, you were at Roncesvalles. You had a bad back!'

'*Oui.*' I nod confirmation and smile at the French pilgrims.

They join us and the discussion turns to the day of the storm on the mountain, then on to the trip to Bilbao and the Guggenheim museum. The French group speak as little English as I speak French, so the German acts as our interpreter. On the bus, the German sits next to me and we discuss languages and cultures. One of the Frenchmen, who's seated alongside us, offers us his opinion on French culture.

'In the middle-ages, French was the language of the royal courts in Europe. As a result, French people give culture to the world, they don't take it, and generally tend not to speak another language.'

The Frenchman's viewpoint is interesting. I ask the German why, in his opinion, most Germans seem to be very multilingual.

'Germany, in comparison with France, is a small country. Because it is surrounded by other countries, Germany sees itself as being almost in the centre of Europe. Therefore, it's influenced politically and economically by world events. In my opinion, Germans feel it's necessary to be able to speak the languages of its neighbours as well as the language of business, English.'

I'm fascinated and delve into the topic with my companion, before shifting the subject back to the Camino. The German suggests I send anything in my backpack, that's not absolutely necessary, to the post office at Santiago de Compostella to await my arrival and then enquire at every refuge for a local masseur, which he suggests will free up energy blockages in my muscles, if done regularly. He also recommends I use a backpack carrying service for the next few days and only walk a short distance each day until my body heals.

'If you can get through the first week, then you'll be fine. The Camino doesn't want you to fail, it's just testing you!'

It sounds like wise advice. I feel the Universe arranged our meeting, sent the German with a message of encouragement to keep me going.

The bus pulls in to Bilbao and we pour out, say our goodbyes, and go our separate ways. With renewed confidence, and stronger motivation, I decide to take the German's advice, tomorrow morning I'll unload unnecessary items from my pack and post them to Santiago de Compostella post office for collection on my arrival.

That evening back in Pamplona, I ask the concierge at the hotel for directions to a doctor. He directs me to the hospital. No-one at the hospital speaks English, so with dictionary in-hand, and only a few words of Spanish, I use lots of gesturing and body language to indicate—*I'm walking to Santiago de Compostella and have hurt my back and feet.* My painful hips are probably a typical pilgrim complaint, so I don't try to describe them to the nurse. I wait several hours in the waiting room before the very friendly staff indicate it's my turn to see a doctor. They're all rather perplexed with how to communicate with me, but they try.

I wonder if hospital staff in Australia would cope with a non-English speaking patient as well as this team are coping with me? The doctor gives me an injection, wishes me *'Bon Camino'* and sends me on my way. I try to pay for the treatment but a lady indicates that the office is shut. At least, I think that's what she says.

The next morning, I rise, determined to shed half the weight of the contents of my carefully planned backpack. Before I left home, I'd researched the absolute minimum requirements to take on my great walk. I wanted as light a load as possible, so I'd only packed what I thought—at the time—were the bare-essentials. Now, some of those *bare-essentials,* need to go. The German had advised me to keep my sleeping mat, though I am tempted to get rid of that too.

'You might need the mat if a refuge is full. Get rid of everything else that you can possibly do without,' he'd advised.

I remind myself that he'd walked the Camino; he knew first-hand. I keep the sleeping bag and sleeping mat; shampoo for washing hair, clothes, and body; the head torch for night-time visits to the toilet; toothbrush and toothpaste, comb, blister dressing, a single change of clothes, a quick-dry towel and lip balm.

Everything else: my first-aid kit, medicines, vitamins, other toiletries, my sketch book and pencils, a thermal top and half my supply of mixed fruit and nuts, goes into a cardboard carton at the post office. I post it *all* off to myself—care of the Santiago de Compostella post office.

I feel profoundly liberated as I leave the post office. Lightening my pack so drastically, fills me with renewed enthusiasm and optimism that I'll be able to complete my journey to Santiago de Compostella. Singing to myself, I go in search of either a physiotherapist, acupuncturist, chiropractor, masseur, or even all four—if that's possible.

I need all the help I can get to be physically able to continue the walk.

The people at the tourist information centre are not terribly helpful; they take a cursory look in the yellow pages and present me with a list of acupuncturists. They tell me they can't find any physiotherapists, chiropractors or masseurs. I have the impression they didn't look beyond "A" for acupuncture and are pleased to get rid of me.

I hobble all over Pamplona, from one address to the next, only to find they are either non-existent or the inhabitants have signs saying they are on holidays for the month of August.

I make my way back to the hospital to pay the bill for yesterday's treatment. Despite the unsuccessful morning, my attitude to continue the walk remains positive. One of the things the German said to me reverberates in my brain, 'There is *no rush,* take it *slowly,* just do ten kilometres a day, only do what you can manage.' I buy some pain-killers from a pharmacy and seal my determination to set off tomorrow.

I will walk through the agony in my back and foot, take a slow stroll across Spain, there's no hurry–I reassure myself–programming my mind to stay positive and focus on the goal ahead.

CHAPTER 10

Larry-Confronting Change

EIGHT WEEKS AFTER I'D COME home from hospital, Amy and Eddy still visited twice every day to see if I needed anything. I still had to be lifted out of bed in the morning and assisted to the toilet. Our house nestled into the side of the hill on three levels; the lower level was my area; all my meals were brought down to what had formerly been the TV room.

If there was no visitor who could give me lunch, Amy and Eddy came up from the office at noon and made my lunch. Amy helped me to the toilet and Eddy stoked the fire in the potbelly–morning, noon and night. Although it was officially Spring, the weather was still wintry. Even under a thick quilt I was constantly cold. I just couldn't seem to get warm.

Each night before he retired, Eddy would look out of his window to see if my bedside light was still on. If it was, he'd pop over and load more wood onto the fire to make sure it stayed lit through the night.

Larry had arranged for Amy and Eddy to fly to the UK to meet with him; he needed help on a trade show in Birmingham. In the past, it would have been my job to be his assistant. Now Amy and Eddy would fill in for me. I was concerned about them leaving Serena and I alone.

How will I cope without them?

Eddy and Amy asked if I would dog-sit their two little dogs while they were in the UK. I couldn't imagine how I could look after the dogs, but I agreed. I was concerned the dogs would fret and bark and distress me and there would be nothing I could do about it.

'Please tell the dogs, Eddy, that they'll have to stay with me, and behave and not bark. Tell them when you'll be coming home, please Eddy?'

Eddy stifled a grin, but agreed to my request.

On the day of their departure, Eddy brought the dogs to my room and sat them both down side-by-side. Very sternly Eddy told them the schedule for the next month and what was expected of them. The two little dogs sat motionless, looking up at him with adoring eyes, listening intently.

When the taxi arrived to take Eddy and Amy to the airport, the two dogs watched through the window as they loaded their suitcases into the taxi and watched as the taxi pulled away.

Not once in the following month did either of the dogs bark, fret, or try to go next door to Amy and Eddy's cottage. They sat quietly doing exactly what they were told, apart from one thing, they would not stop scratching. I'd been especially worried that Tobee, the eldest of the two, would fret and become a problem, but he was a little angel, well almost. Tobee taught the other two dogs one very bad habit. He sat and licked his genitals all day long. Within thirty hours, he had both the other dogs doing the same thing. I scolded them several times a day, demanding they stop. They'd stop for a short while, but would soon get bored and start again. Dreadful though the slurping noise was, I eventually learnt to tune out to the noise.

With Amy and Eddy gone I needed someone to come each day to feed me and help me to the toilet.

'We can ask the neighbours to do a roster while we're away,' Larry suggested.

'No way!' I could think of nothing more embarrassing or humiliating than asking neighbours to help me to the toilet.

'Well what do you plan to do?' Larry sounded exasperated.

'I'll ask family to come and visit on a rota. If I need to ask anyone for that sort of help, I'd rather ask family.'

Before she left for school each morning, Serena put a supply of nuts and dried fruit for me to nibble on throughout the day and a jug of water beside my bed. Family came and assisted me to get out of bed and helped me to the toilet. With the soft dish-washing brush I washed myself after performing my necessities and managed to maintain some dignity.

Nine weeks after the accident and with the family still away, the strain began to take its toll on Serena. She worried about me and refused to go out and leave me alone. It was a big responsibility for a young girl to have to look after her mother. She could see that my spirits were lagging and had grown concerned. I urged Serena to go to visit friends on weekends, to take some time out, but she refused.

I looked around for Marcus. He was standing at the window gazing outside.

'Marcus, what am I to do about Serena? It hurts me to see such a young girl taking on so much responsibility and being unable to go and have fun with her friends. What can I do to help her?'

He walked over to my bedside and sat down.

'She refuses to leave your side out of love for you. Don't try to force her to leave you. That would distress her more. Her friends could come to visit Serena. She'd be happy to be here with you and happy to have friends come to stay.'

'Thank you, Marcus. Of course! Why didn't I think of that?'

'You are focusing each day on dealing with your own pain. It is difficult for you to think of solutions for someone else's pain.'

'Thank you, Marcus. I'll call her now.'

'Serena!'

Marcus disappeared as Serena came running.

'Serena, why don't you call a friend and invite her to come and sleep over?'

Serena considered it a moment, then ran off and phoned a girlfriend. That evening the two girls chatted and giggled while they had a cook-up in the kitchen.

I'm glad I can't see the mess in the kitchen, I smiled to myself as I listened to their delighted laughter.

The feeling of tension had dissolved and the house was once again filled with gaiety and joy. I relaxed into my pillow and drifted in and out of contented sleep as the weekend went by.

The following week Art took me for my next monthly visit to my GP. Dr Derovi told me I could begin to try to get out of bed myself without being lifted.

'You can also begin to walk around a little on your own now. Just take it slowly and only a little way at first until you get steadier. Don't overdo it,' he warned.

I was thrilled with every little piece of progress. I mentally ticked it off the list of achievements that were part of the journey on the *long road back*.

'You're traumatised,' Dr Derovi told me. 'There's a book I want you to read. It's called, *On Death and Dying*.' Read the book, you'll be able to work out how to deal with the PTSD yourself.'

'PTSD! What's that?'

'Post Traumatic Stress Disorder. That's what you're suffering from. Get the book, read it and you'll understand what to do.' Dr Derovi had been my doctor for many years and knew me well.

There's that trauma word again.

'I'm not traumatised. Accidents happen and I believe everything happens for a reason. I think I'm dealing with it well,' I told him.

'The first stage of trauma is denial. Get the book and read it. You'll understand what to do. I know what you're like. You are obsessive compulsive, like me.'

Obsessive compulsive! I had visions of Jack Nicholson, in the movie *As Good As It Gets*, where he skipped down footpaths dodging paving lines, and each time he washed his hands he used a new bar of soap and threw it in the bin afterwards. *I wasn't like that!*

I rang Larry that evening and sounded off about doctors telling me I was traumatised. I didn't mention the obsessive-compulsive comment to Larry – I was still in shock over that and pondering the veracity of the comment. I felt all my doctors had assumed I was traumatised and that I was handling things extremely well. I believed my doctors simply didn't understand where I was at. Larry got an earful of my thoughts and complaints and listened patiently.

That night, once I'd calmed down, I looked around for Marcus. I wanted to ask him if I was obsessive compulsive. He wasn't there.

Larry arrived home from the UK just after midnight. The following morning he brought me breakfast, then ate his in the dining room before going down the pathway to our office. At lunchtime he brought me lunch, then disappeared to the office to eat his.

I've been lying here alone and lonely for nine weeks. I thought, as I listened to the sound of Larry leaving the house. He left me so quickly each time he brought a meal to me there wasn't enough time to ask him to eat with me. I looked around for Marcus but couldn't see him; I needed to talk. With closed eyes, I calmed myself, focused my mind, and meditated–seeking him.

'Marcus, tell me what to do? I feel Larry has abandoned me. What am I to do?' Marcus appeared before me.

'Linda, you are focusing on your own issues. Move your mind to Larry's world and consider life from his perspective. You'll see that he, too, is struggling. His world has crashed around him and he's not coping with the changes. The only way that he knows to handle personal problems is to withdraw. Confronting Larry won't achieve the results you seek. Confronting him will only make him withdraw further. It's going to be up to you, though, to take the initiative to build a bridge for him.'

'How am I to do that?'

'Use an approach that he won't expect.' With that advice Marcus was gone.

That evening after Larry came home from work I asked him to come and sit with me.

'Tell me a story,' I asked, surprising myself by the words as they rolled out of my mouth.

'A story?' He was surprised by the unusual request.

'Yes, tell me about your day and your trip.'

'Oh! He sat down on the bed and began to chat about what had happened in Birmingham, how the trade show had gone, and then what he'd been doing that day. I felt soothed that I finally had some time with him. I was unsure how many barriers I'd be able to break down, but I was happy that a start had been made.

CHAPTER 11

My Spirit Guides

Pamplona

IN MY HOSTEL BED IN Pamplona the memories flood in with the morning light. I rouse myself from the recollections and, refreshed from a sound sleep, I'm overflowing with renewed self-confidence and determination. Having posted my things ahead to Santiago, I set off with my now ultra-light-weight pack to rejoin the Camino.

'No rush, I can do this,' I tell myself happily. And this time I believe it.

Rather than back-tracking to where I know the Camino is, I decide to take a short cut to where I think it will exit the city, but it's not there—I'm lost. I walk around in circles looking for the track, growing ever more stressed; I back track and still can't locate the markers. Anxious and annoyed with myself for getting lost I cross the road to ask a couple directions, they point me down a street and I head off in that direction.

A little way along I find some Camino trail-markers and am relieved to be back on track. I focus my thoughts on the route ahead, trying to calm myself down.

Marcus speaks. 'Linda, remember your resolution to take it slowly. This should be a slow stroll across Spain, it's not a rush. Let your body flow with the rhythm of the universe.'

Yes, you're right. If I'm going to get through this, I must let my body flow with the rhythm of the universe. My heart races with anxiety. *It's alright, I can do anything I set my mind to. Stay calm, focused on the goal. Remember why I'm here. Keep positive.*

The mind controls destiny, success, failure. Control your mind and you control your destiny.

'Linda,' Marcus interrupts my thoughts. If you are going to succeed, your mind and body must work in harmony, and you must listen to both. The mind is the software, the body the hardware. The software will run all the programs of the body provided the hardware can function. The mind can tell the body what to do but the body must be respected, listened to and cared for, for the whole unit to function at its optimum.

I think back to the first day on the Camino, I'd placed my mind in control and forced my body to listen—only my body couldn't do it. It reached a point where no matter how much my mind urged my body it was just physically too much; my body simply said, 'Enough!'

I consider Marcus' advice and recall Marissa's words at Roncesvalles. 'Salsa as you walk,' she'd said.

My mind must listen to my body. I must Salsa when I walk, so my body can flow to the rhythm of the universe. I head off along the Camino trail. Focusing on those thoughts, I try to find the rhythm and discover that, as Marissa had suggested, I need to swing my hips wide from side-to-side. It seems to help with the weight of the backpack. By exaggerating the swing of my hips and relaxing my muscles into the rhythm of the stride, I begin to feel I am indeed flowing with the universe. I tune in to that flow and feel the physical stress melt away. Every now and then I become aware that my mind has regained control. When that happens I lose the rhythm and an ache resurfaces. Marcus gently whispers as he walks alongside, 'Linda, listen to your body.'

Oops, that's right, the rhythm of the universe, the rhythm of the universe. I remind myself until I flow in tune again.

'Take your focus to the pain, Linda, visualise it, ask your body to cooperate with you,' Marcus advises.

I mentally focus on my hips and visualise the pain there. *Please hips, please grow strong, please carry me to Santiago de Compostella.*

'That's it, Linda,' Marcus encourages. 'It's a two-way function. You cannot force your body to undertake marathon tasks. Your mind must listen to your body and your body must listen to your mind. It must be a harmonious relationship with the two working together; flowing with the rhythm of the universe.'

I've already crossed one range of the Pyrenees to reach Roncesvalles. Now, leaving the Basque town of Pamplona, nestled in a valley, the Camino takes me up another range of the Pyrenees. I'm pleased with myself to have reached the top of the first mountain, but then the steep descent tests my fitness. My thighs and calves tremble and scream with every downward step.

The rhythm of the universe, the rhythm of the universe, I tell myself over and over as I carefully pick my way down that stony mountain. As I walk a song begins to play in my head, repeating the same lines over and over:

> *Walk on, walk on*
> *With hope in your heart*
> *And you'll never walk alone*
> *Walk on, walk on.*

I watch every foot placement on that rocky track to make sure I don't twist an ankle or stumble and fall. When I look up I see I'm not alone; I now have four Spirit guides, including Marcus—walking with me. Rodney: my brother now in spirit; Hans: an old school-friend; and my Mum. 'Hello. This is a pleasant surprise. Are you all going to join me on this trek?'

'Yes, we're here to help you,' Rodney replies. 'I'm going to guide you so that you don't get lost.'

'Great, thanks, Rod.'

'I'm going to protect you and keep you from harm,' Hans tells me. 'I always travel with you as your protector, particularly when you travel overseas.'

'Yes, I know you do. I appreciate your protection. I know you saved me from being knifed in Sulawesi a few years ago. Thank you.' I turn to my mum. 'Mum, what is your role going to be?'

She smiles lovingly and knowingly at me. 'I'm here to comfort you when you need comforting.'

'That sounds ominous.' Mum just smiles.

I'm going to need comforting? What's going to happen that I should need comforting? I look to Marcus.

'My role, Linda, on this journey, is to teach you. I'm in charge of your spiritual development.'

'Thank you, Marcus. Thank you Rod, Hans and Mum.' I nod to each of them in turn. Thanks for helping me make this journey.'

The climb up the second peak in the range is steeper than the first. My injured foot burns with pain.

Rhythm of the Universe, I remind myself. *Feel the rhythm. Flow with the Universe.* It's getting harder. My breathing's labored as I push myself up the mountain.

'Let go of control of your mind,' Marcus urges. 'Let your body flow with the rhythm. Your mind has taken control again.'

I do as he instructs. The racking pain eases a little. Two hours later—physically strained–my mind wants to push on but my body does not.

'Stop and rest. Take a seat on the rock. Have a drink and eat some nuts,' Marcus advises.

I do as he suggests. A cool breeze wafts up over the mountains. My body enjoys the rest and when it's ready, I continue.

'Now, you're beginning to listen to your body and work in harmony with the Universe. The mind can send requests to the Universe and to the body. It is the body that must flow in rhythm with the Universe. It is a three-pointed triangle: the mind talks to the body and the Universe, the body flows with the Universe, and the Universe responds to both. Never allow your mind to force its control on the body. It is something you often do, Linda, and it creates disharmony. Use your mind to send its requests to the Universe and to your body but never try to force it, then allow your body to find the rhythm. That is what meditation does. It quiets the mind and allows the body and the spirit to find balance with the rhythms of the Universe.'

As I listen to Marcus, it's clear that in the past I've always forced my body to do my mind's bidding. This is a new lesson for me to learn.

We walk on in silence. My foot has swollen and turned blue from the injuries on day one. Now my hips, knees and thighs are groaning with the unaccustomed long-distance assignment. The training done to prepare for this walk had only been a maximum of three hours a day and none of that had been over mountain ranges. The distance I'll be capable of traveling today won't be great. My muscles are quivering with the strain of the descent. I've only traveled sixteen kilometres from Pamplona when I walk into the tiny village of Uberger, but my body says, 'Enough!'

I find an *albergue* and check in. I wash my sweaty clothes and as I'm hanging the last of them on the line to dry, a voice behind me asks, 'Are you German?'

I turn. A lady sitting at a table nearby smiles.

'No, I'm Australian.' I smile back and walk over to take her outstretched hand.

'I'm very pleased to meet you. I'm Hilda, from The Netherland.'

'Linda, from Australia.' Hilda indicates for me to join her at her table under the grape arbor. The shady arbor provides welcome respite from the heat of the Spanish summer. I order a soda water and relax in her company. We talk about the Camino, its demands and its impact on life. 'I'm not able to walk very far each day, my feet are in a bad way, and my hips are aching. I'm only walking slowly and doing around ten to fifteen kilometres a day.'

Hilda tells me she is a personal life-coach who uses forest walks to teach clients how to release their problems. She teaches them to approach things from a different perspective, to be more innovative in seeking solutions to their issues.

'People walk so fast on the Camino to reach each recommended rest point that they don't connect with nature or hear the Universe speaking to them. They *rush, rush, rush* and miss the meaning of walking the Camino. In addition, each recommended rest point gets so full of pilgrims and "tourists" that it's often hard to find a bed. Then, if you do get a bed, the *refugio* can be so crowded and noisy it's difficult to find peace for your soul. You are right to walk slowly and only travel ten to fifteen kilometres in a day,'

Hilda continues. 'It's enough. Rest at the end of each day. Take a nap along the Camino as well if you so choose. It gives your body and your soul time to talk to the Universe. It means that you'll arrive at a quiet village, where there's only a few pilgrims and no 'tourists'. Then you can find a bed easily and when you've found it, there's peace also for your soul.'

I feel my meeting with Hilda was no coincidence. It seems she's been sent by the Universe to reinforce Marcus' words and to add another dimension to my lesson. Slowly over the next few hours, tired weary pilgrims trickle in to the *Albergue*, sore from the descent down the mountain. They wash their clothes then treat their day's injuries.

I sit on my bunk and write my diary. I hear a man a few beds away explain in French to a woman nearby about a blister on his heel that's turned into a huge ugly raw sore. The woman commiserates with the man and offers advice in Spanish. Their multilingual interchange intrigues me and I stop my writing to watch and listen.

The woman looks up, sees me watching and indicates for me to join them. I put down my diary and pen and walk over to the man's bunk. The woman explains in Spanish about the man's problem; the man continues his story to me in French. I comment and offer suggestions in English. None of us understand the actual words of the other, but we each understand the gist of the conversation and that's enough. That's the way it is on the Camino.

It's been a week now that I've been walking the Camino. During the night, a tap turns on in my head and my nose begins to stream in a sudden unstoppable outpouring.

Am I detoxing? I wonder as I sit up in the morning. The refuge empties early, before dawn. *I'll wait for daylight before I get up.*

As I set off in the cool welcoming air of early morning the load on my back seems somehow lighter than the previous day.

'Good morning,' I greet my Spirit travelers as we walk along the dusty road leading out of the village. My shirt has been rolled up in my backpack and is heavily creased. My cloth hat has lost its shape and is crumpled. I see the odd shape of it in my shadow on the ground.

'It's a good thing nobody else is going to see me looking so scruffy this morning,' I comment to my Spirit guides, grinning at the peculiar shape of my shadow.

'You'll always be beautiful to those who love you,' Hans replies.

A wave of sadness sweeps over me. His loving words refresh the sense of loss his passing left in my life, a lifetime ago. A tear trickles down my cheek.

'At my age, with my aching joints and lines appearing on my face, that's so comforting to hear. What pathway would life have taken if we'd married all those years ago?'

'Don't, Linda. It's too painful to think about. All I ever wanted was to be with you. Now I am, I can protect and be with you whenever you need me. Don't go down the "what if" road. I'm with you now, that's all that matters.'

Another tear traces a joyless path down my cheek.

'Linda,' Marcus interjects. 'You've always worried about what other people think, whether they like you, about being approved of. Lines on your face, or greying hair, are of no importance. It's time you gave up your need for approval. Learn to love the person you are this day, this moment, this second. Don't worry about what other people think, whether they like or dislike you. Just be yourself. Don't worry about appearance unduly. Those who love you, love who you are inside, they see the beauty that is within. The beauty on the outside fades in time, the beauty within remains. Love who you are today! You speak of your age, Linda,' Marcus continues. 'You cannot stop aging. It is a natural process. Life is fleeting, temporary. Every living thing will die. It is important to live life to the full; to appreciate every moment, savour every second. Appreciate the sunrise in the morning and the way the morning sun glistens on the leaves of trees and plants. Be thankful for the coolness of the morning breeze in summer. Be grateful for friendship and value family. These are the things that matter in life, the riches. Money is not richness and material possessions are not wealth—they do not enrich the spirit. Love and joy are what enriches the spirit. Family and friendships are the foundations of love and joy.'

We pause on the trail. In the distance there is a motorway with cars rushing along it and a village with farms around it.

'Look at the village in the valley,' Marcus continues. 'Look at the motorway that passes through the village. See the green fields that surround the village and the animals grazing quietly in the fields. See the humans in their cars *rushing* on the motorway—hurrying from one place to the next. They race through the villages along the road. *Hurrying.* Hurrying to work. Hurrying through life. Hurrying towards the end of their lives. The vast majority of people do not live in the present. Their minds are occupied with their future, with their day ahead, with their problems, with the coming week. Some are occupied with the past, with problems from yesterday, or last week. They're not living in the present moment. They're living either in the future, or in a time past. Their present moment is slipping silently away from them. This present moment is the most important time in your life. Don't let it slip past, it may be all you have.'

We stand and watch the cars rushing along the motorway for a few minutes. I watch the humans below rushing through the precious irreplaceable present moment of their lives.

Then Marcus continues, 'It is important to have harmony and balance and place a whole true value on time with family and time with friends, important to enjoy their company. Slow the pace of life down because it's so very short. Cherish every second and never, *ever*, waste it. Remember, all things age and die, only by being aware and focused on this present moment can you fully appreciate and enjoy life. Always live with total focus on the present moment. Cherish what is important in life: your family and friends, your loved ones. Your loved ones are always there for you; their love is the richness in life. Focus your time and energy around your family and friends; give them the essence of your soul. Give them your love.

Past hurts make you hold back your love through fear of further hurt. Expect love and you'll receive love. Expect hurt and pain and you'll receive hurt and pain. Let go of fear and open your heart to allow love to flow.'

As he speaks, tears stream down my cheeks. His words are sharp and honest. I know I've developed a distrust of people, afraid if I allow people to get close to me I'll be hurt. Marcus is right. It's time to lower my barriers and give the world another chance.

The day is hot and challenging. By the time I reach Cirauqui, my aching screaming feet and body are shouting for me to stop. I find an *Albergue*, called Malatoxl, and check in for the night.

My streaming cold has intensified. I need medication and search out a pharmacist in the village. With the help of a dictionary, some body-language and a bit of acting, I try to make myself understood.

'*Aqui mal.*' I point to my nose and frown, trying to indicate that my nose is a problem. '*Este tableto?*' I hope the pharmacist will understand I need some tablets to stop the water streaming from my nose.

Smiling and patient, the indulgent pharmacist appears to ask if my throat is also a problem.

'*Throat peceno, nose mucho.*' I gesture *little* with my fingers towards my throat and make a *large* sign towards my nose. The pharmacist seems to understand that my throat is only a little problem but my running nose is a much bigger problem. The pharmacist supplies me with tablets and explains in Spanish with lots of hand-gestures, how to take the tablets. I take the medicine and leave.

What a kind and understanding lady. She put up with my abuse of her language and solved my problem too.

Late in the afternoon, a German girl in her twenties arrives in the *Albergue* to share my dormitory. We dine together and exchange business cards before we retire to our bunks for a hot and restless night.

The roasting night heralds a searing dawn. I set out as soon as night's intense black grip relinquishes its power to morning's light. Even so, many pilgrims had already left the refuge when I rise. Afraid of not being able to find path-markers in the blackness and wandering lost in the wrong direction; I prefer to wait until morning's first light. Each morning, I walk in anticipation of the first glimpse of the sun peeping over the distant horizon. Slowly at first, its tendrils of light creep across waiting fields, then fingers of warmth caress my body as they race across the hillsides. It's a joy I look forward to every morning on the Camino.

Sharp rocks on the path leading out of Cirauqui test my tortured feet. I'm grateful for the support my boots give my ankles, but still they twist and roll as I pick my way carefully along the track. As my hips and feet scream with pain, I find, by focusing on the pleasures of the morning, listening to the rhythm of the universe, and swinging my hips in a salsa to that rhythm, I can tune out most of the pain–for the time being at least.

As the sun rises higher in the sky, summer's heat intensifies, notching the temperature higher and higher. The sun's ferocity burns through my hat and sucks the fluid from my body. Wetness trickles between my shoulder blades and soaks my shirt under the sticky backpack.

I reach Lorca in time for a late breakfast. A young man at the *Albergue* smiles as I approach, then steps forward and helps me remove my backpack.

'*Hola.*' He points to himself, 'Jose.' Then he indicates for me to share his table. I smile at his kindness and pull a chair up to his table.

'*Hola. Gracias,*' I thank him as I sit down. Then I point to myself and respond, 'Linda,' before I bend over and begin to take off my boots and socks.

'It helps to stop often.' He seems to want to chat. 'It's good to remove backpacks and shoes.'

'Yes, it's very good.' I'm relieved he speaks English. 'My feet are hot.'

'It's good to let the feet dry in the warm sun, it helps them to heal and helps stop blisters. Blisters come if the feet are wet,' Jose informs me.

We chat amiably over breakfast until I notice grey clouds gathering overhead. Fearing another storm, I excuse myself, hurriedly don my socks and boots, gather my backpack, farewell Jose, and leave.

The threatening clouds blow over without emptying their contents and my anxiety eases. It occurs to me that I'm terrified of getting caught in another storm.

What could happen? It's just a rain cloud. Why am I frightened of a storm?

'It's not a rational fear,' Marcus interrupts my thoughts. 'You've developed a storm phobia.'

My pace is excruciatingly slow, yet still the pain in my feet intensifies. I try hard to ignore it, but today my focus is lost. After five to six hours I can walk no further. I hobble into the World Heritage medieval town of Estella around lunch time, find the Municipal *Albergue* and in agony, check in.

I sit on my allotted bunk and pull off my boots and socks to reveal two deep-purple toes and a third raw toe; a skinless, oozing mess. I treat it and leave it uncovered to dry out, sliding my feet into a pair of sandals.

A sign on a wall states a backpack carrying service is available. I ask a volunteer at the *Albergue* to phone the carrying service for me and arrange for my backpack to be carried to the next refuge tomorrow. It's a relief to have no pack to carry the next day.

I hobble off to find a restaurant for lunch. Estella sits on the River Ega, with the Church of San Miguel set above the town on a hill. It's a pretty city and one I would have liked to share with Larry.

I know Larry would enjoy the long leisurely Spanish lunches too. A three-course lunch with a carafe of red wine is a Spanish tradition I'm delighted to be growing accustomed to. It adds a very pleasant dimension to my journey. A long slow lunch, followed by a siesta on a hot summer afternoon is most pleasurable. The Spanish tend to eat very late at night, far too late for an early rising pilgrim. By finding a small snack in the early evening I can go to bed early, as do the other pilgrims.

As I prepare for bed an Italian man two bunks away sits staring at me. He stares *so* brazenly for *so* long that it un-nerves me. I do my best to ignore him and after showering I settle down on my bunk to write my diary. The Italian's persistent gaze reminds me how vulnerable and alone I am in this foreign land. I turn my back on the Italian and try to focus on my writing. I wish Larry was with me, I want the security of his presence now. To ease the feeling I picture Larry wrapping his arms around me, making me feel safe. Comforted, I think about the things I still want to do in my life and begin writing a list of things to achieve. As I ponder my list Marcus interrupts my thoughts.

'It is better to have a dream and fail trying to achieve it rather than never trying because of fear of failure. You must accept that it is okay to fail. By trying, you allow yourself the opportunity of success. To deny yourself that opportunity would bring great sadness and lifelong regret.'

What you say makes a lot of sense, Marcus, but to have a dream and fail trying to achieve it, destroys the dream. I think that fear of failure, of losing the dream, is very powerful.

'Accept your fears, and do it anyway. If you fail, at least you've tried. To never try would be a greater shame and a life denied. To fail is to lose *nothing*. To never try is to lose *everything*. It is to lose your life's dreams.'

I run his words through my mind.

He's right. To never try would be a lifelong regret. I don't want to reach the end of my life and have regrets.

I look over my list again before tucking it into my backpack and lying down.

Regrets... I've had a few regrets over the years... not too many... I try to live my life without regret.

I mentally wander through events in my life before my thoughts turn once more to my family. I miss them deeply. It is hard being away from them. Even though I email them each evening and collect news from home, it doesn't ease the longing to be with them.

I wonder what they've been doing today? Their day will be over in Australia. Thank goodness for email. Still, it's not like speaking to them. I miss Larry and the girls so much. It is the early hours of the morning in Perth now. Too late—no, too early—for them; for me to phone them now. I'll phone them tomorrow. ET phone home.

I pull the sleeping sheet up to protect me from buzzing insects, imagine Larry beside me, mutter goodnight to him and drift off to sleep.

CHAPTER 12

Finding Healing Where You Seek It

IT'S BEEN TEN WEEKS NOW since the accident. I don't know how much longer I can take it. Constant pain enveloped my body and sapped my mental reserves.

'Go and see this lady,' one of my brothers-in-law insisted, as he scribbled her details on a piece of paper. 'She's a witch doctor. I don't know what she does, but it works. We use her all the time. She's very busy though, it can take two months to see her.'

'Is she a kinesiologist?' I asked.

'Yes, that's it! Kinesiology. Hocus-pocus stuff if you ask me, but it works.'

I recalled his words with a smile. I'd often been to kinesiologists in the past and not always found them effective. My brother-in-law was not a spiritual person; he was very black and white, very stick-to-the-facts, if he believed in this lady then she was undoubtedly very good. But I was afraid to have anyone touch my back. I needed certainty I could trust her not to hurt me further.

I looked around for Marcus. I was alone. I meditated and focused my mind, taking myself upward to the *Godzone*—the place where communication with Spirit Masters is possible. When I reached the *Godzone* I approached the Spirit Masters.

'Should I see this kinesiologist that has been recommended to me?' I asked them. 'Will she be able to do anything for me?'

'There are many pathways to a destination. Your journey is to read the signposts and make your own interpretations. There will be many helpers along the way; each will have something to offer you. Take from each what you need and give back where you are able. All souls give and receive in the ebb and flow of Universal energy. You will find healing where you seek it.'

I decided I had nothing to lose and booked an appointment straight away. I waited two months for the appointment.

I don't know what she can do to help me, I thought as I entered her waiting room. *But I'm prepared to try anything. I'm prepared to do whatever it takes to get back to normal – whatever normal will end up being.*

'What is it you want to get out of this session with me?' the lady asked.

What a strange question. I thought about it a moment. *I don't believe that kinesiology can 'fix' my back, but some relief from the pain would be welcome.*

'Pain relief.'

For one and half hours the kinesiologist worked on my damaged body.

'Now stand up and walk towards the door.'

As I walked to the door and back, I could barely believe what I experienced. A smile spread across my face.

'The pain's gone!' I was delighted.

For the first time in ten weeks, I was without pain. The pain stayed away for almost two weeks and those two weeks were wonderful.

I continued my visits to the kinesiologist every ten to twelve weeks; which was the earliest appointment available with her each time.

Twelve weeks passed. I'd settled into a routine of seeing Dr Derovi every month. At the next visit to Dr Derovi I had to decide about seeing the fusion specialist, Dr Wong. I'd put the decision off as I was strongly opposed to spinal operations unless they were an absolute last resort. I didn't feel I was at my "last resort," and I didn't want an operation on my spine. But, the neurosurgeon had said, if I still had lower back pain, then I must see the specialist for a decision on the operation.

'I'm still in a lot of pain, but I don't want the operation,' I told Dr Derovi.

'It might not be necessary, but it would be best for you to let the specialist make that decision.' Dr Derovi was understanding and tried to reassure me.

He wrote a referral for me to take to the fusion doctor.

'I'm still getting over you telling me, on my last visit, that I'm obsessive compulsive,' I began, as he handed me the letter. 'I walked out of your surgery with visions of Jack Nicholson skipping down the footpath dodging the lines of the pavers, in the movie *As Good as it Gets*.'

'That was an extreme example of obsessive compulsion,' Dr Derovi smiled. 'It's a continuum that we are all on. Some people never achieve anything in their lives, they have no drive, and they're at one end of the continuum. The range then goes through the majority of people sitting somewhere in the middle, through to high achievers like you and me. We need to have a degree of obsessive compulsive nature to get things done and achieve as much as we do. Then it goes through to the extreme where it becomes a disorder, like the character Jack Nicholson played.' He was grinning widely now, as he explained.

'I'm obsessive compulsive. That is why I can recognise it in you. We have to be a little *obsessive compulsive* to be good at what we do.'

'Well, you had me really worried,' I grinned.

'It's not a problem for you, it's a good thing.' Dr Derovi chuckled.

I felt a lot happier as I left his surgery.

I need to build my argument now, against having the operation, ready to present to the fusion doctor.

Two weeks had passed since Dr Derovi had told me that I could start to get out of bed on my own and walk around a little without assistance. But I was still not able to do it. I was frustrated that I still needed assistance. Then stubbornness, fierce independence, and a reluctance to ask for help–unless avoidable–led me to make a very stupid decision.

I decided I would just do it. I'd go ahead and get out of bed, alone. I rolled myself over to the edge of the bed and, rigid in the metal brace, tried to swing myself into an upright position. I couldn't get my balance. The room tilted sideways. I reached out to grab the table in front to steady myself, but couldn't reach. Falling sideways, I tried to grab a chair to save myself but I missed the chair and toppled sideways. Crashing through a second chair, I hit the floor with a thud. Wedged on my side against a cupboard I was unable to move. My arm was pinned beneath me exactly as I'd landed at the time of the accident. Frightened I'd done more damage, I tried to roll over and get off my trapped arm. I needed to get some sort of leverage to roll myself back. But I couldn't budge. I was stuck.

'Serena!' I yelled.

Sobbing with self-pity, frustration and pain all rolled into one, I needed my daughter to help me. There was no response.

'Serena!'

Serena came running.

'Oh no!' The sight of a crumpled weeping ragdoll mother wedged against a cupboard on the floor frightened Serena.

Uncontrollable sobs shook my body as Serena carefully lifted me up and helped me back to bed. I had hit emotional rock-bottom. *It was the end. I couldn't continue. It was too hard.* I couldn't even try at that moment to mask my despair from my little girl. *I'd reached the gates of hell.*

'Oh, mum!' Serena held me in her arms on the bed and let me weep.

The next morning I was too afraid to try to get out of bed. Marcus was standing in the doorway watching me. He smiled and nodded as I stirred, then walked towards my bed and sat down next to me.

'Good morning, Linda.'

'Good morning, Marcus.' Memories of the previous day flooded back. Sick heavy despair pulsed through me like a living creature.

'Marcus, what am I to do?'

'Linda, be gentle with yourself. You always push yourself. Ask too much of your body and judge yourself too harshly. Nurture yourself, Linda, with the same love and understanding you give to others. Be kind to yourself, and then *surrender* to the Universe.'

'That is easy to say, Marcus, but hard to do. I don't know that I'd ever be able to ease back. I always have to push.'

'Take a step back and look at yourself. See where you've pushed yourself to at this moment.' He stood, his face glowed with love as he smiled and walked out of the room.

Serena brought my breakfast and propped me up against a wedge pillow, then left the room. I lay there until mid-morning when the phone rang. It was Eddy. He asked a question about a computer program he was having a problem with. I needed to have my laptop open with the program running in front of me to be able to talk Eddy through it.

'Give me fifteen minutes, I'll get myself out of bed, put the computer on, and talk you through it on the intercom.' I'd committed myself to get out of bed. It was the incentive I needed.

Pushing aside the fear, I edged my legs gently to the side of the bed. Easing around from the propped position on the pillow I slowly and carefully pushed myself upright. I was wobbly, but carefully shuffled to the table, took my laptop and then worked through the computer problem with Eddy. Pleased with myself, I was unaware of the dark gloom that lurked beneath the surface.

Now that I'm up I could have a shower. I haven't had a proper wash for a few days. I think I should be able to do it alone now. I'll put myself in the shower chair.

Once the water temperature was nicely warm, I carefully removed my metal brace, lowered myself into the shower chair and surrendered to the soothing cascade. As the water coursed over my body the warmth seeped deep inside. It penetrated my bones, and drew something up that I'd suppressed deep inside. It exploded to the surface in a dirge of wailing tears. A torrent of raw emotions rose to the surface and then gushed out. *Self-pity, frustration, pain, incompetence.* When the grieving was spent I turned the shower off and dried myself, dressed and then climbed back into bed.

When I woke the next morning I felt different. *I felt great.* It wasn't a physical improvement it was a mental one. It was as though the desolation and despondency that had been pent up inside me had been purged and a heaviness had lifted. I felt capable of dealing with life again; lightness replaced gloom and a sense of calm had returned.

Holidays were over and Serena had returned to school. A blue wren tapped at my window as Marcus walked into my room.

'Good morning. The world seems brighter today, Marcus, I think I've turned another corner.'

He radiated understanding, his lined old face a portrait of love. 'Nurture yourself, Linda. You ignore your own needs, you must acknowledge your needs in order to restore your soul and replenish your reserves. Remember to nurture yourself, Linda.' Then he was gone again.

I thought about his words for several minutes.

Nurture myself? I'd been 13 weeks in this bed. I felt scruffy. I need a haircut and colour.

I picked up the phone and booked an appointment with my hairdresser, Howie, who always made me laugh. I asked Art to drive me to town that afternoon for the appointment. Howie, though, was full of his own problems and I returned home feeling lower than when I left.

Thursday was the day of the appointment with the fusion specialist. Art drove me to the doctor's rooms and did his best to calm and reassure me. I was anxious about the visit. I feared I'd be told that I needed to have the operation. I armed myself with Sarah Key's book, *Back in Action*. I was prepared to argue against having the operation. I wanted to try every possible natural alternative first rather than have surgery on my back.

But there was no need to worry or protest. The specialist, Dr Reid, was sympathetic and understanding.

'In my opinion, fusion operations should only ever be an absolute last resort. We should try all other means first, such as hydrotherapy and physiotherapy, to see if we can solve the problem.'

My relief was audible as I exhaled the tension from deep within.

'I can see, though, that you are still traumatised by the accident,' he added.

I was too relieved about not needing the operation to be annoyed by that "T" word again.

Larry, who'd been away for three weeks, arrived home just after midnight. I told him about my wailing outburst in the shower and about the visit to Dr Wong and Dr Reid, saying I didn't need the operation. I was babbling.

'Perhaps you should get the book on trauma that Dr Derovi told you to read,' Larry broached the subject gently.

'Maybe you're right. Maybe I should. I cry on and off all day now for no apparent reason. Can't seem to stop. The grief doesn't seem to be in my head. It feels like it's in my gut. If it was in my head, I could switch it off and switch on some positive mental attitude, but I can't do that. *I'm a weeping wreck; a complete emotional mess.* I've reached rock bottom, all over again. Yes, okay, I'll get the book.'

Friday was the day of Trudy's funeral. I was determined to attend even though I knew it would be too much for me. It was important for me to pay my respects to Trudy. It was the same week I had the accident that Baxter rang me in hospital, telling me that Trudy had a stroke. Now, within thirteen weeks, she was gone. Trudy's death confused me. I was deeply saddened she'd lost her battle and at the same time I felt guilty to still be here when she wasn't. It seemed a signal for me to keep fighting.

Marcus was standing looking out of the window across the valley.

'Marcus.' He turned and walked towards my bed.

'Marcus, why do I have such conflicted emotions about Trudy's passing?'

'Each soul's journey is unique. Where the journey ends is not for you to know. Each soul travels its own pathway. Your journey continues. You have much to do.'

'But why do I have feelings of guilt, Marcus?'

'Each soul chooses its own time to begin and its own time to leave, what lessons it wishes to learn and the type of life it will lead. One soul's journey is linked to those of the souls around them. Your journey is not yet over. You still have much to do.'

Then he left. I still didn't understand why I had feelings of guilt, but knew I would get no further explanation from Marcus for now.

The long drive in my tiny sports car was excruciatingly painful. The seats were not designed for a driver with a back injury. I'd made a couple of short drives on my own in the past two weeks, but this long drive was just too much. I knew it, but I was determined to go to Trudy's funeral. Leaning on the walking-frame for support, I dragged and pushed myself into the crowded little church. Pains shot like hot and cold arrows through my ever-suffering body. The service, a moving celebration of Trudy's life, drained me so totally that I felt faint with the effort to stay upright. As soon as the service ended I made my way through the crowd to Baxter, offering him my condolences at Trudy's passing.

Then I struggled back to my car. Close to collapse when I arrived home, I climbed into bed, took painkillers and sank into a black oblivion of *cold searing pain.*

CHAPTER 13

The "Mad Hatter" Frenchman

Estella to Los Arcos

MORNING LIGHT OF DAY NINE on the Camino plays across my eyelids, coaxing them open. In semi-wakefulness I remember the staring Italian of the previous night and without lifting my head wait for the sounds that indicate he's gone before I get out of bed.

The municipal refuge in Estella, unlike most refuges, provides a pilgrim breakfast. At €3.50, the dry bread, jam and coffee is excellent value and the breakfast room buzzes with noisy pilgrims enjoying a rare communal meal.

Great, I have a chance to break bread with fellow travelers this morning. I do miss my normal breakfast of fruit and yoghurt though. From this evening onwards, I'll buy fruit and yoghurt each evening at an "Alimentacion" store for the next morning's breakfast. That way I can set out early each day and eat my breakfast of choice on the road.

I'm pleased that I'm beginning to learn how to manage my life on the Camino.

It's still dark as; with breakfast finished I go outside to find the bag-carrying service Jacotrans' trailer. I've got the numbers of the combination padlock to open the trailer and deposit my bag. The trailer is outside the refuge, but someone has placed the padlock on upside down. There isn't enough room to turn the padlock over and it's too dark to see the numbers on the underside, so I can't open the lock.

A Frenchman, seeing me struggling, comes to my rescue. I explain to him that I can't turn the lock over, or see the numbers to open it, and I need to put my bag inside. He twiddles the numbers on the combination lock until it opens.

'*Merci.*' I thank him.

'You're welcome. *Bon Camino.*'

As I put my pack in the trailer, I feel slightly concerned about the reliability and security of this service, especially as it seems that everyone using it is given the combination to the lock. Yet I've not heard any bad rumours about the service, so feel I should trust that my pack will be at the next refuge when I arrive.

I close the lid of the trailer and slide the combination numbers around a few times. I ask my Spirit guides to take care of my pack and head off into the still quiet blackness of pre-dawn.

It's cool and crisp with a freshness in the air; a great morning for walking. Ahead of me on the route out of town is a Spanish woman who has lost the trail at an intersection. She is standing–puzzling–trying to find the Camino-markers to show which road to take. I catch up to her and–like a pair of sniffer dogs around the intersection–we search together.

'*Aqui.*' I signal to the woman that I'd found the marker and we set off again. In the darkness it's difficult to see the markers, so we stay close to each other, walking in silence. Twice in the next hour we lose the trail leading out of Estella and sniff around until one of us finds a marker, calls to the other, *aqui*, and we set off together again.

An hour and a half after leaving the *Albergue*, as I'm passing a camp site, nature calls. I go into the camp office and ask for the *servicios*.

'*Non abri.*' Not open, an unfriendly caretaker informs me. I give him a pained expression, clutch my belly and bend over, acting out how desperate I am to go to the toilet.

'*Abrir nuevo hora.*' Open at nine o'clock, he indicates, pointing to his watch.

Miserable sod. I turn and make my way back out of the campsite. *Fine, I'll have to foul the countryside! Did he care about the countryside, or prefer that pilgrims fertilised it?*

I head off to a clump of bushes by the track to relieve myself. I carry a stash of rolled-up toilet paper in my panties for emergencies such as this; it's handier, I've learned, than fossicking through my backpack. When I emerge from the bushes, no other pilgrim is in sight; the Spanish lady has disappeared over the horizon.

She must be far ahead by now. It's daylight anyway, so we no longer need each other for security or company to find the markers.

A few kilometers further on I come upon a pilgrim resting against a boulder under a small spindly tree by the roadside. It's Toni, the New Zealander I met at Cirauqui.

'*Hola*, Linda,' Toni calls and waves cheerily as I approach.

I squat beside Toni and we chat for a few minutes before I continue on, leaving her resting in her tiny piece of sparse and dusty shade.

By late morning the heat is blistering and a toe on my right foot is throbbing excruciatingly. The instep on my left foot, where I was later to find out I'd broken a bone on day one, feels as though burning knives are tearing through it at every jarring step.

I need to take my boots off and rest my feet but I'm passing through a barren treeless stretch of countryside and there's nowhere shady to rest. I've no choice but to carry on.

It's almost noon on the hot open plain when I reach a shady tree-lined creek. Its grassy dappled banks look very inviting as it meanders–snaking through the dry plain. I head for a shady spot on the bank and drop my waist-bag and camera in the dry grass. It's a relief to lower my aching body to the ground and pull off my boots and socks. Lying flat on my back in the grass with my feet freed is pure bliss. I inspect my wounds and massage the soreness.

A cluster of vultures, drift lazily, high overhead. I lay and watch their circuitous journey. They look so peaceful hovering, seemingly aimless dark spots in a clear blue sky. I envy their serene manner of travel. Soft white clouds compete with the black vultures for floating space.

Other walkers approach the creek in pairs. They too are enticed away from the dry scorching track to the cool allure of the shaded river bank. Soon there are four of us, all women, lying on the dry grassy bank. We shelter in the sparse shade, boots off, packs off, enjoying some respite from the stifling midday sun.

'That looks like a great idea,' I hear someone say, as footsteps approach. I lift my hat off my face and look up. It's Toni. She grins as she drops her pack on the grass, pulls off her boots and socks, and collapses beside me. We chat briefly then lay silently watching the white clouds skidding across the sky and the vultures circling on updrafts. The reprieve from plodding the dusty track beneath the scorching sun is heavenly. Then there is silence, as all we five women on the shady oasis, drift in and out of peaceful exhausted slumber.

All too soon, the white clouds are replaced by threatening grey clouds, and the dark intensity rapidly deepens. The wind picks up, rushing over and waking us. We sit up.

'Looks like rain.'

'Yes. We should get going.' Toni reaches for her boots. 'We should try to get to Los Arcos before it rains.'

We pull on our socks and boots, gather up our backpacks, dust off our trousers, and stride off quickly, hoping to avoid being caught in a downpour. The dark and ominous clouds pass overhead without emptying their loads. They leave behind instead, a light blanket of cloud that shades us from the strong sun. Along with a cooling breeze our journey becomes a great deal more bearable. Los Arcos is visible in the distance when a motor home pulls alongside Toni and me. The driver puts his head out of the window.

In a strong French accent, he asks, "ave you seen a man sitting on the side of the Camino, 'e cannot walk? I was told 'e was 'ere, somewhere, and needed 'elp. 'ave you seen him? Do you know where 'e is?'

The driver is Hemingway. I'm delighted to meet him again.

'Hello there, it's my friend from Roncesvalles. It's good to see you again. Toni, this man was like an angel who came to my rescue in Roncesvalles. There was a terrible storm on the mountain the day before; I hurt my back and feet in a fall and could barely walk. He organised a taxi to take me to Pamplona where I rested for a couple of days.'

'Hello, very nice to meet you, I'm Toni.'

"ello.'

'No, we haven't seen anyone sitting by the roadside. Sorry! We've seen a lot of pilgrims limping, but everyone has been mobile.'

'Bon, 'e must be walking. Then you will share tea with me, non? And a piece of cake for two weary pilgrims?'

'Fantastic!' Toni responds enthusiastically.

Hemingway pulls his motorhome off to the side of the road and jumps out. He pulls out two folding chairs, indicates for us to sit and disappears inside his van. When he reappears he has a small folding table that he opens and carefully places in front of us. Then he disappears inside his van again, talking constantly as he goes. He rushes out, spreads a clean white table cloth on the table and bustles off again.

I smirk at Toni. It's rather odd, sitting at a table with a tablecloth, at the Camino edge, waiting while a strange man makes us tea. Toni grins back.

In a few minutes Hemingway appears again carrying a tray with three cups of tea and a plate of cake, all of which he places carefully on the table in front of us.

'Eat, 'ave some cake, you need to keep your strength on the Camino.' He offers the plate to Toni.

'Thank you very much, this looks wonderful.' Toni takes a slice and closes her eyes in pleasure as she bites into the moist chocolate slice.

He offers it to me. 'No, thank you very much. I'm fine. I'm sorry, I can't take sugar.' I'm embarrassed that I can't accept his cake.

He takes a piece himself, sits down, hungrily munches on the cake, and asks me, 'Where's your backpack?'

'My back and feet were aching. I arranged a carrier at Estella to take my pack to Los Arcos for me.'

'Who did you use?' Concern showed on his face and in his voice.

'Jacotrans.'

'You 'ave to be careful with your pack. You shouldn't let it out of your sight. There are many thieves around.'

'They sounded reputable.'

'I've 'eard of them. But even so, you can't be too careful.'

I nod knowingly and catch sight of Toni smirking at me as I sip my tea. The curious circumstances amuse us; if a talking white rabbit in a vest had hopped past, it would have completed the illusion of *Alice in Wonderland*.

Is this the Mad Hatter that we are supping with?

'I'll carry your pack for you, if you like,' Hemingway suggests to Toni. 'I'm going to Los Arcos. You can take it from me when you get to the village. It's easier to walk without a pack. Much better for your back, you can walk faster too.'

Toni accepts and hands over her pack to the stranger. 'Thank you so much. Where will I meet you?'

'I'll meet you at the *Albergue*. I'll park out front. I know the manager there. I'll ask 'im where the Jacotrans trailer is parked. 'e'll know.'

I bristle, piqued at his presumption of taking charge of locating my pack. 'I was told the trailer would be outside the *Albergue*.'

He brushes aside my annoyance. 'I'll 'ave a look and find it before you get into the village.'

It doesn't sit well with me, but I override my irritation, as it's not worth spoiling a great day over. It is, however, the first sign of trouble and I *should* have taken notice of my instincts regarding this "Mad Hatter".

'Off you go then, I'll see you in Los Arcos.' He throws the pack in the back, climbs into his van and starts up the engine. The van kicks up sharp pieces of creamy grey gravel as the wheels bite for traction amongst the powder and stones.

'It's wonderful to walk without a pack,' says Toni. 'I feel so light.'

I grin at my new friend. 'Where did you start walking the Camino?'

'Le Puy. You?'

'St. Jean Pied de Port.'

Light and gay, without the burden of our packs, we enjoy the novelty of having someone to share the adventure with. We stroll off happily, powdered dust rising as we amble along. We share stories for the last few kilometers until walking into Los Arcos.

We've barely entered the village when Hemingway rushes toward us, waving his arms in the air, his brow is creased in worry. We stop and stare at him.

'There's no Jacotrans trailer outside La Fuente *Albergue*.'

My heart hits my belly with a thud and my gut churns anxiously.

'I've been looking everywhere for the trailer. It's not in the village.'

Annoyance that he's overstepping the boundary rises again; I hadn't asked him to hunt out my pack. Anxiety gnaws in my gut. Now my pack is missing. Or is he over-reacting? He's flustered and fussing and I can't think clearly with him babbling at me. I need to be able to think logically. I want to tell him to "shut up" but that would be unkind. He is, after all, only trying to help. I hold up my hand for him to stop.

'I was told to ask at La Fuente *Albergue* for my pack,' I say slowly, thinking through the situation. 'That is what I'll do.'

'I've had a look in the *Albergue*,' he rushes. 'There's no packs inside.' He's clearly agitated but I don't want to buy into his stress. I need a clear head to think through a solution. Again I hold up my hand for him to stop chattering. Unspeaking, I head towards the door of the *Albergue*. He steps in front of me, wringing his hands. 'I've had a look in there. There's no packs there.'

Struggling to keep myself from taking on his anxiety, I give him a look that implies, *I'll deal with this,* and walk around him and inside the *Albergue*. Striding with a confidence I don't feel, I walk up to the manager's desk.

What will I do if my pack has indeed gone missing? One thing at a time, Linda, I tell myself.

'Jacotrans have carried my pack,' I tell the manager behind the counter. 'They told me to collect it here.' I force my voice to sound calm as I feign a smile to the man at the desk.

All the packs are inside.' The smiling overseer guides me inside the *Albergue* dormitory to collect my pack. Relieved and annoyed that Hemingway had caused me to worry unnecessarily, I thank the overseer, don my pack and head back outside.

'It was inside,' is all I say to Hemingway and Toni who are waiting wide-eyed and anxious in the sun.

'I'll get your pack,' Hemingway says to Toni over his shoulder as he rushes off. 'It's in my auto.'

"As he disappears inside his motorhome, Toni and I roll our eyes at each other, silently conveying our incredulity at his over-reaction. His uncalled-for panic caused us to stress enormously. Hemingway emerges and runs towards us with Toni's pack in his hand. As he hands it to her he asks, "ave you seen Eunate Chapel?'

'I have,' Toni responds. 'I sang in it. *It's amazing!* It has the most fantastic acoustics.'

'The steep descent down the hill put me off,' I reply. 'My feet and hips couldn't handle it and I couldn't see how far away it was, so I didn't take the detour to the chapel.'

'It's a twelfth century Knights Templar chapel and well worth seeing. I can take you in my van to see it. I'm sorry, my name is Louis.' Hemingway extends his hand to me. 'It's far on foot, but quite close in a van. You shouldn't pass without seeing it. We can be back inside an hour.'

'It's certainly worth seeing,' agrees Toni. 'It's an amazing building, you should see it.' Toni kisses me goodbye and then with a cheery wave, she's gone.

A gnawing discomfort tugs in my belly at the thought of going off in this stranger's van. Besides, it doesn't seem right, getting into a car to go anywhere; I've come to Spain to walk this pilgrim trail. Toni has practically dropped me into seeing the chapel with this man.

Still, he helped me out in Roncesvalles and Toni did say I should see the chapel. I don't want to offend him. He has been kind. While my mind processes these thoughts my gut continues to churn.

'Okay, but I must be back here …' I began.

'Certainment,' he interrupts. 'We will look at the chapel and come straight back, if that is your wish.'

'Yes, thank you ...' I begin.

'Or, we can take a short detour to look at …' he cuts in, before I stop him.

'No! No detours. I want to come straight back to the *Albergue*.'

'Certainment. If that is your wish.'

'Yes. It is my wish. Thank you,' I respond curtly.

The chapel is further away than I thought it would be from Louis' description. He said it was close and yet it takes about twenty minutes to drive there.

It's a long way if I have to walk back.

The tiny stone chapel is nestled at the base of the hill.

Strange place to build a chapel. Churches are usually built on top of a hill, not at the foot of it.

It's octagonal with fine alabaster windows and ornately carved stone walls. It's surrounded by fields of tall, swaying, sunflowers whose golden full faces glow as they nod happily towards the sun. Louis pulls the van alongside the chapel and parks.

'Templar Knights on horseback used to ride around the outside of the chapel in worship. It saved them having to get off their horses,' he tells me.

I step through the arch onto the entry stone, worn deep by a million seekers footsteps. A mystic mantle of a thousand years of devotion permeates the sacred space. Despite the heavy heat outside, inside the chapel the air is light, crisp and cool. Silence rings in my ears. Awed, I move quietly to a worn dark wooden pew and sit down. Profound spirituality numbs and captivates me.

What sights have these ancient walls witnessed through the centuries?

A rapid fleeting movement near the altar distracts me. I look up just in time to see a spirit in a long faded fawn-coloured gown, scurry away.

Roused from my thoughts, I stand slowly and walk outside into the hot brilliant sunlight. It's past 2.00 pm, I'm hungry and keen to get back to the refuge. Louis is waiting at his van.

'I was just about to prepare a salad for lunch. I planned on lunch anyway and I 'ave plenty in the auto. Would you care to join me?' It's a statement more than an invitation as he's already set out one folding chair and is in the process of setting out a second.

I'm not comfortable with this. He's very presuming. I don't want to be in his debt. But he's already setting the table for two. I'm a long way from the refuge. Too far to walk to get back before nightfall. I've got no water or supplies with me. He has been kind, maybe this is just kindness.

'I really should get back to the refuge …'

'I'll take you back after lunch,' he cuts in. 'We eat first. Red or white?' He re-emerges from his van with a bottle of red wine held high in offering.

There's no point arguing, he's made up his mind we're eating here.

'Red. Thanks.' I sit down.

'Take your boots off, let your feet dry.'

I don't like him telling me what to do. Shall I refuse to take my boots off? Don't be silly, I am longing to get them off.

I bend over, unlace the boots and ease them off, releasing my sweaty, aching bruised and blistered feet to the soothing fresh dry air.

Aah, what a relief. Louis pushes a glass of red wine into my hand.

'Now, I'll just throw us some lunch together.' He disappears back into the motorhome singing as he busies himself inside.

How odd. I'm sitting here, sipping red wine while some strange man prepares my lunch.

I sip. *Spanish wine is excellent. I've not had a sub-standard red wine since I've come to Spain.* I take another sip. *Short of being rude, I've got no option other than to try to conceal my discomfort, relax and accept Louis' hospitality.* A few minutes later, Louis reappears with a fresh salad and a loaf of crusty bread. He sets everything on a little folding table next to the van and disappears inside the van again. He returns with a large bowl of warm salty water.

'Soak your feet in the water while you dine,' he instructs, laying the bowl at my feet before sitting down.

Crisp fresh lettuce, large plump sweet-tasting tomatoes, huge black succulent olives and slices of red onion dressed in a just-made olive oil and balsamic vinaigrette–it's outstanding. The crusty bread is a superb accompaniment to the meal. *The joy of Spanish red wine, apart from the excellent flavour, is that it can be consumed like water; half a bottle with a meal is a true pleasure. I can't drink Australian wine at midday like this; I'd be drunk on the second glass.*

The warm sun bathes the fields in a golden glow. A balmy wind tickles the faces of the thousands of sunflowers in the fields circling this holy site. Louis is a walking encyclopedia on the Camino. He relates its history and many stories of his experiences over lunch. Louis adds more boiling water to the foot bath to keep the water warm as we dine.

When lunch is over, he disappears inside the van. He reappears with a towel and kneels in front of me, then lifts my feet out of the water and to my deep embarrassment, dries them gently.

'I can show you another chapel,' he offers as he finishes drying my feet.

'No. Thanks, Louis. It has been a lovely lunch, but I need to get back to Los Arcos.' I pull my socks back on, slide my feet into my boots and tie the boot laces. 'I've not yet secured a bed at the refuge. I'm concerned that if I leave it much later, I may miss out.'

'I 'ave a spare bed in my auto. You may 'ave that,' he offers coyly.

'No. Thank you. I'd like to go back to Los Arcos now if you don't mind.' My gut churns. I think of Larry far away. *I wish he was here now.*

I stand and begin clearing away the lunch dishes. 'Shall I pop these inside the van?'

'Oui. Yes… please. Put them on the sink, I'll wash them later. Thank you.'

Louis packs away the chairs and the table. I take one last look at the rolling hills, at the million smiling sunflowers nodding farewell, I breathe deeply and suck in the peacefulness of this tranquil scene. Charming Eunate Chapel has planted its tendrils into my soul. I climb into the van. *Farewell dazzling sunflowers, farewell Eunate Chapel.*

Louis starts the engine, turns the van back up the hill and onto the main road towards Los Arcos.

It seemed so far on foot, yet it's so fast in a vehicle. The scenery rushes past. *We miss so much in a car. I can't see the tiny flowers on the side of the road, or feel the warmth of the breeze on my face. Walking is such a pleasant experience. Driving in a car is convenient, fast and easy. But my goodness, we miss such a lot in a vehicle.*

Louis interrupts my thoughts. 'The road from Los Arcos to San Sol is the beginning of a very difficult section of rocky hilly country that lasts some kilometres. It will be very 'ard on your back and your feet. I 'ave a recommendation. Tomorrow, I carry your pack in my auto to San Sol. You walk to San Sol with no pack. I will meet you there. Then I drive you through the rugged stretch. Once on the flat land again, you can walk again. It is best … because of your feet.'

His suggestion sounds reasonable; he knows the area very well. He's been very kind and gentlemanly. Perhaps I have been a bit paranoid about his intentions.

'Thank you, Louis, that's very kind of you. You obviously know the terrain ahead. If it's no problem for you to carry my pack, that'd be wonderful. Thank you.'

In no time we are back in Los Arcos.

'Thank you so much for lunch Louis, it was delicious and thank you for showing me Eunate Chapel. It's an incredible chapel. It's been a lovely day.'

'I'll make us dinner tonight in my auto …' he begins.

'No. Thank you, Louis. Eunate Chapel was amazing and lunch was fabulous. But no, thank you.' I clamber down from the cabin, open the rear door and gather my pack and poles from the van.

'Bye, Louis.' I wave him farewell, stride off and check in to the *refugio*.

I wish Larry, or one of the girls, was with me now. If they were with me, Louis would not have approached me and I wouldn't feel so vulnerable, or so frightened.

I look around at the small groups and couples in the *refugio* that evening. An ache for my family tightens inside as isolation and aloneness clouds thickly around me.

Make yourself busy, Linda. Shut out the loneliness.

Anxious to get my clothes washed and on a line quickly to allow time to dry I busy myself with my laundry. Line space is always at a premium at refuges, and pegs non-existent, so it's a competition to find the best spots for spreading clothes. The hope is always that they'll be dry by morning.

A pilgrim's evening routine involves: first of all securing a bunkbed in a *refugio* at the end of a day's walk, by spreading a sleeping bag on the selected bunk once registration has been completed; the next most important action is to shower away the day's sweat, then wash that day's clothes and hang them out to dry; finally it's finding a meal, or if there's a kitchen at the refuge, cooking one. All this should be done soon enough so that you can retire for the night before lock-out time at the *refugio*.

The dormitory is large and spacious and relatively quiet tonight. After washing I creep out of the refuge and, trying not to be seen by Louis, venture in the opposite direction of his van, then circle back into the village centre to find a restaurant to get a meal.

The restaurant is crowded with couples and families. Sitting alone in the restaurant I feel the intense pain of being separated from my family. I know it's exacerbated by my fear of Louis' attention. Thoughts of quitting the walk and going home haunt me. I push them aside.

Louis is just being friendly, I assure myself. *You're over-reacting. He is quite safe, stop worrying.*

By the time I leave the restaurant my loneliness has settled into a gloom. I head back towards the refuge. Louis' van is still parked out front. I circle around again, away from it, and surreptitiously slink back into the refuge to avoid him seeing my return.

Climbing onto the bunk, I slide into my sleeping bag. Miserable with loneliness and anxious about Louis' intentions, I pull the sleeping bag over my head, turn my face into my pillow and weep for Larry's company. I desperately want him with me and my thoughts again turn to giving up walking the Camino and going home. To soothe myself to sleep I imagine Larry by my side with his arms wrapped around me.

CHAPTER 14

Catching My Own Jumbo Jet

I RECALL THE MORNING BACK home four years ago, when fifteen weeks after the fall, in a state of fatigue, I welcomed dawn's light at the window as it brought with it a temporary end to the night's black dreams. Back then, nightmares had become a regular intrusion into the dark loneliness of sleep. *Vivid, heart-pounding, off-the-wall nightmares* plagued me; shaking me out of my slumber every night. That morning was no different. When I woke, Marcus was sitting nearby.

'Why am I having nightmares, Marcus?'

'You've suppressed your emotions, Linda. Denied your fears. They must be faced. They must be dealt with.'

'Oh Marcus, I'm too exhausted to do that now.'

Sixteen weeks after the accident I was beginning to become a little more mobile. I stubbornly refused to register for a disabled permit which would enable me to park close to the shop entrance. *I'm not disabled!* I retorted whenever anyone suggested I apply for one. The sharpness of my response discouraged friends and family from taking the conversation further.

Larry had arranged a treat; he'd bought tickets for the theatre. As we made our way there, Larry and Serena looped their arms into mine and side-by-side they helped me into His Majesty's Theatre in the city centre. Sitting was one of the most painful experiences. I carried my pillow with me wherever I went and used it either to sit on, or as a back support. I was aware I looked a bit of an oddity as I walked through the Perth city streets in a steel brace with a pillow tucked under my arm. But it was the only way

I could survive an outing. I was glad to be getting out of the house and it felt wonderful to be experiencing city life again. With Larry and Serena's support I held my head high and delighted in the sights, sounds, smells, and the cool wind on my face as we made our way to the theatre. I reveled in the colour and gaiety of the shop windows and the laughter of people passing by on their way to their big night out. It was my big night out too and I smiled with pleasure.

The following Monday I had my next monthly appointment with Dr Derovi.

'It's time to start doing some hydrotherapy,' he told me as he wrote out a referral to a physiotherapist.

I left his surgery elated to be able to start doing something constructive to repair my body. Commencing hydrotherapy would be another step on the journey back to normality; the very thought supercharged me.

I was so excited at the prospect of making progress that I thought I could start trying to do something useful around the house too.

I'll have a go at doing some cooking.

But I didn't have the strength to stand long enough to stir a pot and had to sit down. While I was sitting, the saucepan boiled over and somehow the cooktop exploded–bursting into flames. I managed to douse the flames with water but there was mess all over the oven, the wall and the floor. I wiped at what I could reach; but unable to bend or stretch, had to leave the mess on the floor and the walls. The kitchen was blackened and mucky and I couldn't do anything about it. Frustrated, disappointed, and annoyed at the mess I'd caused, I dropped my head into my hands and burst into tears.

I am useless! I sobbed to myself. *This is a pattern, I cry all the time. I can't cope with anything, I'm a wreck, an emotional mess.*

I went back to bed and lay sobbing–miserable, sorry for myself and frustrated. My morning high had quickly evaporated. A grey blanket of depression settled over me; suffocating and pushing me down. It pinned me to the bed and held me prisoner in my room. When night came, the blanket gave way once more to tormenting nightmares that plagued me with their horror.

'Marcus, tell me what to do?' I wept into my pillow, not listening for an answer.

Two days later I started hydrotherapy and mentioned the nightmares to the physiotherapist.

'They're typical PTSD, Post Traumatic Stress Disorder.'

There's that 'trauma' word again! Everyone keeps saying that 'trauma' word to me. I don't like it.

The twenty-five minute round trip three times a week to the physiotherapist was agony. But I was determined to do whatever it took to get well again and I could drive myself now, although maybe not legally. I had to reaffirm myself every morning that the hydrotherapy was doing some good, because the effort of pushing through the pain barrier to reach the pool drained me totally.

The water in the physiotherapist's pool felt hot when I first stepped into it but after a few minutes of working my way through the exercises, it seemed only tepid. The warmth of the water, the soothing buoyancy and its gentle resistance gave mild relief from the pain. I drove my body up and down the pool carrying out the prescribed exercises. At the end of the hour my legs were heavy as I climbed out of the water. I picked my way cautiously over the slippery floor tiles to the dressing room, robotically dressed and strapped myself back into the steel brace before carefully making my way outside and easing my body into the tiny car for the excruciating drive home.

Once home I took extra painkillers and slid wearily back into bed. That was my routine three times a week. I always needed more painkillers after a visit to the hydrotherapy pool.

Seventeen weeks after the accident a new agony began. My teeth began to ache, not one or two, but all of them. I changed my toothbrush to a new soft one. I bought Listerine to gargle with, but found it too painful to gargle. Nothing seemed to help. My whole mouth throbbed so much that the pain in my mouth took over and dominated every waking moment. I wanted to cry but tears wouldn't flow. I was fed up with everything–*myself, my relationship, the pain, my life.*

'Help me, Marcus. Tell me what to do?'

'Linda, this is just another part of your journey. It'll pass with time. There's something else for you to consider. The issues that confront you, puzzle Larry; he struggles to comprehend your highs and lows. Each day seems to present a new challenge in his eyes. Just when he thinks he's beginning to comprehend what's happening to you, a new issue arises and he feels lost once more. He doesn't know how to react to it or what to say to you. Be clear with him, Linda. Be clear what it is you need and what it is you want from him.'

When Larry returned home I told him I felt he'd been avoiding and neglecting me, that I felt deeply hurt by his actions and that I wanted him to talk to me. I needed to share my feelings with him and I wanted him to share his day with me.

'I am finding it very hard to cope, but I hadn't intended to avoid you, Linda. I just don't know how to deal with the situation.'

Larry made an extra effort to be present after that. He tried hard to understand and be loving and to give me what I needed.

'I just want life to return to normal, Larry.'

'Do you think you can manage a visit to the cinema? I could take you to see a movie.'

'I'd love to see a movie. I'll have to take a pillow to sit on. I'm not sure that I'll be able to sit through a whole movie, but I'd love to go out. Yes, let's give it a try.'

That week Larry took me to see James Bond in the movie *Die Another Day*, and it was just what I needed. It gave me another boost of inspiration to motivate myself. In the movie, Halle Berry chased a jumbo jet down a runway and jumped in the plane before takeoff. I'd read an article about how hard she'd had to train to be fit enough to play the role in the movie. As I watched Halle Berry chase that plane I promised myself that if Halle could get fit enough to chase a jumbo jet down a runway and jump in before takeoff, then I could get fit again too. As we drove home after the movie I told Larry my thoughts.

'Have you heard about computer enhancements in movies? She wouldn't really have chased a jumbo jet and jumped in. It was just a movie.'

'That's not the point. I know she trained very hard for that movie. Whether she chased and caught the jumbo jet, or not, is not the issue for me. If she can get fit enough to play that demanding role and appear to catch the jumbo jet, then I can get fit enough to lead a normal life again. I'm going to catch my own jumbo jet!'

Larry grinned, reached over and took my hand, and gave it a squeeze.

With each day that passed the pain in my teeth increased until I could no longer eat. Even something soft like a banana was agony. I couldn't drink room temperature water without the ache growing greater. I woke one morning crying with the pain.

'Well, go and see a dentist!' Larry was exasperated with me again.

'I can't stand the pain any longer. I can't eat, I can't drink. It's not temperature related,' I explained to the dentist.

He looked at my teeth and took some x-rays.

'Your teeth are fine. There's nothing wrong with them.'

'What's causing the pain?'

'The nerve endings in your teeth are being aggravated by the spinal injury. There's really nothing that can be done about it.'

My mood plummeted as I left the surgery.

The pain is seriously getting me down. I can't take much more. I've had enough. My back aches, my neck hurts, my mouth is driving me nuts.

I climbed into my car, rested my forehead on the steering wheel and once again the tears flowed. Marcus appeared next to me in the car.

'What's happening to me, Marcus? Tell me what to do?'

'Linda, you must deal with this, you can't ignore it. Your doctor told you to read a book; find the book. It's time to act.'

OK. I admit the time's come. I need to find that book on trauma, Doctor Derovi told me to read. You're right. I need to know what I'm facing here and how to deal with it.

I wiped the tears from my face, started the car and drove home. Once home I switched my computer on and searched the web for the book while Marcus stood beside me and watched. I located a copy on the library database at Curtin University just as Art knocked on the front door.

'Hi, Linda, how you doing?'

'I'm a mental wreck, Art. My back aches, my neck aches, and now even my teeth hurt. I can't eat without pain, I can't drink without pain; yet the dentist said my teeth are fine. He said it's the nerve endings in my spine making my teeth ache, that there's nothing that can be done about it. *I'm a mess*! I need to get that book on PTSD that Dr Derovi told me to get and then decide what to do. *I'm falling apart!* I've just been on the internet tracking it down and Curtin University library has copies.'

'I'll go and get a copy for you, if you tell my where to go and what to do.'

Art is so kind. But he can't deal with crowds or crowded spaces; he leaves a party when more than a handful of people arrive. He's very sweet to offer but he'd never cope with the crowds at the university, he'll totally freak out. I can't do that to him, can't put him through that.

'Thanks, Art, but without knowing your way around campus, you'd never find the library, least of all the book.'

'How will you get the book then?'

We discussed the problem at length, trying to think of someone who knew their way around the University campus who could get the book. We couldn't think of anyone. We finally agreed that the only solution was for Art to take me to the campus and help me to the library to locate the book.

Art had never been to Curtin University, it was an entirely new experience for him. Once inside the library he paused to look around.

'Where are all the Australian students?' he whispered to me, awed by the unfamiliar surroundings. I looked around the library, trying to see it through his eyes. There were hundreds of multicultural students sitting in the café and filing in and out of the library. We were the only Caucasians in sight. Art had never been in a situation where, as an Australian in his homeland, he was in the minority. To answer his question, I pointed to myself.

'Here.'

Art smiled at the joke. 'Don't Australian students study at Uni anymore?'

'I think foreign students are far more committed to put in the extra effort than Australian students. Foreign students have more expectations placed on them to do well, by their families back home. They seem to spend a lot more time in the library than most Aussie students. Their diligence puts us to shame.'

We reached the area of the library I was looking for. Apart from the one book that Dr Derovi had recommended, I selected an additional five books, all on Post Traumatic Stress Disorder. On the way back to the car, delighted with my find, I showed Art the books.

'Look, I found six books on PTSD!' He smiled as he took them to carry for me.

I chattered away excitedly as he helped me walk back to the vehicle.

'Dr Derovi said that once I've read the book I'd be able to figure out how to deal with it. He knows me, knows my personality. He knows I need all the facts. He said I'm obsessive compulsive.' I stopped in midsentence and gasped.

'Oh dear!'

'What's wrong?' Art looked worried.

'Maybe that's being obsessive compulsive!'

'Maybe what's being obsessive compulsive?' Confusion masked Art's face.

'Getting six books instead of one. Maybe that's being obsessive compulsive. The doctor told me to get one and read it—I got six! *Oh dear!* Maybe that's what he means. I couldn't just get one, I had to get six. *Oh no!*'

'It's okay. It doesn't matter; one book or six. It doesn't matter, don't worry,' Art tried to reassure me.

'You're right. There's no point in stressing. I just need to read them all and figure out what on earth's happening to me, and how to deal with it.'

Art drove me home and after he left I settled back into bed and began reading the tomes. Eddy came in and I told him about my trip to the university; how I'd selected six books and then fretted that it might've been a sign of being obsessive compulsive. Eddy grinned and then took pity on my stressed state.

'Would you like me to do some reflexology? It might help ease the pain and maybe help you relax a little?'

'Eddy, you're a star. You've got healing hands, I could never turn down an offer of reflexology.'

'I know,' Eddy grinned and settled down to work on my feet.

I relaxed immediately and he worked on every painful problem point until the tension released and the pain dissolved. The session eased both my pain and stress.

I finished reading all the books and wrote a summary of what I'd learnt about PTSD.

- Trauma is cumulative.
- Trauma must be acknowledged and permitted to be felt.
- Trauma must be discussed and the sooner the better.
- Trauma affects the whole family and loved ones and this must be acknowledged, permitted, and discussed. Everyone around the person involved is affected by the trauma in some way.
- It must not be swept aside and people must not be told things like, "put it behind you and move on", "put it out of your mind" or "get yourself together".
- Unresolved trauma can manifest in many ways: physical and emotional illness, nervousness, irritability, anger, confusion, insomnia, nightmares, restlessness, feelings of vulnerability, etc.
- Everyone involved needs to sit down together and discuss their own feelings honestly; by airing their feelings they can release them.
- It is alright to admit feelings of anger, in fact it is advisable to admit whatever feelings are felt. When the feelings being experienced are acknowledged they are not internalised: they are released.

I put my notes down and thought through what I'd learnt and how it related to me.

I've had many traumas over the years. I simply buried them and got on with life. I thought it was weak to dwell on problems and therefore didn't talk to anyone about them. Now I see that I hadn't dealt with them at all; they sat beneath the surface simmering all this time—until now.

I've been in denial. I was traumatised; angry and frustrated with myself for being in this situation. I haven't been dealing with the pain, even though I tell myself and everyone around me I'm coping. I'm not! I'm not coping! I'm denying it. That's not coping.

I resent Larry for not being more supportive yet I'm not giving him the understanding he needs either. He's suffering too. He's been affected by my disability and I'm not making allowances for that. The accident didn't just happen to me, it happened to my whole family. Everyone's been affected by it.

We've never sat down and talked about how we all feel. We've talked about coping mechanisms, but we haven't talked about any emotional issues. I've been thoughtless and selfish thinking that I'm the only one affected.

I crossed the eighteenth week off my calendar; as if by scratching that week out could erase all the mistakes I'd made, and I resolved to try and talk about feelings with those around me.

My routine of hydrotherapy sessions three times a week continued. I enjoyed the way the warmth penetrated and coaxed muscles to relax. I worked my way, almost trance-like, up and down the pool, taking temporary relief from the intense pain. A young female physiotherapist had taken over supervision of my routine.

'You do understand, Linda, that once you have *recovered* from this, the management of your back will be a lifetime commitment. If you don't keep up the exercises, it will all *lockup* again. You'll need to take up swimming, every week for the rest of your life, to maintain mobility.'

Her words shattered me.

I'd set myself a goal of doing everything I could to get back to *normal*. I'd not dreamed that I'd have to keep up the grueling routine for the rest of my life.

That night, I crumbled. 'I can't deal with it any more–*I've had enough!*' I buried my face in my pillow and wept. Once my tears were spent I lay thinking of my dilemma.

I need to control these feelings of having had enough and not being able to deal with things. Dr Derovi, the neurosurgeon, the physiotherapist, all told me. They said I'm traumatized; suffering Post Traumatic Stress Disorder. Now that

I've read the books I understand they're right. I've been in denial all along. I need a resolution.

I drift into a troubled sleep. Night was once again filled with monsters, demons, and people chasing me–trying to kill me.

Sunday's clear blue sky hinted at summer's approach. Cheeky pink and grey galahs chased a flock of white cockatoos, as they circled overhead. I could get myself in and out of the car and drive a short distance, but the pain was always excruciating.

Coming home from hydrotherapy along the near deserted freeway, my thoughts turned momentarily to the naughty galahs. When I glanced back to the dials in front of me, the car's temperature gauge was up too high.

It's overheating! Oh damn!

I pulled off the freeway, got out of the car, rang for roadside assistance, and then burst into tears. I stood shaking and distraught on the roadside waiting for help to arrive.

I wish this problem would just vanish; I can't deal with this, can't handle it!

When assistance arrived, the mechanic looked under the bonnet of my car, only to re-emerge minutes later shaking his head.

'Did you stop straight away?' A strangling lump in my throat prevented me from speaking; I nodded instead. He shook his head again and looking at the ground to avoid meeting my tear-filled eyes. 'The head-gasket might be damaged. It's going to cost a fortune to fix. You will need a tow truck to tow the car away. I can call one now for you and give you the paperwork …' he was still talking but I didn't hear any more.

I want to walk away from it all, leave the car and forget about it. I ring Celeste.

'My car's broken down,' is all I managed to get out before I started sobbing again.

'Where are you, Mum? I'll come right away and wait with you.'

Standing on the roadside, in physical pain, crying uncontrollably; I wished I could wake up and discover this was just a bad dream.

I feel such a fool standing bawling on the roadside. It's not so much the fact of the damage to the car that's distressing me; I just can't handle the problem.

Celeste arrived and tried her best to console me while we waited for the tow-truck driver. *It was a new experience for Celeste to see me weeping like a baby. I'd always been the strong one, now I was a whimpering mess.* Celeste was at a loss as to how she could help. Being Sunday, all the car repair yards were shut, so the tow truck driver towed the car to Celeste's house. It was closer to the repair company than my home.

Next morning I arranged for my formerly, much-loved little red car, to be towed from Celeste's to the repair yard. That afternoon I received the prognosis; the car needed a new head-gasket at a cost of nearly three thousand dollars. I authorized the repairs as the car had to be fixed.

In my fragile mental state, that car breakdown was so traumatic for me that I was never emotionally able to drive the car again—*I was afraid of it.* The sight of the car sent me into a panic attack. *I just couldn't get in it.*

Tuesday morning the gas fitter arrived to install the new gas stovetop to replace the one I'd exploded. I just wanted to run out the door and escape the seemingly escalating problems.

I forced myself to stay and talk to the gas fitter. He saw my fragile state and worked cheerfully and without fuss; minimising my anxiety over the damaged stovetop. My insides churned; emotions surged through my body. *I felt sad, frightened, depressed, anxious,* and yet unable to pinpoint why. My attention span was down to seconds and anxiety in my gut made me nauseous.

I hate these feelings. I can't explain them to anyone because I can't make sense of them myself. I *want to run into the forest to escape from it all.*

Everything around me caused more stress.

I'm trapped. But mostly I feel trapped inside myself. It's really me I want to run away from.

Sick inside, I forced myself to sit down at my computer and analyse the notes I'd typed from the books on PTSD.

I must heal myself, but where do I begin? I need to sort my thoughts into some kind of order.

I began to type my thoughts.

'I accept that Dr Derovi, Dr Reid and the physiotherapist were right. I realise that I'm traumatised and that I've been in denial. I admit that

I'm suffering PTSD. From the books I've learnt that Post Traumatic Stress Disorder results from a culmination of traumas, sometimes over a long period. One more trauma can throw a person over the edge. My current emotional *fragility* probably had its roots in a hostile encounter twenty years prior. The recent accident was the final thing that sent me over the edge.

Even though I now understand what PTSD is and accept that I'm suffering from it, I still don't know how to deal with it. It's in my gut and not my head. I can't *think* myself out of it through controlling my thoughts. I collapse emotionally at the smallest stress. I cry at the tiniest thing. The resolution of this is ...'

I paused in my typing and thought about my situation. I thought about what I'd read in the books. I thought about how I felt inside. I knew I was about to crack. It's not only breaking my back that sent me over the edge; it's all the traumas of my life rolled into one. All those things together were making me feel incompetent, vulnerable, fragile and frightened. But how was I going to work through it? I looked around for Marcus. He wasn't there.

I need a counsellor. I don't know how to do this.

I picked up the phone and rang two local counsellor. I got an answering machine each time and left messages asking them to phone me urgently. I was desperate to get help. Crying and tense, I could feel myself unraveling.

I can't live like this.

I paced the room like a caged and frightened animal, then phoned the counsellors again. Answering machines. Night fell. Lying in bed I knew I was at crisis point.

I must do something. I can't go on this way.

I looked for Marcus.

Can't see him. Need help. Need guidance from the Universe.

I close my eyes, focus my mind and enter into a deep meditation, traveling upwards to the *Godzone*.

'Please help me. I need help to work through this.'

Marcus appears. 'This way child, come with me,' he gestures for me to follow. Marcus walks me back, one step at a time, through each traumatic event in my life. It was like walking through movies. He led me to one major issue that I clearly hadn't resolved.

'Marcus, I see that I haven't dealt with this. Would you please counsel me and help me work through this one?'

The night became an emotional roller-coaster. Marcus took me back, not just through that one issue, but made me re-experience every major trauma I'd ever suffered. He took me through the emotion, fear, stress and anxiety; he made me relive each major ordeal–moment by moment. I *sobbed relentlessly* as I experienced each occurrence and accompanying pain all over again.

At the end of each trauma, Marcus thoughtfully encouraged me to genuinely forgive those involved in causing me harm. He showed me why they did what they did and what they were experiencing in their lives at the time. The knowledge and the visions severed my emotions and freed me from them, liberating me from the pain. My repressed emotions I'd been holding onto–buried deep in my soul–no longer belonged to me; they were gone.

Then I reached the major trauma I'd identified to Marcus; the one that had destroyed my belief and trust in others. I paused, afraid to step into it.

'Go on, Linda, keep going.'

I hesitated, reluctant to participate. The pain was still deep and disturbingly raw after so many years. I was a child when it happened and now as a woman I was afraid to go back.

'Go on, Linda,' Marcus urged.

I inhaled deeply, put my trust in Marcus and stepped back in time. As I did so, my father approached in spirit and stopped me. *'I'm sorry, Linda. I never intended for you to suffer. I made a mistake. I had no idea it would affect you this way. May I have your permission to change the "events" of that time in your thoughts to that of a loving supportive outcome? Please, Linda?'*

I stood and wept. The anguish had surfaced again. I was eleven years-old once more. My uncle, mum's elder brother, was standing before me. I was frozen in fear as he stroked my tiny breasts and slid his hand inside my panties.

'I'll give you some loving, Linda. You meet me down by the bridge on Saturday afternoon. Don't tell your mum. Come down under the bridge, I'll be waiting for you. I'll give you some loving. I know you want it. I know you don't get enough love at home.'

Terrified, it took a couple of hours to muster the courage to tell Mum. It seemed to trigger a cold hidden rage in her. A calm accommodating woman, Mum threw the vacuum cleaner up against the wall, took me by my shoulders and sat me down.

'Tell me exactly what he did.' Her icy tone chilled and frightened me. Trembling, I told her exactly what he said and did.

'You stay here. I'm going to tell that dirty pig a thing or two.'

With that, Mum took off her apron, threw it on the chair, got the keys to her car and drove off. That evening I heard Mum and Dad shouting at each other and arguing. Dad sounded very angry.

'He wouldn't do that sort of thing!' I heard Dad yell. 'The kid must be lying!'

'It is exactly the sort of thing that dirty pig would do!' Mum yelled back. *'Linda is not lying!'*

I could hear the fury in Mum's voice; it was not a tone I'd ever heard from her before. Their quarrelling petrified me.

'She's lying. He just wouldn't do it.'

'Yes, he would!' Mum was almost screaming.

I was too frightened to listen any longer. I ran outside and hid in my secret hiding place, the place I went too when life got out-of-control. My stomach knotted and I struggled against an urge to urinate. Mum and Dad had argued before, *but never like that.*

Dad said I was lying. He didn't believe me. Why did Dad think I was lying?

His disbelief confused me. Their angry words frightened me. I was terrified of my uncle; afraid he would come looking for me and punish me for telling Mum what he'd done. Dad's angry words made me feel I'd done something very bad, but I wasn't sure what it could be.

I must have done something very bad to make Dad so angry with me.

Guilt, like a cold black mantle, settled over me. It wrapped itself around my heart and my gut, held me prisoner, penetrated my body through to my bones and *crippled me*. That mantle of guilt was never to leave me. *It stayed with me for life.*

The door slammed as Dad stormed out of the house. Fury swirled around him as he strode past where I was crouched, concealed in my hiding place. I watched him march off down the lane and out-of-sight. Like a dog with its tail between its legs, I crept back into the house, being sure to avoid being seen. On tiptoes, I skulked into my bedroom, crawled under the blankets and hid in the dark and lonely safety of the bed covers.

I listened to Mum storm around the house banging things and slamming cupboards. Mum and Dad didn't speak to each other for days. The air in the house was so thick it was hard to breath. I knew it was all my fault. I knew I'd done something *bad, very bad.*

Mum told my uncle he wasn't welcome at our house and not to set foot on our property again; it was twenty years before she spoke to him again. In the weeks that followed that awful day, Dad scowled every time he saw me and growled angrily at me. My guilty feelings deepened, cementing themselves into my soul. Like a frightened animal, I avoided Dad whenever possible. I was the bad person in his eyes. That day my relationship with him changed forever.

I learnt two important survival lessons that day. Never tell anyone when something bad happens–because somehow it will become my fault, and don't trust anyone except Mum to be on my side because people will turn against me if I reveal my fears or problems. But, even with Mum, I could no longer tell her my anxieties, because she'd tell others, and the "others" would turn against me and it would become my fault again. I learnt to bottle everything inside me and deal with problems myself–I closed everyone out of my life.

Now, decades later, Dad is standing in front of me in spirit, saying he's sorry and asking if he can change the "events" of that time, in my head. The old pain is back.

I still can't trust anyone to support me in a time of crisis; have to fight my demons myself. What do I do?

'Linda? What is your decision?' Marcus pushes for an answer.

'Please, Linda?' Dad implores, but my throat has squeezed tightly shut. 'I was so wrong to react the way I did–I'm so sorry–I had no idea what I was doing. Please let me change the "events" to how I wish I'd reacted?'

'Linda, it's your decision.' Marcus prompted.

I couldn't speak. Blinded by tears I relented, nodding agreement. Dad and Marcus re-ran the "events" of the time, however changed Dad's reaction to believing Mum. He took me onto his lap and asked me gently what happened, consoled me quietly, hugged me. He reassured me that it was not my fault and that I did the right thing by telling Mum. He kissed my forehead and handed me over to Mum, then left to deal with my uncle himself.

A tsunami of emotions containing decades of guilt and self-punishment gushed from me, washing away the chains that incarcerated the child inside the woman. Un-acknowledged heaviness in my heart dissipated and was replaced by a lightness I had never known.

'I'm sorry, will you forgive me?' I heard dad asking.

I nodded slowly. 'Yes,' is all I could manage to croak through mingled grief and joy.

'Linda, because of that *dreadful mistake* I've been able to guide you in spirit these last few years; to help you feel "looked after" and "safe". I failed to keep you safe as a child, allowed you to grow up feeling threatened, afraid, forever vigilant and listening for sounds of danger, and never knowing trust. In spirit I've come to help you, to make amends.'

Marcus spoke, 'Linda, you developed a deep distrust and hyper-vigilance because of that incident. You maintained your body in a constant state of "fight-or-flight" and that has caused both psychological and health issues. Your adrenals are constantly over-active, causing your pancreas to over-produce insulin and that has brought on hypoglycemia. At your father's judgment time, he has seen the results of his actions and has chosen to return to care for you; to help you with the problems he's caused.'

It was a harrowing night of grueling spiritual counselling and when morning came I was exhausted, but had a lightness in my heart and gut that I couldn't recall ever having experienced before. I stepped out of bed, stood and opened my bedroom curtains as I did every morning. But that morning something was different. The world outside looked *brighter*. The leaves of the trees *greener*. The colour of the flowers *more intense*. Everything seemed sharper, clearer, more brilliant. I felt lighter, more alive–a crushing burden had lifted off me.

Mary, the counsellor, phoned over breakfast. I told Mary that I'd been trying to reach her for help and explained what had happened regarding the car breakdown and my feelings of being unable to cope. I then explained about the Spiritual counselling during the night.

'It sounds like you have sorted out the problem, Linda, but if you still need to talk to me, give me a call and we can book you in for a session.'

'Thanks, Mary. I don't think I need it now.'

I re-read the notes I'd written from the books on Post Traumatic Stress Disorder and thought through the events of the previous night. *It seems the Universe intended that I shouldn't reach a counsellor; that I should learn the process of self-analysis, to meditate on my problems, ask Marcus to counsel me and show me how to resolve things myself. Facing and re-experiencing those painful memories was difficult but it seems to have released them. I hope the nightmares are finally behind me.*

CHAPTER 15

A Long-Term Goal Beyond Recovery

IN SPAIN THAT NIGHT, MY thoughts once again drift back to the healing journey that brought me to walk this pilgrimage. I think about one of my visits to Dr Derovi. He's been my doctor for twenty years, he understands me and knows I'm not one to complain.

'You leave things far too long, Linda. Why didn't you see me about this sooner?' he often scolds.

'Well, things usually heal themselves. Why should I waste your time and mine complaining when they'll probably get better on their own?'

A high pain-threshold, a stubborn independent nature and a preference for natural healing means that prior to the accident I'd been an infrequent patient; visiting him only when it was unavoidable. After the accident, however, the constant physical pain had become too much to bear; it had driven me back to him.

'It's getting worse. Now it's my mouth. It's full of aching teeth. I can hardly bare to eat. I went to the dentist and told him all–not just one–but all my teeth are aching. He had a look, took x-rays and told me there's nothing actually wrong with my teeth. He advised the pain was most likely caused by aching nerve endings resulting from the spinal injury.'

Dr Derovi listened attentively and nodded, agreeing with the dentist's prognosis.

'In the last couple of weeks I've begun to have severe menstrual cramps.'

He gave me a puzzled look, as I continued my uncharacteristic moaning.

'How can I have menstrual cramps when I don't have a uterus? I've had a hysterectomy. First my teeth ache so much I can hardly eat and now I have period pains when I don't have a uterus.'

My world was crashing down around me. I wanted a reprieve from the pain but instead it was escalating—I felt distraught. I noticed my doctor desperately restraining a smile; it amused him that even now, at my lowest ebb, I was unable to complain without making a joke about my lack of a uterus. But, he knew the joke was masking deep depression and quickly regained his composure.

'The feeling of having menstrual cramps is the nerve endings feeling pain where the uterus was removed. A spinal injury can create the feeling of pain in nerve endings, I'm afraid. You may get pain elsewhere in the body too.' His voice had become full of sympathy and understanding.

'Oh, great! That's just what I don't need.' It was five months since the accident and it had become a struggle to keep my spirits up. I felt I was a burden to those around me, a dead weight dragging others down. How could I say I felt fine when someone asked how I was? I didn't feel *fine*—I felt *awful*. I wanted to tell people I felt awful. But they didn't really want to know; they were just being polite. It's just a game we play. I tried to smile and sound genuine when I answered, 'Fine thanks.' How could I tell them it was hard just to keep going? They wouldn't understand. But it must be hard for them too; putting up with me being unable to do everything I once did; having to make adjustments for me.

Each morning I worked at the physiotherapy exercises at home and every night I repeated the exercises again. Three times a week I drove to the hydrotherapy pool and pushed through the water. I was doggedly determined to get my strength and mobility back but felt like I was walking and balancing on a tight-rope between two mighty canyons. On one side of the chasm was my resolve to do whatever it took to get better. On the other side of the chasm was mounting opposition, pain—the feeling it was all getting *just too hard*. I was beginning to doubt I could reach my goal, thought I might get no further than half way.

At the second visit to the kinesiologist the treatment eased the pain slightly, but not as dramatically as it had the first time. The pain was much more localised and the kinesiologist eased the pain in those specific areas only a little. Still, it helped a bit, as did the hydrotherapy; it all seemed to work together and even a small improvement was another hook-hold on the mountainside for me to mentally pull myself up.

After the accident I had trouble reading. I couldn't retain the words on a page; they floated away after a sentence or two. I re-read the first couple of sentences of a novel—over and over—but each time the words drifted away. I'd put the book away but when I went back later the same thing happened. I tried several times before giving up.

'Marcus, what is wrong with my brain? Is this inability to hold onto words due to the bump on my head when I fell?'

'You need to nourish your brain, Linda. Use your pendulum. Dowse to build a list of what you need.'

I mulled over his words, trying to determine how to dowse on what I needed. I drew up and dowsed on a list of food categories. I divided these into food types and dowsed again. The food types I divided into individual items and dowsed again. It all took several hours. Finally, *exhausted* from the mental effort, I had a collection of twenty-seven grains, fruit and nuts.

'Okay. Now what do I do with the list, Marcus? Do I snack on them, cook them or what?'

'Make them into a snack without cooking them.'

'Hmm.' I pondered a bit, then decided to process them. I processed them into bars, balls and muesli. It was fiddly and the ingredients expensive, but the result was delicious.

I hope this gets my brain working again, if it does it'll be worth the cost.

Every so often, I'd have a good day when the pain would be less. Those good days brought *golden sunshine* into my life but, by contrast, made the bad even harder to endure.

'You can slowly try to wean yourself off the back-brace,' Dr Derovi suggested. 'Wear it for half a day and leave it off for half a day.'

I felt vulnerable and frightened without the brace but I wanted progress so agreed to try.

'Mum, there's an acupuncturist in Kalamunda who's very good. Why don't you try him? He might help with the pain,' Amy suggested.

'Amy, I know acupuncture doesn't hurt, I had it done in the past many years ago but at the moment I have so much pain to endure, that right now I'm not ready to have anyone stick needles in me.'

'Mum, why don't you come with me on my next visit? I spoke to the acupuncturist about you. He suggested you come with me and watch my treatment, so you can see what happens. It'll sort of break you in gently to the idea.'

'Okay.' Amy seemed determined, so I agreed to go with her. Friday arrived and Amy picked me up. I sat and watched the acupuncturist stick needles into her.

That night Larry came home from his overseas trip, giving me a brief outline of how it went.

'How are you feeling?'

'Fine,' I lied.

I doubt he's interested enough to listen to me moan about how I really feel. He's only interested in his work, too busy to have space in his life to care about how I feel.

I was too miserable and sorry for myself to give Larry the opportunity to share in my life.

The next morning, the mechanic rang as the repairs to my car were finished. It was ready to collect but I fretted over picking it up. The thought of driving it made my gut churn and my heart race, and it filled me with dread.

'Don't be silly, Linda, you can do it.' I tried to talk myself out of the anxiety that engulfed me. It didn't work. I just *couldn't* bring myself to drive the car. I rang Amy and Eddy and asked if one of them would collect it for me. They were delighted to have an opportunity to drive the sports car and quickly agreed to bring it home.

The next week, I crossed twenty-one weeks off the calendar and continued my routine of exercises and hydrotherapy; but didn't seem to be making any progress. Each day I took the brace off, as Dr Derovi suggested, and tried to endure without it, but the pain was way too bad. Without the brace, it felt like I couldn't hold myself upright; felt like I was going to collapse. Frustrated, it was hard to stay cheerful and I was growing less tolerant. Deep down my mood was darkening—I resented Larry for not helping me more, resented him for going away to work. In the depths of my mind he became responsible for my problems, and I shifted the blame for my situation onto Larry.

'Linda, Larry is not to blame. Hold your focus on your goal. Larry has issues of his own,' Marcus warned me. 'He's struggling too. He's struggling to deal with the changes in you, with the changes to his relationship with you. In times of trouble he immerses himself in his work, it's is his way of maintaining stability in his life, the only constant he has. Acknowledge that your despair is your own. It belongs to you.'

It's easy for Marcus to say that Larry's not the cause of my problems. Rationally I know he's right, but emotionally I resent my situation and I resent Larry for not being a source of strength for me.

I wasn't ready to accept Marcus' advice just yet.

I'm tired of the pain, tired of Larry burying himself in work and tired of trying to get back to a state of health I doubt I'll ever reach.

I didn't discuss my feelings with Larry, so he was unaware of the turmoil in my mind.

I crossed twenty-three weeks off the calendar. It was only two weeks to Christmas and I'd begun to resign myself to being permanently in a brace. Daily physiotherapy and weekly hydrotherapy were still my routine. I told people I was going to make a full recovery, but deep down I doubted it. I no longer had faith that I'd get back full mobility. A return to "normal" seemed beyond me but I kept that thought to myself.

Evening came and I picked up a book to try to read. Relief dawned, like the *spreading light of morning*, when I found I could retain the words as I read.

It's my Brain Food! It must be the snack food I'd dowsed that nourished my brain and enabled me to remember the words. I smiled to myself before dropping off to sleep. *Yes, it must be my "Brain Food" working.*

The months rolled past and I had an occasional good day. On a good day I woke, looked out my window and gave thanks for being alive.

'Thank you, God, for this beautiful morning, for the fresh air we breathe, for this moment, for this life.' On a good day–I had a deep appreciation for simply feeling good. I'd lay and listen to the trilling of the honey eaters as they sipped from the long-stemmed red flowers of the Kangaroo Paw outside my window. I'd marvel at the intense blueness of the morning sky and the brilliance of the colours around me.

Some days the clarity of beauty of the landscape outside my window held my heart with such passion that it was unbearable and I'd weep. On those days—I felt like nothing in the world could hold me down. I'd rise with lightness in my step and joy surrounding me. I felt radiant and others around me responded with delight and laughter. On those days–I felt I'd returned and could tackle anything. Those days–I felt I could take the brace off.

I'd take the steel brace off, and painful dark miserable agonising days would follow. Depressing days, where it was difficult just getting up in the morning.

Wonderful highs followed by crashing lows tortured my psyche.

I'm going to have to learn to take it easy when I feel good. But it's hard to hold back when the world shines invitingly.

At least I can read whole novels again.

At my next visit to Dr Derovi I unloaded my problems. 'I have aches and pains everywhere. I know I broke my back, but why do I have aches and pains all over my body? I feel like a truck has run over me, *I ache everywhere.* Why do I have a pain in my side when the break is in the centre of my back and the collapsed lumbar is in the base of my spine? It is twenty-seven weeks; will I ever be without pain?' I pelt him with questions.

'Here is where the break was.' He patiently explains and draws me a picture of my spine. 'Your spine goes straight down to where the break is.' He drew a big circle to show where the break was, then a line coming off at an angle from there. 'Basically, your spine is crooked from where the break is, and your muscles have to cope with having to stretch further around in some places, and not as far in others. As a result you have pain in several places.'

I sighed heavily. It made sense when he explained it like that. I felt both reassured and frustrated as I left his surgery.

Is it ever going to be over?

The following week was time for my first acupuncture treatment. Steve, the acupuncturist, checked my back and told me it was crooked.

'Yes, I know, my doctor told me last week.'

'I think three visits and we can get that straightened.'

What a load of rubbish. How dare he tell me he can straighten my spine? The last thing I need now is false hope. I felt patronised, but said nothing. During the treatment, I stewed over his words.

He really shouldn't tell people that sort of thing, some people may actually believe him. They'd get their hopes up, only to be disappointed when it didn't happen. It's just not right.

I visited Steve once a week.

'Right, Linda,' Steve told me at the end of my third visit. 'Your spine's straight now.'

What rubbish! How could sticking a few needles in my back straighten a broken crooked spine? He really shouldn't say things like that. It's enough that I'm feeling better this past week. He shouldn't give people false hope.

But I said nothing. I thanked him quietly, paid my bill and left. As I walked out of his office I noticed the pain was a lot less. My weekly routine became acupuncture, kinesiology, physiotherapy and hydrotherapy; I made an all-out effort to get pain relief and healing.

A week later, it was time for my next monthly check with Dr Derovi. I stood topless in front of him as he ran his fingers down my spine.

'Your spine's straight!' he sounded shocked. 'What've you been doing?'

'Well … I've been having acupuncture.'

'Whatever it is you're doing–keep doing it–because it's working.'

I smiled to myself. *The acupuncturist was right. He did straighten my spine. I owe him an apology for my thoughts.*

'Doctor, I'm feeling very low.' I moved on with my problems. 'I can't seem to wean myself off the brace any further than every second day. Whenever I try to increase the time without the brace to three days, the fourth day I end up back in bed in excruciating pain. Also, I have a lump growing on my back.'

He inspected and prodded the lump. 'It's a cyst, the least of your worries right now. We need to get your back healed before we worry about that.'

'I've got this one too.' I showed him a second lump growing on my left hand. 'It's very sore and incapacitating.'

'Oh dear! That's a ganglion and relatively minor. Again, it's best to leave this until your back is sorted out. All these things are due to the spinal injury. The spine holds the central nervous system, and an injury to the spine upsets the entire nervous system. All sorts of things can result from such an injury.'

I felt even lower when I left his surgery. The dark hole in my mind was getting ever deeper. *Will I ever get through this?*

One thing after another keeps piling on top of me. My list of things to deal with just keeps getting longer.

I was close to tears.

How much more do I have to endure?

Another week passed as I crossed thirty-three weeks off my calendar.

I weep constantly, am unable to think clearly, unable to get out of bed without the brace on, and most days even with the brace—I'm in agony.

I began to think about the bridges in Perth, analysing their heights in my mind, for potential jump-off points.

It would have to be high enough to make sure I don't just do more damage than I have already done. I think about where I can park my car near a bridge and what time of day will be best to jump, to make sure nobody sees me.

I can't risk anyone trying to stop me.

Marcus appears before me.

'Linda, this is not what you want. You've reached a crisis point. You need help to get through it. See your doctor!'

'I simply can't keep on pushing and getting nowhere, Marcus.' But I know Marcus is right. I need help. I ring the doctor's surgery.

'*I need an emergency appointment,*' I tell the receptionist. She makes me an appointment for a couple of hours later.

'I feel so depressed lately, I really can't go on. I just *can't* do it anymore. I've come to get some anti-depressants. I really feel I can't keep on trying.' Dr Derovi listens as I pour out my feelings of frustration and desolation. 'I've tried and tried to extend the time without the steel brace, but I just can't get past two days. The pain is too great. If I push further than two days I collapse in agony,' I sob.

'That's why you are doing the weight-bearing exercises at the physiotherapist.' His tone is gentle as he continues. 'The weight bearing exercises are to build up your strength so that you can support yourself without the brace.'

'What weight-bearing exercises?' I didn't understand.

He sat up straight in his chair. 'Well, aren't you doing weight-bearing exercise at the physiotherapist?'

'No.'

His face flushed red. 'Well, what are you doing at the physio?'

'Hydrotherapy, and gym-ball at home.'

In a rage, he threw his prescription pad against the wall. 'I shouldn't have to tell people how to do their job! They're supposed to be professionals! They should know what they're doing! I shouldn't have to be on their backs ensuring they're doing the right thing by their patients!' He hurled his pen against the wall to join his pad on the floor.

'Well, actually, the other thing I wanted to ask you for was a referral to another physiotherapist, who has been recommended to me.'

'Who's that?' he asked, calming down.

I told him the name.

'Alright, but those people you've been seeing should've been doing their job properly. You'd be a lot further along now if they had.' He wrote a referral letter for the new physiotherapist and handed it to me.

When I arrived home, there was a message on the answering machine from the current physiotherapist asking me to call her and make an appointment for a review of my program.

She must have received a blast from the doctor as soon as I walked out of the door.

I rang the new physiotherapist first thing the next morning and made an appointment, then rang the current physiotherapist and made an appointment for the program review, just to hear what she had to say.

Eight months passed after the accident before my first visit to the new physiotherapist.

This new physio is my last hope; if he can't help me to progress, then I've exhausted all avenues and I'll be doomed to life as an invalid.

I was nervous, hopeful, and frightened as I walked into his clinic.

'What hands-on work have you had done?'

'None.'

'What weight-bearing work have you been doing?'

'None.'

'What manipulative work have you had done?'

'None.'

He shook his head in disbelief.

'Which physiotherapist have you been going to?'

I told him.

'I used to work there–but I left. Alright, let's just forget whatever you have been told before and we'll start from scratch.'

'Yes, please. Let's get started.' I felt a glimmer of hope flicker in my heart.

He looked over my spine and began working on me with his hands. Nobody had done that before. My tight aching muscles and rigid joints screamed at each touch. From that very first visit I felt a slight but immediate improvement. I pulled my exercise chart out of my wallet and showed it to him.

'These are the exercises I'm doing every day.'

He studied it a moment. 'If you could do all these exercises properly you wouldn't be here now. Next week, wear your gym gear and we'll look over the exercises. I'll show you how to do them properly.'

I visited him twice a week. He cancelled the hydrotherapy, eliminated all but the very first exercises on the chart, and gave me gym-ball exercises to do at home.

'Once I show you how to do these exercises *properly*, you won't need me.' It took me several attempts to do them to his satisfaction. He showed me how to breathe, to turn on the muscle around my spine, and tilt my pelvis–properly. It was a struggle to breathe, turn muscles on, tilt my pelvis and perform the exercises according to his strict instructions. I folded after only one exercise.

He grinned at me. 'Like I said, if you could do these properly, you wouldn't need me.'

I tried again, and again I collapsed.

'Take it easy,' his voice soothed. 'Slowly, there's no rush. Just get it right.'

I like this man. I felt a confidence in him I'd not felt with any of the other physiotherapists. 'Will I ever get back to normal?'

I've been told so often in the previous eight months about all the things I'll never be able to do again, I want his honest opinion. He'll be straight with me, he seems to understand what I need to do; what my recovery will entail.

'Normal? What does normal mean?' He mused a moment. 'It depends on how much you're prepared to put into it. If you're prepared to do everything I tell you to do, and work at it with one hundred percent effort and determination, then I don't see why you can't get back to living a fairly-normal sort of life. It depends on you though, on how much you are prepared to work at it.'

I appreciated his honesty and felt confident he'd continue to be straight with me. I had a renewed sense of purpose, a new drive.

I'm going to make it! If there's a possibility for a return to some sort of normality, then I'll do whatever it takes to make that possibility a reality.

I knew I had to believe it and had to keep a positive attitude. That evening I started work on the new exercises. When I finished I noticed Marcus watching me.

'It's going to be alright now, isn't it?' I grinned at him. He smiled back at me.

'Set yourself a long-term goal, Linda, a goal beyond recovery. Something you can aim for.'

I nodded in agreement, but wasn't sure what sort of goal to set.

'You've talked of long-term goals in the past, Linda.'

I sat puzzled, trying to think through what he meant. He mentally showed me an image of a lady I met five years prior, in Indonesia. She was British and in her early eighties. The lady had backpacked alone from Britain across the Middle East, down through Cambodia and Laos and into Indonesia. She planned to continue to Australia and then New Zealand, as she circled the world on her way back home to England. The lady had so impressed me that I declared I'd backpack around the world one day too.

I grinned at Marcus.

'Backpacking around the world seems a fairly remote possibility at this point in time.'

'It's a long-term goal, Linda.'

He fixed his gaze on me and I felt him urging me to take up his challenge. I remembered how inspired that woman had made me feel. I thought about it for a few minutes before answering.

'If she could do it, so could I.' I only half believed it. I thought about it for a moment longer and was aware I needed to strengthen my determination.

'I'm going to backpack around the world.' I made a tentative promise to myself and to the Universe. I knew I needed to create a positive mental attitude, although deep down I wasn't certain I'd be physically capable. Mentally, I threw another pick up ahead of me, on the difficult mountain I had to climb. Every step a challenge on the road to recovery from the crisis in my life. I needed the "hooks" to hold on to, to steady and pull myself up out of the deep black holes that I kept falling into. I worked with intense determination on the new exercises *every* morning and *every* night.

I held the idea of returning to a "normal" life in my mind. With every movement of every exercise I held the vision of walking normally. As the weeks of exercising turned into months, I forgot the promise I made.

I continued to see the new physiotherapist and with his guidance through the exercises; his coaching, coaxing, and gentle hands-on manipulation, the muscles holding my spine strengthened. Within a few weeks I was able to lengthen the time without the brace. Each morning I meditated, asking the Universe for the strength and determination to re-build my body, spirit and willpower, so I could tackle the months ahead and the physiotherapy exercises.

CHAPTER 16

The Promise

IT TOOK THREE YEARS OF exercises: physiotherapy, acupuncture, and kinesiology, to release me from the metal brace. I graduated to an elastic brace and underwent a couple of operations on the lumps, cysts and torn tendon in my shoulder. It was a long journey and progress was slow.

I had practised Reiki and Theta healing for many years prior to the accident, performing the spiritual healing on family and friends. During my recovery period I had time to resume my practice and studies of Theta healing. Theta is a type of spiritual healing using particularly slow brain-wave activity. I joined an advanced Theta healing class to further my studies and relished the company of like-minded people, reveling in the calm energy that filled the room.

One warm Sunday afternoon in a Theta class of ten students, we sat in pairs and practised channeling. My partner, Mairin and I, had not met before but I enjoyed her radiated spirituality and intelligence. It was Mairin's turn to channel for me.

'Your Spiritual Master is here.'

'Describe him for me.' I wanted her to verify she was seeing Marcus, not some other Spirit guide.

She described Marcus' long white hair, long flowing robes and his radiant feeling of love and compassion. 'He looks like he must be one hundred and twenty years old, at least.'

I knew immediately it was Marcus she was seeing. 'Go on.' I prompted her to continue.

'He says you must do the Camino next year.'

'Camino? What's the Camino?' *Sounds like some sort of dance; Tango–Camino.*

At that moment, another woman from the class was walking past us. She stopped and spun around.

'Camino! Did you say, "What's the Camino?"' She looked stunned.

Mairin and I gawked at her. 'Yes.' We were surprised that she would interrupt our channeling.

'I have a book on the Camino in my bag. Here.' She reached inside her bag, pulled a book out and handed it to me. Mairin and I stared at each other, stunned by the exchange.

'Thank you.' I took the book and scanned the back cover.

'The Camino is a pilgrimage, an ancient trail across Europe. It leads to Santiago de Compostella in Spain,' the woman explained.

As I read the book cover, I recalled the promise I'd made, and promptly forgotten, two and a half years earlier.

The Universe is calling on me to fulfil my promise, the long-term goal I set to "backpack around the world".

Mairin and the other woman watched me silently, waiting for my reaction to the spiritual interchange that had just occurred. I sat nodding my head, reading the back cover of the book, absorbing what I was being told to do. I looked up at the waiting women.

'Thank you.' A strange energy and deep sense of peace had enveloped me. 'Yes.' I was still nodding. 'This is what I must do.' I explained to the women the story of the promise I had made and that I was being called to act on it.

That evening at home I researched what and where the Camino was and sought out books and information on the pilgrim trail. At the end of the next week, I told my family I would walk the Camino the following year. At first, they were in disbelief. The girls were shocked when they understood I was serious. Larry was horrified.

'There's no way you can walk across Spain, least of all carry a backpack!'

'If Mum's decided to do it, Dad, there's nothing you can say or do that'll change her mind. You know that.' Serena was supportive and encouraging.

Larry spent the next six months trying to talk me out of my "foolish idea".

'Be realistic ... for goodness sake. There's absolutely *no way* you can walk this Camino. You've only just learnt to walk again. You've had a broken back. You don't have the strength. There's no way you can carry a backpack eight hundred kilometres. Be sensible about this. You'll put yourself at risk all over again. It's ridiculous to even consider it!'

But I'd made a promise. Now the Universe had asked me to fulfil that promise, I was determined to do it. *Alone!* I had to do it, but had no idea if I could actually succeed.

When Larry realised he couldn't talk me out of it, he tried another tactic. 'Well, if you're determined to do this, then we must get you fit enough to be able to do it. We have to get you into training.'

Larry drew up a grueling training regime. Every weekend he took me walking, with a loaded backpack, on the nearby hilly and rugged Bibbulmun Track. Every morning during the week, before work, he took me walking with a loaded pack up nearby hills for two hours. He gradually increased the weight of my backpack so that after two weeks the pack weighed eight kilos.

I knew Larry was trying to prove to me that I wasn't up to the task. I was tired and sore on those early walks and often struggled to reach the day's target. But I was going to walk the Camino; it was *not negotiable*. By trying to show me that I couldn't do it, Larry succeeded in getting me fit. After four months Larry's attitude changed. He'd seen my determination and accepted that I was going to walk the Camino. He began to coach me on how best to carry the pack and manage the difficult terrain. Now he wanted to help me succeed.

CHAPTER 17

Traumatised by Louis

San Sol to Viana - Spain

WAKING EARLY AFTER A DEEP sleep, feeling *vulnerable* and *on-edge*, I stay in bed waiting until almost everyone has gone; especially the staring Italian man who unnerved me two nights ago. Nervous about Louis, missing Larry, and my girls and Eddy, leaves me feeling emotionally withdrawn. At 6.30 am, when the refuge is almost empty, I climb out of bed. It's still dark as I dress. I roll up my sleeping bag, pack my backpack and walk out into the darkness.

Lights illuminate the compound. It's cool as I stroll out of the *refugio* towards the street. My mind relaxes and wanders in the peace and calm of the ambient moment. Then a familiar voice snaps me back to the present.

'Linda, I 'ave porridge cooking and your coffee is 'ere.'

I'd momentarily forgotten about Louis parked outside.

He's been watching and waiting for me. The ball of anxiety knots again in my belly.

'Good morning, Louis.' I try to conceal my disappointment that he's still here.

Handing me a cup of coffee, Louis motions for me to take a seat. Over porridge, he reminds me that he'll take my pack to San Sol in his vehicle and meet me there.

"ad you forgotten?' he asks, without waiting for an answer.

'I'll drive you over the difficult section. It's rugged and very undulating. I'll put you down at the beginning of the flat terrain. You can walk the rest of the way from there. But first I take you to look at another 'istorical chapel in a village nearby.'

'No. Thank you. I'm keen to get going. Thank you so much for breakfast and for offering to take my pack to San Sol. Thank you, Louis. See you in San Sol.'

I clamber out of the motorhome, swing the trekking poles into motion and set off at a brisk pace. 'Bye.' I wave, trying to achieve a polite level of friendliness, without seeming too friendly.

The coolness of the summer morning swirls around me. Its unexpected crispness sends imperceptible shivers through my body. It's not long before sunrise lights the dusty track. A fresh clear blueness washes across the sky, banishing the cool darkness and lifting my mood. Concerns about Louis evaporate as my heart dances with the peaceful expanse of the countryside and the rolling hills. The carefully cultivated landscape is denuded of crops. As the Camino meanders between sleepy farms the freedom of not carrying a backpack feels delicious.

A couple of kilometres before San Sol a figure appears in the distance. The figure is walking towards me. As the shape draws closer, I recognise Louis. His arms are out-stretched and as he walks towards me, I see he's grinning broadly. My heart sinks. He greets me with a kiss on each cheek and wraps his arms around me like a lover. I pull back and push him away but he doesn't seem to notice my brusqueness.

Louis knows I'm married, what's he thinking acting like that? How do I handle this man?

We walk to the outskirts of town.

'There's something you must see.' He steers me to a balcony of a church.

'Look, down there,' he points, indicating a remarkable view of Torres del Rio far below. *It's stunning!*

I would have missed that view if Louis had not pointed it out. He certainly knows the area well.

He leads me to the van, we climb into the cabin and he starts the engine.

'I need a woman in my life.' He smiles at me.

That does it! I need to get out of this situation. Anxiety clenches my gut. *It's time to consult my Spirit guides, but first I need to lose some tension so I can hear them.* Breathing deeply, I close my eyes, focusing to slow my brain down and relax my body, so I can communicate with them.

'Hans, what should I do?'

'He's dangerous. Get rid of him–*quickly!*' I'm taken aback by Hans' sharp response.

As we reach the end of the rugged stretch that Louis had so well described, he pulls the van over to the shoulder of the road.

'Right, 'ere you go *ma cherie*. I will cook dinner for us tonight. Where shall we meet this evening, Viana or Logroňo?'

My head is pounding.

'Louis, I need to go on alone from here.' I strive to convey a sense of calm.

'To where? Viana or Logroňo?'

'To Santiago de Compostella.'

'What are you telling me?' A pained expression deeply etches his face.

'I'm saying, I need to go on alone from here to Santiago de Compostella. You can relate to that Louis. You've walked the Camino. You understand that this is my spiritual journey. I must do it *alone.*'

A black look masks his face. He drops his head so I can't see his face. He seems to be studying the ground, thinking. He won't look up, but sits silently; viciously picking at the skin on his hands. His sudden dark transformation engulfs me with mind-numbing fear. *I've seen this sort of insane mood-swing before.* The blood coursing through my veins feels icy; I shiver. *I need to be very careful.* When I last saw that black look, Ethan was holding a loaded rifle to my head. Staying calm and not reacting was the only thing that stopped him from pulling the trigger and blowing my brains out. I learnt not to show fear with Ethan.

He's insane. Stay calm Linda. Hide your fear. Fear fuels insanity. Talk him down. He believes we are in some sort of relationship.

My gut churns.

Breathe deeply. Don't panic. Think, Linda, think! Let go of the tension before you speak.

'I really appreciate your kindness and help, Louis. You've been great, a true friend. You've walked the Camino, I know you'll understand that this is my spiritual journey and I must do it alone.'

Still he doesn't speak. He picks at his hand ever-more violently. My knees begin to quiver, visibly, and I try to relax them; to stop them shaking.

When Ethan behaved like Louis is now, I had to fight for my life. Terror tightens its grip in my belly. *I think I'm going to throw up. Don't show fear– fear's a trigger. Stay calm–think of a way out of this ... Keep talking–talk your way out. Compose yourself ... Gather your things slowly. Start walking ... Walk away slowly ... Don't run.*

A steel belt of anxiety tightens around my lungs making it difficult to breath—a feeling of light-headedness leaves me swirling. My legs wobble jelly-like as I stand; they're barely able to support me.

'Thank you, Louis, for your kindness. You've been amazing.' I go to the rear of the van and fetch my pack and trekking poles. I stumble as I return to the cabin.

'You're a good friend, Louis. I really appreciate your friendship.' I climb down out of the van with as much composure as I'm able to muster.

Louis continues to tear the skin from his hand as I close the door. *Terrified*, I stride away from the van in the direction of Viana. I want to run, but know I mustn't. I want to look back, to see if he's coming; but force myself to look ahead. Hyper-alert at every sound, I'm afraid he'll try to run me down.

I've gotta get off this road.

I look for a track leading away from the road; body tense, ready to leap sideways into the ditch should he try to run me down. I see a track and make for it. Shaking uncontrollably and fighting down nausea I push through the bushes.

A vehicle door slams and heavy footsteps stomp on gravel. I start running. Someone is crashing through bushes behind me–I don't look back–I have to escape. I'm fit. He's not. The awkward heavy pack on my back slows me down as I run, stumbling in panic. The crashing grows louder.

Have to hide. Have to get off this track. Is that a ditch in the bushes?

I leap off the track through the bushes and hurl myself into a deep ditch. I lay on my side so that my bright blue pack might not be seen.

My breathing is labored. I try to hold it so it won't be heard. My bladder's ready to burst.

Please help me. Please help me. Please help me. I focus my brain on the Godzone.

The crashing noise is upon me. Then it passes. I daren't move. The crashing noise carries on into the distance.

Please help me. Please help me. Please help me. Still focusing my mind.

He has to come back to get to his van. I can't move until he's gone.

I lay and listen. The sound of crashing footsteps has gone. I wait for him to come back. I need to empty my bladder. I daren't move.

'Linda!' There's a roar in the distance.

I nearly wet myself in fright, but lie unmoving in the dirt. I wait for him to come back. He doesn't. It feels like a half an hour passes but it's probably only minutes.

I think I hear a motor start and a vehicle pull away. I wait and listen. Silence. I get up onto my knees and stretch carefully until I can peep out over the top of the ditch. It seems safe. I ease up onto my feet to see if I can see him. My breathing is loud in my ears. I climb out of the ditch and walk a short way to see if I can see Louis' van through the bushes. I can't see it.

He might have made his way back to the road on another path, gone to his van and driven off looking for me. I think I've lost him. For now.

I jump back into the ditch, drop my trousers and empty my bladder. Relieved, but with my head pounding from the tension, I need to think through my situation.

I don't know where I am. He may still be coming after me. Maybe he's driven to where this path leaves the bushes and rejoins the road. Maybe he's waiting in Viana or somewhere further along the track. He knows all the tracks and villages, he could hide and wait for me anywhere.

I throw up silently into the bushes, wipe my mouth, take a sip of water and spit it out.

If he finds me he'll kill me. He thinks I'm a lover who's walked out on him. He's totally nuts. I want to be home with family. I need to talk to someone to have company and reassurance.

Fingers tremble as I dial home on my phone. The phone rings and rings and then goes to message bank. Serena's voice asks me to leave a message–I hang up.

It's best not to leave a message and tell them I'm frightened and in fear for my life. No point worrying them, they can't do anything. It would've been good to talk to them though.

Hearing Serena's recorded voice comforts me a little. I take a couple more deep breaths to steady my nerves and slow my breathing, then ring Serena's mobile phone. I know I won't be able to reach Larry, he's traveling somewhere. He usually has his mobile phone switched off anyway. Serena's phone rings a couple of times.

'Hello, mum!' I feel comforted immediately.

'Hello, love.' I hope she can't hear the tremor in my voice. 'How was your day?' If it was either of the older girls, they would've instantly heard the fear in my voice. But Serena's younger, less experienced, she doesn't pick it up. I don't want to frighten her by telling her I'm in trouble. I just want the comfort of listening to a loved one's voice. We chat for a few minutes and I keep my problems to myself.

Feeling a little calmer, I assess the situation.

I need a plan. Louis might lie in wait for me somewhere. If he murders me I need to leave some clues to his identity.

I take out my voice recorder and record details of what's just happened and give a lengthy description of Louis and his van. If I go missing I hope this'll help the police track him down. I hide the voice recorder amongst my things.

Alert for any odd sound and watchful for any nearby movement, I continue on my way. The track leads straight into Viana. Still concealed, I scrutinise the roads before I emerge from the bushes. The road into town seems clear and the motorhome nowhere to be seen.

Perhaps he thought I'd keep on going into Logroño?

I trudge nervously up the stone street into Viana, studying every door and laneway I pass, in case Louis is lurking somewhere. Toni is sitting outside a café quietly drinking tea and waves a welcome as I approach.

'Hi, Linda, please … join me.' Toni points to her table.

Relieved to see a friendly face, I make my way over to the café, and pull out a chair.

'Mint tea, please.' I give the waiter my order as I drop my backpack to the ground and sit down.

Toni is shocked but sympathetic when I relate my escapade with Louis. Telling her is extra insurance should I "disappear" on the trail in the coming days or weeks. Once I unload my story my trembling eases.

'I told Louis I planned to stay in Viana tonight, but now I want to get out of Viana as quickly as possible. I'll go on to Logrono tonight.'

Toni nods agreement. I finish my tea, hoist my backpack on and pick up the trekking poles.

'Bye, Toni, safe travels.'

'Bon Camino. Stay safe my friend. See you further on the track, Linda.'

CHAPTER 18

The Staring Italian

Logrono (The Province's Capital)
I SET OFF OUT OF Viana, watchful of every motorhome that passes. At every bend I fear I'll see Louis parked. Not far from Logroño there's a "detour" on the Camino. It leads into a forest and is so badly signed I lose the trail. There are many tracks—I try several. Each time I'm forced to retrace my steps and try another. I can't find any Camino-markers. Panic in my belly rises again. I'm close to tears.

Calm down—think. I must rationalise my position. I'm fairly sure I know the direction to Logrono, all I have to do is find a track. Otherwise I'll have to walk all the way back to the detour sign and try to find the other pathway.

I climb to the highest point I can find and scan the horizon. I'm about to head off in the general direction of where I *think* Logrono is, when I see a pilgrim in the distance. He hasn't taken the detour.

Did Louis put that sign there to confuse me? You're getting paranoid, Linda.

Scrambling down from my vantage point, I hurry through the forest toward the direction of the pilgrim. Crossing a field of tall grass, I stumble onto the concealed track. Relief flows through me, washing away my anxiety. Breathing deeply to exhale the tension, I follow the trail. The other pilgrim is quite a long way ahead.

In the distance, the pilgrim notices I've joined the track. He stops.

Oh no! Has he lost the track too? Oh well, it's going in the direction of Logrono, so at least it's the right way. Perhaps there's someone coming along behind me that he's waiting for.

When I get closer to the waiting pilgrim I recognise him.

Oh no! It's the staring Italian from a couple of nights back. Damn!

When I reach him I nod politely and keep walking straight past. The trail is clearly marked and I follow the markers. As I pass him he begins walking again.

Was he waiting for me?

The Italian follows silently.

Oh hell!

It feels like two bricks are crushing my temples together. Anxiety swirls again. There's no other person or building in sight. I'm still at least an hour away from the outskirts of Logrono.

A German pilgrim I met a few days ago told me she'd been pursued for several days by wild dogs that had terrified her. She had walked the same track at much the same time as me, but I'd not seen any dogs at all. I thought at the time that the dogs might have represented inner-demons she was being forced to face on the Camino. Now I wonder if I'm being forced to deal with my own demons.

Do men represent my own inner-demons that I have to learn to deal with? What is it specifically that is the problem I have to learn to overcome? Is it me? Is it manipulative men? Is it men that try to control my life?

I look around for Marcus or my other Spirit guides but they're not in sight. I feel too tense to calm my mind enough to speak with the Universe now, so I trudge on with a heavy heart, wondering what it is that I need to learn. After several kilometres I call again, for Marcus.

'Marcus! Have I faced my demons? Did I deal with my demons in the way I handled Louis?'

'Yes, you did. You've passed that test now.'

'Thank you, Marcus.' My chest heaves with relief that he's with me again. 'Is this a new demon I have to deal with?'

He doesn't answer.

I guess I have to figure it out for myself. Think, Linda, think. Perhaps I am just plain paranoid now.

The staring Italian catches up with me and wanders alongside as I hobble heavy-hearted down the track. I ignore him as he walks by my side. An Irish girl I met on the Camino a few days back, and her walking partner, catch up with us. The Irish girl greets both of us warmly. The staring Italian and the Irish girl discuss the route ahead like old friends.

Perhaps he isn't the demon I thought he might have been. I begin to relax a little. The Irish girl and her friend stride ahead much faster than I'm capable of and the staring Italian and I are soon alone again.

I think he's probably safe. But I don't have the emotional energy to talk to him now. The drama with Louis and then getting lost in the forest has drained me. I continue to ignore him as we walk side-by-side.

White and pink campanula line the roadside. Thyme, lavender, chamomile, buddleia, thistles and dandelions are abundant. Blue cornflowers and unrecognisable herbs mass the edges of the road.

It's like a cottage garden. Its beauty absorbs me. Hobbling along, I spot a small grey bush beside the road.

What is that? I hobble over and pull a few leaves, crush them in my hand and lift them to my nose to smell. I know many of the plants, but this one's strong fragrance is unfamiliar. *It looks herbal, but I don't know what it is.*

I drop it and walk on.

The staring Italian watches then walks to the same shrub, takes a few leaves, crushes them between his fingers, holds them to his nose and smells them.

'Ah, bella! Bella!' He grins at me and puts the leaves in his pocket.

I chuckle at his actions. He says something to me in Italian about the plant. I point out another plant and go over to it.

'Buddleia,' I tell him as I smell its flowers.

He smells it, 'Ah, bella,' and discusses it in Italian.

The ice is broken. We're friends now and we walk on discussing (him in Italian and me in English), various fragrant plants along the way.

On the outskirts of Logroño, the province's capital, we catch up with the Irish girl and her friend. They are lying, restful with their hiking boots off, on a patch of green grass under a shady tree, waiting for us. Seeing us approach, they quickly pull their boots on and join us. The four of us travel the last couple of kilometres into town together discussing the day and what we've seen. I don't mention Louis to them.

I'm relieved to be walking with a group of people into town as I fear Logroño could be the place where Louis might be lying in wait for me. If I see him or his motorhome, I'll tell my new friends what happened. Otherwise I'll keep it to myself. I want to forget it now–put it behind me. We're approaching the point where the Camino enters the city. This is where I fear Louis might park. I look around–Louis is nowhere to be seen.

Whatever that demon was that I had to deal with, it's been put to rest, I delude myself and heave a happy but misguided sigh. *I wonder if it means I'll have no more 'man' troubles in my life now that I've dealt with this symbolic demon. I hope so.*

CHAPTER 19

Friendships on the Camino

Navarette to Ventosa

THE IRISH GIRL AND MY Italian friend lead the way to the *Albergue*. I'm allocated a top bunk.

I don't like top bunks. I don't like having to climb up over someone else in the lower bunk to get in to or out of bed.

But pilgrims have to take what they are allocated, there's no negotiation. Once we've completed the check in, the Irish girl and I, soaked with sweat, go off to have a shower. It's a great relief to get my boots off. I inspect my feet. One of my toes is a deep, plum-coloured purple. Its nail is surrounded by a huge black blister. It's throbbing painfully.

I think I'll lose that nail.

On returning from my shower, the staring Italian has been checked-in. He's been allocated the bunk beneath me. In Italian and using gestures, he indicates that if I prefer the bottom bunk he's happy to change. I accept gladly and we swap. I wash out my sweaty clothes and put them to dry before going for a walk around town to buy supplies for tomorrow's breakfast and lunch.

It's easy to distinguish a pilgrim on the Camino. They're the ones limping.

When I return to the *Albergue*, the Italian, who's about to head out of the dormitory with a shopping bag, introduces himself as Italo. I understand enough of what he says to comprehend he's hungry and is going to the kitchen to eat. I'm surprised to learn there's a kitchen in the *Albergue*.

'*Cucina! Questa Cucina?*' Kitchen! Where's the kitchen? I ask him.

Italo indicates to follow him and leads me to a fabulously equipped kitchen in the heart of the *Albergue*. He talks too rapidly to follow much of what he says. I gather he's bought a lot of food for tonight and tomorrow and that it's going to be too heavy to carry. He invites me to share some with him. Nodding and pointing, he puts a tomato on a plate with a knife and pushes it towards me. I understand it's for me.

Breaking bread? Okay.

'*Una momentito,*' I rush off to the dormitory.

I collect some of my provisions and bring them back to Italo's table. He slides a tomato, olive oil, vinegar and salt, towards me. I offer him bread and fruit. I discuss the weather over the meal. I think Italo discusses the weather too. We chat away in our respective languages, enjoying the food all the more for the spirit of companionship and adventure in which it's shared.

One of the greatest pleasures of the Camino for me is conversations where actual words are often not comprehended, but context, body language and intent, bring people together in happy meetings of mutual understanding. Being able to speak the languages of other pilgrims matters little; it's the act of communicating that is the joy. Pilgrims often use a captivating mish-mash of languages and body language to get their meanings across.

'Thank you, Italo. It was a lovely meal and it was lovely to talk with you. I'm going to get an early night now. I'll see you in the morning. Good night.'

'*Grazie. Grazie,*' he begins and chats on in Italian. I think he says he's going to take a walk to look at the church, but I really can't be sure. I nod and smile, say goodnight again and leave him to it.

Refugios are locked at 10.00 pm each night and unlocked at 6.00 am so eager pilgrims can make an early start. During the night a sore throat and a cough develops and I spend most of the night trying to smother my coughs in my pillow so as not to disturb anyone.

Italo in the bunk above stirs at 5.00 am and quietly packs to leave. Wistfully, I listen to him preparing to leave, my early apprehension of his watchfulness has grown into an appreciation of his company. I feel safe walking with him. Friendships on the Camino are fluid and fleeting; people meet, make friends, then go separate ways, in accordance to walking speeds, abilities, personal preferences on start and stop times or desire to travel certain distances each day. It's still dark as Italo leaves.

It's hard enough to see the trail markers during daylight hours. I don't want to try to find them in the dark. It's different for a man. I feel safer in the daylight.

I wait until the blackness of night lightens before I set off. It's crisp, cool and quiet on the cobbled streets of Logroño as I head out of the *refugio*. The Irish girl catches up with me.

'Good morning,' she tosses the words brightly as she strides past.

'Good morning. *Bon Camino.*'

The girl turns down a street.

'Hey, I think that's the wrong street.' I shout a warning in the dim loneliness of the still empty city.

'No, I am sure this is the right way,' she calls back, continuing on.

I see a local on the other side of the road and call out in my now adequate Spanish and ask which road is correct for the Camino. His cheerful answer indicates I'm right. The Irish girl hears the exchange, calls her thanks, changes roads, waves me a grateful farewell and walking much faster than I am, is soon out of sight on the right road.

I've been going pathetically slow. Even though my toe is still a black blistered mess, it's not slowing me down so much. I'm a lot fitter now and feeling really good today. I think I can speed up, got some time to make up.

I stride longer and increase my speed. Last night, in my planning for today, I calculated I could travel fifteen kilometres to Navarette and stop the night there. But today, having sped up, I reach Navarette by 10.00 am.

It's far too early to stop for the day. I'll have a cup of mint tea and a few minutes rest here and then continue on to Ventosa, it's only another seven kilometres.

Everything's shut in Navarette on this sleepy Sunday morning. The empty silence of the village is rather unnerving so I don't stay long. I'm fatigued when I reach Ventosa; my coughing is worse and my blackened toe is throbbing.

It's just after midday when I check in at the *Albergue* San Saturnino. I eat the *bocadillo* (cheese roll) that I prepared last night, shower, wash my clothes, hang them in the sun and collapse on my bunk. I feel dreadful. My chest is heavily congested and my throat is so sore I can barely talk or swallow.

The Spanish volunteer checking me in at the refuge, is clearly worried about me. He sends a woman who speaks a little English to look in on me.

'Are you ill? Pedro asked me to come and see if you are alright? Do you have a fever?'

'I'm fine—just a cold. Thank you.'

The woman seems truly concerned, but leaves me to a restless coughing sleep. A few hours later I wake, chilled, and rug myself up with blankets. Then hot and sweating I throw all the covers off. Later, faint with hunger, I stagger downstairs to find a place to get something to eat. I want a tomato salad for dinner. I didn't see a shop when I walked through the village on my way in to the *Albergue*.

'Is there somewhere in the village where I can buy tomatoes?' I croak to the lady at reception between bouts of coughing.

The lady appears to misunderstand my question and begins to discuss with her Spanish colleagues the challenge of getting me to a doctor.

With my head spinning, blackness hovers, I lean on the table for support. I don't have the strength to interrupt the conversation to reiterate that all I want is some tomatoes for my dinner. The chap at reception who'd checked me in, offers to drive me to a doctor if necessary, but first he wants to look down my throat.

Much discussion (all in Spanish), follows each of our gestures. I have very little idea of exactly what's going on, but know they're all *most concerned* about my state of well-being. The man pulls a kit that looks like a dentist's kit, out of a cupboard, and extracts from it a device to examine my throat. I now feel extremely nervous about the direction things appear to be heading.

I hope he's not planning on extracting one of my teeth.

He gently probes the glands in my throat then feels the heat of my forehead as the gathering in the reception area, now numbering four, look on. I think he tells our audience that I definitely have a fever, as he looks down my throat. After several of his Spanish *"Arrs"* followed by several of my strangled English "Arrs" he announces I have pharyngitis. Much discussion and looking in dictionaries amongst the group follows. I realise they are trying to find out how to say *faringeetus* in English, to explain it to me.

'Do you mean pharyngitis?' I enquire.

'*Si!*' He's relieved that I understand.

'How do you say it in English?' the woman asks.

'Pharyngitis.' I grin at them.

'Oh, is the same?'

'*Si*. Is the same.' I grin again.

The audience heaves a collective sigh of relief. The man, it turns out, is a male nurse, an *infermo*. He disappears for a few minutes and then reappears with tablets for me to take. The woman interprets his instructions to me on how to take the tablets, declaring 'You will be well in 24 hours!'

'*Gracias.*' I take the proffered tablets and swallow them, washing them down with a glass of water the woman hands me.

'Is there anywhere in the village I can buy tomatoes?' I ask meekly once again.

'*Si. La tienda*. The shop in the village.' The woman gives me directions to the village shop.

I love Spanish tomatoes. They look like they've been grown in the villages, imperfect in shape, with extraordinary sweetness; just like the tomatoes mum grew in our garden when I was a child, without any artificial anything added. Tomatoes, when I was a child, had so much flavour; not like insipid supermarket tomatoes today. I buy some large deep red, succulent-looking ones. There are no other fresh salad vegetables in the tiny shop, so I buy a jar of asparagus, a bread stick and order one hundred grams of cheese, because that's the only measurement I understand how to order in Spanish. Everything I order is one hundred grams – meat, cheese, whatever– 'One hundred grams please.' There's nothing else in the shop I recognise or know the words for, so I gather my tomatoes, asparagus, bread and cheese, and go back to the *Albergue*.

Back in the *Albergue* I cut up the tomatoes into a bowl, add the sectioned asparagus, some cheese, and sprinkle it all with a little salt. It's absolutely delicious and quite sufficient along with the bread stick for my meal. The rest of the bread and cheese I make into a *bocadillo*, a Spanish sandwich for tomorrow's breakfast, and stash it away. Alone in the dormitory I re-plan the next few days' journey before I climb into my bunk and fall into a very deep and very early sleep.

CHAPTER 20

The "Humpfing" Woman

Azofra (Province of La Rioja)
WHILE I SLEEP, THE DORMITORY fills with pilgrims. I wake in the middle of the night as water trickles, then pours onto my face. I leap out of bed in fright. In the darkness I feel the bottom of the mattress of the bunk above me; it's saturated. A young man is sleeping peacefully on the wet mattress, I shake him gently.

'There's water pouring onto my face underneath.' I whisper to him, pointing to the bunk below.

A Japanese lady in the bunk alongside makes a very loud and annoyed *"humpf"* at being disturbed and turns over angrily and noisily in her bunk.

The young man in the bunk above blinks at me a couple of times, looking rather startled and very sleepy. It takes him a moment to wake fully and take in what I've just whispered. His eyes widen and he quickly pulls a water drink bottle from under his pillow. The little water still left in it pours onto his bed; its cap had become unscrewed during the night. Water had been trickling out and had saturated his mattress before washing onto my face and pillow on the bunk below.

'Sorry! So sorry!' He tightens the lid on the bottle.

I climb back into the soggy bunk. The inundation had been electrifying. I turn the soaked pillow over to the less-wet side and settle back down to sleep again. The Japanese lady's angry *"humpf"* and exaggerated body-toss irritates me.

I was very quiet when I leapt out of bed. I whispered quietly. I could have screamed in fright. That would've thrown a few people out of bed with the shock of it. Most people would've made a lot more fuss than I just did if they woke to water pouring onto their face in the night. What's she performing so angrily for?

My heart is still thumping from the fright as I try to settle back to sleep.

At 5.00 am the *"humpfing"* woman in the bunk next door rattles, bangs, drags, snorts, sniffs, and scuffles for forty-five minutes as she rises and packs her gear on her bunk.

I listen to the noise she's making and grow even more annoyed with her. Pilgrims are generally extremely considerate of others in a refuge. There's an unspoken rule not to rise before 6.00 am and when they do rise, they do it quietly or pack their things outside of the sleeping area. Often I don't hear anything at all, they're just not there anymore when I wake.

I'm tired from the water torture during the night, and the *"humpfing"* woman's noisy lack of consideration for anyone else irritates me enormously. Come morning, several pilgrims mutter their displeasure about the woman's too early, noisy departure.

I hoist on my pack and wearily head out of the Ventosa *refugio* at 7.00 am. It's a steep dusty track going down the hill out of the village. I trek for forty minutes before I realise I've left my trekking poles back at the *refugio*. Exasperated, I scold myself for forgetting them, then mutter and scuff the dust all the way back up the hill to the refuge to retrieve them.

Camino-markings here are neither abundant, nor clear, and I lose the trail several times. Each time I lose the trail, I do my tracker dog act; sniffing around and hunting to pick up the trail again. It's gentle undulating countryside. There's a lot less difference between the highs and lows and a lot less ruggedness than in recent days. At the last *refugio* they told me the hardest parts of the Camino were behind me. I hope so.

The province of Navarra is behind me now, this is La Rioja. La Rioja is famous for its red wine. Its hillsides are striped with meticulously straight and neatly tended rows of grape vines. The Camino meanders through the vineyards, in every direction the vines are heavy with masses of tight bunches of succulent-looking, black grapes. The crops have been thinned; there are just as many bunches discarded on the ground as still on the vines.

Soft dry dust rises as I walk. The temperature climbs steadily through the morning. It's mid-morning and I'm hungry when I reach Najera. At a bar, I order some tapas and a cup of *poleo menthe* (mint tea) for a second breakfast. Pulling off my boots and socks, I give my feet an airing in the sun to dry them off. I'm hot, tired and sore, but it's much too early to stop for the day. After ten minutes of rest and refreshments I pull my socks and boots back on, hoist on my backpack and trudge on.

Shade trees have disappeared from the landscape. The countryside is drier and the temperature hotter. The hard dusty barren earth reflects the heat back up in a quivering haze, drying the air. I suck warm water often from the tube of the hydro-pack inside my backpack. Water fountains in villages are welcome sights. Greedily I slurp their cool fresh water and splash their blessing over my red and steaming face. I soak my cotton hat in the coolness, wring it out and pull it onto my head. The sun's rays burn through my shirt. My water supply is diminishing rapidly. I trek from village fountain to village fountain. Azofra is only another 5.5 kilometres but seems a very long way.

How much further? I climb over one hillock after another.

Then, from a hilltop I see a church steeple in the distance nestled amongst ancient roof tops of a small village.

That must be Azofra. A welcome sight.

Dusty and red in the face, I trudge into the compound of the *Albergue* at just after midday. A straggle of sweaty, tired-looking pilgrims have already gathered in the compound and are waiting for the *Albergue* to open.

'*A uno!*' A pilgrim man calls to me as I approach, indicating that the *Albergue* will not open until 1.00 pm.

Too fatigued to speak I nod acknowledgement, drag a chair under the shade to sit on and then another to rest my aching feet on. Unhitching my waist bag, camera and backpack, I drop them to the ground. Slumping into the chair, I join the exhausted bedraggled bunch waiting for opening time.

At one o'clock the refuge opens. Registration in refuges is done one person at a time. Pilgrims wait silently and patiently. When it's my turn to register, I'm allocated a room with a Swiss woman, Elizabeth. We're both delighted when we see only two bunks in the room. To share a whole room with only one other person is a rare treat; most refuges have ten, twenty, thirty or one hundred bunks in a room.

I may not need my earplugs tonight. I unpack my things and lay them on the bed. *Then-again the walls here are quite thin, and the snorers can be incredibly loud, so perhaps I'll wear the earplugs anyway.*

My earplugs are indispensable little treasures on the Camino and they, along with my eye mask, have caused many envious comments over the past weeks. I do my showering and laundering and head off to find a restaurant for my evening meal.

The entry into the refuge is almost invisible from the street outside– nothing more than a hole in a large stone wall. It's only visible when you're directly outside it. I step through the gap in the wall onto the street and see the *"humpfing"* woman has missed the entrance and has walked past down the road. Her friend, trailing way behind her is approaching the entrance and is startled as I pop out of the hole in the wall in front of her. Grinning at her look of shock, I give her a nod as I step onto the road. I feel ever-so slightly avenged that the *"humpfing"*-one has missed the entrance. If it had been anyone else, I would have called to them immediately to let them know they'd missed the gate. But I hesitate for just a moment, and in that moment the *"humpfing"*-one's friend calls to her and points out the gate. I'm grateful that someone else saved the *"humpfing"*-one for me.

I find a restaurant with a sign out front saying *Menu Peregrino,* (Pilgrims' Menu) for nine euro. Pilgrim menus are too good to pass up; they consist of three course meals, often with wine included, and are always fresh local produce cooked in a nourishing traditional recipe. Today's menu consists of a first-course of salad, a second-course of calamari and chips and then a desert of fresh melon slices. Wine in La Rioja is cheaper than water. Water here costs extra; wine is complimentary and superb. After the meal I return to the refuge, curl up on my bunk and succumb, happy and contented, to the pull of a well-earned sleep.

CHAPTER 21

Spiritual Energy of the Camino

Santo Domingo de la Calzado to Vilora del Rioja

NAVARRA, THE FIRST REGION THE Camino passes through in Spain, is steep and craggy. While it is ruggedly beautiful, it makes walking hard. In La Rioja, while the undulating counterpane–covered with straight, evenly-spaced, neatly-trimmed grape vines–makes walking far less strenuous, the lack of variety of the landscape is monotonous.

The land, denuded of trees, offers no respite from the searing sun scorching the hard baked earth. No boulders or crags to shelter under. No places to sit or rest. The intense heat is relentless. There is no alternative but to trudge on over the tough stony path.

Bang! Bang! There it is again. For the last couple of weeks I've heard that noise on a daily basis. It sounds like gunshots somewhere in the distance. I look around, studying the hills, trying to see where the noise is coming from. On a distant hill a man with a shotgun on his hip strolls through a field with two dogs. He pauses and waits. His dogs startle a tiny bird from the field. As the bird rises into the air, the man raises his rifle and fires.

Bang! The tiny bird falls to the ground. The bird is so small I cannot imagine it will provide more than a morsel of meat. It's hard to believe such tiny birds are being shot for food. I've seen so few birds and so little wildlife in Spain, perhaps this is the reason–hunters.

This morning I set out with a plan to walk 21.5 kilometres to Grañon. I've just reached Santo Domingo de la Calzado and I've only traveled fifteen kilometres, but my feet are screaming for me to stop. I check in to the refuge at noon. I'm done for the day.

After a welcome shower and the ritual laundering I limp off to find a restaurant for lunch. Los Caballeros offers a traditional three-course pilgrim menu that consists of a jug of excellent red wine, a basket of crusty bread, paella for the first-course, pork and chips for main-course, and yoghurt for desert. It's divine.

Weary to the bone, I use the internet at the refuge and email my daily report home before settling down for a much longed-for nap. But sleep doesn't come. An angry raised red rash has developed on my feet and legs. Its burning itchy irritation prevents sleep's blissful relief carrying my cares away.

The inflamed rash coupled with aching feet is unbearable, I have to do something.

A good hard foot massage might free up some of the pain in my feet.

A pilgrim along the way told me there's someone in most villages that will do massages for pilgrims quite cheaply. All you need to do is ask the *hospitalero*, the volunteer host at the refuge, and the *hospitalero* will arrange it, the pilgrim had said. I ask the *hospitalero* if there's someone in town who can do a foot massage.

Knowing the word for massage in Spanish is *masaje* (pronounced *mas-a-kee*), but not knowing the word for the person who does the massage, I take a guess at *masajero* (and pronounce it *mas-a-kee-ro*). I ask the *hospitalero*- '*donde ese uno masajero?*' (my intended question being 'where is there a masseur?') The *hospitalero* gives me a puzzled look and I know immediately I've got it wrong.

'*Masaje,*' I say, acting out quite a good demonstration of a massage.

'*Oh, masachista!*' The *hospitalero* proclaims with confidence.

I don't feel very reassured. The suggestion of a masochist bothers me.

'*Si,*' I nod hesitantly, dubiously wondering what I'm getting myself into.

The *hospitalero* promptly pulls a card from his desk that's clearly for a physiotherapist, and hands it to me.

'*Masachista?*' I ask uncertainly, pointing to the card.

'*Si,*' he nods confidently and turns, giving rapid instructions to two young girls who are helping him. The two girls speak a little English and offer to take me to the *masachista,* who, they say, doesn't speak any English. On the way to the masochist, just to make sure there's no misunderstanding of what I'm seeking, I explain to the girls that my feet are very sore.

'I need a good foot massage to ease the pain.'

They smile and nod at me. Once we arrive at the masochist's rooms, the girls, I hope, explain that I have sore feet and an appointment is duly made for later in the evening.

On my return to the refuge, Birgitte, a Danish pilgrim, calls me over. Earlier I gave Birgitte twenty minutes of my pre-paid internet time. Now she reciprocates by inviting me to join her for a picnic meal and wine. I sit with her happily drinking wine, comparing sore spots and aches as we contemplate how long it will take our wounds to heal. Then it's time for me to visit the masochist.

The masochist puts a lamp of sorts to glow on my feet, wafts an infrared thing over them and finishes off by giving them a light rub with some mentholated smelling stuff. That's it. I'm deeply disappointed as I feel all the sore spots need a good firm massage. But not being an expert, I tell myself that perhaps by tomorrow, after this unfamiliar treatment, I might be able to walk properly again.

'Thirty euros,' the masochist demands.

Thirty euros for that! It had better fix my feet. I pay the money and leave. As I walk back into the refuge after my visit to the masochist, the church bell chimes 8.00 pm and the refuge promptly empties. It's time for pilgrims' mass or, in my case–not being catholic, bed.

Grey sky the next morning hangs heavily. I plan an easy 13.5 kilometre hike to Vilora del Rioja, hoping the weather stays fine 'til I get there. Rain begins to sprinkle eight kilometres out of Grañon. I've learnt my lesson; I stop immediately, retrieve my wet weather gear, pull on waterproof trousers and get out a new vinyl poncho, ready to put on if the rain gets any heavier. Prepared for a storm, I hoist my pack on and set off. The rain eases and the clouds pass overhead without discharging their cargo.

Sauntering along, I become aware of Marcus walking by my side.

'Good morning, Marcus.'

'Good morning. Tell me, what have you learnt from the people you've met in the last few days?'

I think about his question for a few moments. 'The people I like the most are the ones who laugh a lot.'

'And what does that tell you?' I consider this new question deeply before answering.

'It tells me that I don't laugh enough. I'd like to laugh more often. I feel joy but I hold it inside.'

'Why do you do that?'

I think long and hard and dig deep into my well of buried emotions before answering.

'Because people will think less of me if I laugh.'

'Do you really think that's true?'

'No, it sounds silly. But that's what came to mind.' I pause and analyse what thoughts or emotions lay beneath that feeling. 'I'll make a fool of myself.'

'And do you really think that's true?'

'No, but again that's what comes to mind.'

'Where do you think those feelings come from?'

Several minutes pass while I dig deeper into my subconscious.

'They seem to come from the time I was ten years old in Mr Jones' class at school.'

'What happened?'

A few more minutes pass while I excavate long forgotten and deeply buried memories.

'I loved school; Mr Jones was my only source of positive strokes in life. The other kids called me "teacher's pet". I was usually top of the class that year and Mr Jones would say things to me like "good girl" and "well done". I lived for his words of praise. My parents didn't give praise, my father was an angry man and mum spent her time "keeping the peace" as she would call it. School was my place of escape and when I learnt that by working hard at school I could get some positive strokes in life, I reveled in it.

I recall giggling in class one day at something someone sitting in front of me had said. Mr Jones made me stand up and insisted I tell the class what I was laughing at. I was painfully shy and totally lacked self-esteem and self-confidence. Standing up and repeating something silly in front of all my classmates humiliated and embarrassed me. I felt I made a fool of myself that day and let Mr Jones down.'

'Is that still relevant to you today?'

'No, it isn't.'

'How are those old feelings making you feel today though?'

'Like there is a heavy weight of fear stopping me from laughing out loud.'

'Visualise that fear, give it a shape, size and colour. What shape is it?'

'Square.'

'What colour is it?'

'Brown. A big square heavy brown wooden box.'

'Now I am going to attach a giant helium balloon to that crate. Watch it lift the box off you. Watch the balloon carry it up and away into the sky.' A few minutes pass as I visualise the scene he's created in my mind.

'Is the crate still attached to you?'

'Yes, there are several strings attached to me.'

'Your Spirit guides are going to cut those strings. Watch as they cut them. Now watch the box as it soars into the sky. Tell me when it's disappeared from your view.'

I watch the strings being cut and the balloon taking the box out of my sight. A few minutes pass. 'It's gone now. A weight has lifted off me; I feel quite floaty.'

'Never be afraid to laugh again. Laughter is good for your soul as well as your body and mind–laugh often. You're attracted to people who laugh frequently; become like them.

'Yes, Marcus.'

As I walk into Vilora del Rioja my body tingles with lightness. It's 11.30 am, which is rather early to stop walking but I promised my feet they'd go no further today, and I keep my promises.

The refuge is run by a Brazilian man and his Italian wife. There are sixteen to eighteen bunkbeds upstairs and a lounge and dining room downstairs. Pictures of Paolo Coehlo decorate the walls, he stayed here in 2005. I check-in, go upstairs and choose a bunk, organise my things and lay down. Wave after wave of chilling cold washes through my body from my head right down to my toes.

I hope I'm not coming down with something else.

That evening the Brazilian host, interpreted by his wife, tells me he's walked a pilgrimage every year for the past fifteen years. He's walked the Camino many times. He's also walked pilgrimages through South America, Spain, France, and many other places.

'The Camino has the strongest spiritual energy of all the pilgrimages I've walked,' he says. 'It is because the Camino in Spain is on a ley-line and has the energy of the ley-line to help pilgrims find direction in life. The ley-line gives the Camino the *spiritual energy* to help see your *spiritual direction* with clarity. Your sore throat is the beginning of your throat chakra opening up. It indicates communication, a need for you to improve your communication. You need to speak out more, be more open and say when you like or dislike something–instead of holding everything inside.'

I have always kept things to myself but in recent years feel I've been speaking out more. I've probably been doing it badly though because it seems I often offend people. I have been thinking recently of returning to my old ways of keeping things to myself. I guess he's confirming that I need to continue to speak out.

'When you find an unpopulated area while walking the Camino; no villages or people, then you must stop and scream. Scream loudly. It will help the opening of your throat chakra. Massage your throat area while you're screaming. Massage it randomly as well, it will help the opening of the chakra.'

The evening meal is communal around the hosts' table with several other pilgrims. That night, my aching feet and sore throat result in another unsettled sleepless night.

CHAPTER 22

Clarity

As the early morning rays of light creep across the countryside I sit up and look out the window. A series of strange "events" had played in my mind during the night. In the first and longest, I was asked to restore three ancient buildings. I was some sort of designer or architect, brought in as a consultant. The person speaking to me was most insistent that I advise and assist in the renovation. It was so vivid I could smell and feel the buildings.

Each "event" that played in my mind during the night was as vivid as the previous. Throughout the night I kept asking *please God, turn it off, I need to sleep.* But they wouldn't stop. Now I'm too tired to think through the meaning of the dreams.

I want to go home! I came on the Camino for spiritual growth and I've had fifteen days of physical agony. I've had enough. My feet are still aching and my sore toe is still incredibly painful. What's the point of going on a six week walk if I can barely walk? Now I've got a sore throat and I'm not sleeping.

I miss Larry and the girls and Eddy and my dog. I miss my own bed and the comforts of home. That's it. I'm going home. I don't need to finish walking the Camino. I just need to walk on to a village where I can catch a bus, to begin my journey home.

I set off exhausted and determined that today I'm finished on the Camino—I've given up the need to walk it. I stride out of Viloria del Rioja to find a bus that'll take me to a city, from where I can fly home.

As I walk, I'm seduced: by the distinctive country aroma of pig manure permeating the air. The smell is so very "back to nature" that the tension in me rises up and floats away. My shoulders loosen and I relax into a comfortable stride; reveling in the rural sensation the smell of pigs has donated to the fresh morning air.

Easing the pace my mind drifts into a myriad of thoughts. Last night's conversation around the dinner table comes to mind. As I reach an area in the middle of fields, I recall my host's advice on opening up my throat chakra. I stop and look around to see if I'm alone. I've left the pigs way behind, there's no-one in sight, no houses, no buildings, no cars. Just open fields.

Self-conscious, I check a second time to make certain no-one's within hearing. Standing still in the middle of the field I mentally encourage myself to attempt a scream. A squawk comes out.

That's feeble.

It's not natural to stand alone in the countryside and scream. *Uneasy,* I look around again to see if I'm alone. There's still no-one in view.

I try again. My second squawk is a little stronger. I'm nervous because someone might misinterpret my squawk and come running to my aid.

I don't want to have to explain I'm practising screaming to open my throat chakra. I fidget from one foot to the other.

A truck approaches on the highway nearby. I wait for it to draw near. As it roars noisily alongside I try again. This time I put some guts into it, and timing—so that it's drowned out by the din of the passing vehicle.

AAAAAAAAAAAAAAAAAGGHH!

It feels wonderful. In fact, it feels so good, I laugh. Four more gutsy screams later, my heart is soaring and I'm filled with joy and giggling.

'Oh what a beautiful morning,' I begin singing the old song that always seems so happy.

Just as well no-one else is around. They'd think I'm totally out of my mind.

Chuckling at the thought, and with a light heart and soaring spirit, I continue on my way through the fields. The cool bliss of almost-dawn envelopes me as the sun peeps over the horizon to bless the surrounding fields.

It really is a glorious morning.

I look up and see I have company.

'Good morning,' I greet Marcus and my Spirit guides.

'Good morning, Linda.'

'Marcus, what was my dream about last night? Was it really a dream, because it felt like I was awake? What was that all about, designing houses? It just kept playing over and over. It wouldn't stop.'

'You are the designer. You are the architect of your own houses and they need renovating. You must redesign your mental, physical and spiritual houses and re-build them.'

'Oh!' Clarity dawns, as the last remaining weight in my belly dissipates like fine dust in a breeze, and wafts away. *He's right. I do need to rebuild.*

Was I given the accident, the broken back, to bring me to this point? I can see clearly now that my life needs to be reconstructed, the Camino has made that clear. I can't quit walking the Camino now, not when I've just found my purpose.

At the very point I felt I'd had enough and was ready to quit, I could see my purpose of walking the Camino. It's not just about keeping my promise, it's about rebuilding my life.

'Marcus, I understand now that I need to re-design and re-build my spiritual life, but how do I re-design and re-build my mental and physical life?'

'You've been in a mental hole, the last several months; you have been in a space that doesn't fill your heart with joy. Because of that, mentally, physically and spiritually you lost your direction.'

I ponder his words for some time as I walk. *He's right. I chose to return to fulltime work in our business because it was necessary as we created a new direction for the business. I chose to do it but it was not a decision of my heart. Not something that filled my heart with joy. It was a rational decision of what was needed at the time. I told myself I'd give it twelve months and at the end of twelve months we'd reassess where we were going with the business and what my role was to be.*

It's not twelve months yet, it's eight. Eight months and I'm finding it emotionally, spiritually and physically difficult.

'How you live your life is totally your choice. Choose how your heart wants you to live your life. Make the decision. Always live in choice.'

'I understand, Marcus. I see that I'm going to have to reassess my direction.'

I've got a few more weeks on the Camino to reassess my direction. I hope the Camino will give me some answers, will tell me how to do that. I can't quit the Camino now.

I know Marcus is here to guide me, but how I live my life is always entirely my own choice. It is up to me to make the decisions. Marcus and the Universe will guide me but I must choose the pathway myself.

I know that sometimes when I'm on a life pathway that's wrong for me, the Universe steps in and forces a change of direction—like the accident. Perhaps the accident was to force me to stop, to re-consider, force me to come to this point here, now.

I recall the negative self-talk that led me to the moment of the accident.

Yes. I was saying in the back of my mind, 'I've had enough.' I must be careful about what I think. I must live in choice. Now I have to decide what my choices are. What do I want to do with my life? It's not about what I feel I should do, or must do, it's about what I want to do with my life.

CHAPTER 23

Bunk Thief

Villafranca Montes de Oca to Burgos (Province of Castilla y Leon)
The changing landscape brings my thoughts back to the present.

It's obvious La Rioja province is behind me; all of a sudden the vineyards have gone.

In their place, the rolling hills of Castilla y Leon are covered with mown straw. Neat regular stripes and tractor furrows on the brown hills indicate a crop has recently been harvested.

Elder flowers jostle each other alongside the Camino offering their crowns of berries up to the midday sun. Blackberries sprawl untidily along the roadside. White butterflies flit from flower to flower. Nearby, pink campanula entice tiny rust coloured butterflies to seek their nectar. Mown hillsides, striped beige and brown are laid bare. The occasional tall stacks of fresh hay mark the fields' recent yield.

An intense-blue, cloudless sky offers no protection from the blazing Spanish summer sun climbing high overhead. The rocky path torments my ankles. Huge trucks rumble by raising clouds of choking dust that blanket everything.

'*Bravo Peregrino,*' (well done pilgrim) a truck driver shouts, tooting and waving as his truck thunders past. My chest swells with pride and my back straightens from his encouragement. Weariness abates–slightly.

The Camino moves closer alongside the road. Like an artist's canvas awash with mauves, violets, purples and lavenders, dainty and diminutive flowers of legumes line the sides of the path.

It's like a cottage garden. I breathe in the beauty surrounding me as I pass through the tiny village of Villa Major to reach Bellorado. Bellorado is only slighter larger than the last village, but it has a couple of insignificant shops while the other villages have none.

I've written postcards and I've been looking for days for somewhere to buy postage stamps so I can post them. A local in the last village told me I could buy postage stamps in Bellorado but I pass through Bellorado without seeing an obvious place to buy stamps.

By mid-afternoon I'm fatigued to the point of dazed automation. The yellow arrows of the Camino draw me onward. *This way,* they beckon, *this way, keep going.* One foot follows the other.

No longer am I walking just to close the door on the years of recovery and fulfil the promise I made; now I'm walking to find a new direction in life.

Will I go back to the life I've left? What changes should I make? Where am I walking to?

I stumble into the refuge at Villafranca Montes de Oca.

That makes twenty-two kilometres today. Is that a new record for me? I can't remember. I'm too tired to care.

After another long hot restless night, morning is not welcome.

That's two bad nights in a row. Don't want to walk today. There's little choice though, can't stay a second night in the refuge; against the rules. Have to push on today.

I massage my broken foot and put blister plasters on the raw spots. I coat my feet and toes thoroughly with Vaseline and pull on first my liner socks, then my thick outer socks. Slipping my feet into my boots, I lace them firmly. I load my backpack and with a somewhat numb, yet reluctant determination, head out into the early morning air.

The route out of Villafranca Montes de Oca (Town of the Franks at the foot of the Oca mountains) is a shock. The narrow Camino track runs straight up the mountainside through dense oak forest. Even though, after sixteen days of walking I'm now quite fit, the mountain is so steep that I'm forced to stop every ten or fifteen metres to gasp for breath. Two thirds of the way up the mountain, my lungs are on fire. *I need some extra stamina*. I stop, retrieve my breakfast from my pack and sit down to eat and rest.

After the energy-boosting break I continue up the arduous mountainside. Further on, the shade of forest trees provides protection from the sting of the blazing sun. On the top of the ridge the path levels out and walking becomes less of an effort. The burn in my lungs eases. A sandy track winds its way for twelve kilometres through woodland into the tiny hamlet of San Juan de Ortega. Saint John of Ortega built the Romanesque monastery here as a place where pilgrims, walking to Santiago de Compostella, could stop and worship. His tomb is in its crypt.

I see a bar as I approach the hamlet. Several pilgrims, their backpacks and boots stacked outside, are resting, eating and drinking at tables outside. They nod as I approach and give a "please come and join our table" gesture. I nod thanks and drop my backpack at one of their tables before going into the bar. I order a cup of mint tea and a piece of Spanish omelet and return to the table. Easing my boots off to let my feet air-dry in the sun; it's a relief to sit down after such a grueling morning. I've no idea what nationality the other pilgrims at the table are, we simply smile and nod; it's easier than trying to communicate when you're exhausted and have no idea what language is spoken.

Out of San Juan de Ortega the oak forest gradually disappears to be replaced beyond Ages with farmers' fields. Atapuerca, a municipality in the *province* of Burgos, Castile and León is my destination for tonight. The *albergue* at Atapuerca is small basic and adequate and the bonus is that there are only three of us in the *albergue* tonight.

'What bliss to have so much space to ourselves,' I comment to two Italian room-mates. They introduce themselves as brothers, Gabriel and Mario, and agree it's a rare treat to have a quiet *albergue*. There's internet access in the bar next door. I check-in on news from home and send my daily report. My toe, though still ugly-looking, has finally begun to heal and my throat is also less painful.

Yesterday's screaming must have done it some good. I smirk at my secret.

Evening comes; I wander into the restaurant next door and see Gabriel and Mario sitting at a table. They gesture for me to join them. They speak only slightly more English than I speak Italian, which is very little but it doesn't matter, we are brothers and sisters on the same journey. A young man walks into the restaurant.

'*Peregrino?*' (Pilgrim?) Gabriel calls to him.

'*Si,*' the young man confirms. Gabriel waves a hand inviting him to join us.

The young man introduces himself as Thomas from Germany. Thomas has just left school and is walking the Camino to give himself time and space to contemplate life beyond school. Thomas speaks German, English and Spanish and can comprehend quite a bit of Italian, so he interprets when comprehension fails between the Italians and me. Over dinner with a bottle of red wine, we share stories and Camino experiences in Spanish, Italian and English.

Mario is walking the Camino for spiritual insight. Gabriel for the enjoyment of the countryside, a "walking holiday" he calls it.

'If I receive any spiritual insight it will be a bonus.'

"A walking holiday"–what a pleasant notion.

'And you, Linda, why are you walking the Camino?'

'I am walking for spiritual insight too.' *There's no need to go into detail telling these strangers I'm fulfilling a promise.*

Vivid dreams trouble my sleep for the third night in a row. This time a man is pursuing me. Every time I try to run away he appears before me. I can't escape. I'm relieved when morning's light begins to dissipate the darkness.

Who was the man pursuing me?

According to my guidebook, the *panaderia* (bread shop) in the village opens at 5.30 am and serves breakfast for two euro. At 7.00 am I bid the Italians farewell and hungrily head for the *panaderia*. It's shut. In Spain, I've found that it's not uncommon for shops not to open or close according to their stated trading hours. My guidebook indicates there are no shops or bars to buy food until Burgos, twenty-two kilometres away.

I've only got a few nuts in my pack as I ate my remaining supplies yesterday on the mountain. They won't last till Burgos–I've got a problem. I'll pass out without breakfast or something to snack on today, my blood-sugar levels won't cope.

None of the bars along the way in the past week sold nuts, or anything I could stock up on for emergencies.

Oh dear! What am I going to do without breakfast? I'd also planned on buying something here for lunch. It's a long way to walk today, I can't continue without the certainty of getting food in the next couple of hours. I'll have to wait here until the panaderia opens. But what if it doesn't open at all? What if they've gone on holiday? I'll have to go to the bar I was at last night and ask if the panaderia is opening today or alternatively ask where I can get food.

I'm considering my dilemma when two American ladies stroll up.

'Is it shut?'

'Yes. I have a problem. I'd planned on breakfast at the *panaderia* but it's closed.'

'We'd planned on breakfast here too,' said the taller American.

'I can't go on without getting some food; I've got low blood-sugar. I have to find somewhere else to get something to eat.'

'My guidebook says there are places to buy food in the villages ahead.'

'Really? I hope your guidebook is right.' I grin at the American.

'So do I.' She grins back. 'My name's Cathy, this is Peg.'

'Linda. Nice to meet you.'

We walk together along the trail heading out of the village.

'I need to find somewhere to get more supplies of snacks, nuts or something.'

'Good luck at that.' Grins Cathy. 'I haven't seen anything like that in the villages we've been through. I think you need a city for that sort of thing.'

'Yes, that's the challenge.'

We stroll off up the next hill, chatting in the cool of early morning. A few hundred metres up the hill, Peg has fallen behind. The hill is steep and she can't keep up.

'I'll have to wait for Peg. You go on. We'll see you further on. Bye for now.' Cathy waves me on and then hangs back to wait for Peg to catch up.

Two hours further on a cluster of pilgrims marks the breakfast stop. Hungry, I drop my pack and poles to the ground and rush inside the bar. A queue of pilgrims leads the way to the food counter. As I'm standing at the bar waiting for my order to be handed to me a woman with a backpack and trekking poles taps me on the shoulder.

'Do you know what that food is there?' She points to the selections under the glass domes on the counter.

'Spanish tortilla. It's like a potato omelet. Very tasty. They are olives of course, and those are octopus.' I point out the tapas on the bar. She gives me a smiling nod as I collect my order and go outside to a table. I put my breakfast down, collect my backpack and poles that I'd abandoned in haste, and lay them neatly next to my chair. I'm enjoying my tortilla and tea when the woman I'd met inside emerges. I wave to her in a gesture of invitation.

'Thank you. My name is Katrina.' She joins me with her breakfast in hand.

'Linda. Nice to meet you.'

'I'm starving. You sound Australian. Or Kiwi?'

'Australian. Where are you from?'

'Norway.'

'I'm starving too. I was worried about getting food.'

'Me too. I have low blood-sugar problems. I have to eat every two hours or I will pass out,' Katrina tells me.

'Hey, me too! It's a bit of a challenge on the Camino. You have to prepare well in advance and then hope that you can get supplies when you run out.'

'Yes, it's difficult,' Katrina agrees.

After breakfast we walk together for a while until Katrina has to answer the call of nature in the bushes and I continue on.

The city of Burgos is the capital of the province of Burgos and sits at the edge of the central plateau. It's my destination tonight. My guide book says there are eight kilometers of noisy bustling suburbia before the city centre. Honking speeding traffic is a hazard I'm not looking forward to.

On the outskirts of the city I see a group of twenty to thirty pilgrims gathered. As I approach on the opposite side of the road they whistle and hoot and call to me in a multitude of languages until they get my attention. Puzzled, I stop and watch them gesticulating to me.

What on earth are they doing?

I make out the words "autobus" and "Burgos" but don't understand what they're trying to tell me. They seem most insistent I join them. Curious, I cross the road to them. Katrina, Mario and Gabriel and two Spaniards I met yesterday, Carlos and Esther, are among the group.

'There's a bus. It'll take us to the city centre and the city traffic can be avoided. It is eight kilometres of dangerous traffic,' Katrina tells me.

"Thank you,' I smile at my friends.

'Autobus is good.' Gabriel grins.

'Yes, very good,' I agree.

Esther gives me a hug, and laughs. I turn to Katrina.

'I thought you were behind me. How did you get in front of me?'

Katrina shrugs. 'You must have stopped somewhere to rest.'

'I did take a rest at one point. I didn't see you pass though.'

She shrugs again and bites into an apple. My Camino friends are welcome faces indeed. We don't have to wait long. Once on board, the luxury of being transported by bus excites us. There is a babel of excited chatter from pilgrims juggling trekking poles and nursing backpacks as bemused locals sit silently studying us. Our excitement grows in parallel to the proximity of our destination.

The bus passes the *"humpfing"* woman, trudging alone through the city streets.

'Didn't anyone tell her about the bus?' I ask Katrina, pointing to the *"humpfing"* woman.

'She's unfriendly,' says Katrina munching into her apple. 'Her friend is nice, but that one is a very rude lady.'

We're soon in the centre of Burgos and the bus disgorges its load of locals and clambering pilgrims, packs and poles, onto the sidewalk. The challenge now is to find the *albergues*. French, Australian, Italian, Norwegian and Spanish all ask passers-by directions to their chosen refuges. A Spanish pilgrim, Paul Antonia, assumes the role of local guide and is kept busy helping everyone with directions. Al Paral is the refuge I've chosen for tonight.

'Al Paral is my choice too,' Katrina tells me. Paul Antonio points us in the direction of Al Paral and Katrina and I set off together through the streets of Burgos to find it. A cool-looking river divides the city and a dense leafy tree-lined avenue hugs the riverbank.

My guidebook lists the refuge as consisting of huts in a park, so we know we're looking for a park. It feels as if we've walked for kilometres and still there's no sign of a park. Katrina doubts the directions we've been given and is just about to turn back when I spot Camino-marker signs and a pointer to the refuge.

At the refuge many now-familiar faces greet us. Paul Antonio, the Spanish couple—Esther and Carlos, the *"humpfing"* woman and her friend, the two American women—Cathy and Peg, are already at the refuge. There are many other pilgrims there too, some of whom I've seen along the way, as well as numerous new faces.

Katrina wants to recharge her phonecard and I still need postage stamps for my postcards. We deposit our packs and trekking poles next to our bunks and hurry back to the city centre to reach the shops before everything closes. It's Saturday; everything shuts at 2.00 pm on Saturdays.

The journey from the refuge back to the city centre seems to take far less time than the journey to reach the refuge. In the city, Katrina rushes to do what she needs and I go my way to complete my tasks.

A magnificent ancient cathedral and cobbled streets define the old quarter of the city. Castle ruins tower above—keeping watch over the surrounding countryside.

This is another city I'd like to bring Larry to one day. I'd like to spend another day here now, exploring this amazing city, but my walking pace has been so slow I haven't covered anywhere near the distance I'd originally planned. If I'm going to reach Santiago de Compostella on the appointed date I need to make up time.

'Linda, you're better off catching a bus from Burgos to Astorga,' Anna and Alberto (pilgrims from Barcelona) advise me back at the refuge. 'It's a desert, flat and boring, and at this time of year, baking hot. With your sore feet, it's best to take the bus over that stretch.'

'Is it? I do need to make up some lost time. I've been walking so slowly I'm behind schedule.'

'Catch a bus.' They both nod agreement.

I hobble to the bus terminal to check on tomorrow's departure times and find that the bus only goes as far as Leon. I buy a ticket to Leon for tomorrow. As I leave the terminal hunger pains lure me into a rather dreary-looking little back-street restaurant that offers a pilgrim menu. As my eyes adjust to the environment I spot Esther and Carlos sitting at a table. They wave to me to join them. The meal is exceedingly good; a sweet luscious melon with delicately sliced prosciutto followed by grilled chicken and flavor-filled fried potatoes. The meal finishes with a large fresh *juicy* peach cut in half. It's all accompanied by lots of fresh crusty bread and washed down with a carafe of superb local red wine.

'It's been lovely to chat,' I tell Esther and Carlos after the meal. 'But I must get my clothes washed, so they can dry before morning.'

'Bye then.' Esther and Carlos grin. 'We leave the Camino tomorrow. We must go back to work.'

'Esther's miserable at the thought of leaving,' says Carlos.

We hug, promise to keep in touch and take photos of each other before I hurry back to Al Paral. I need not have worried about getting my clothes dry by morning; it's such a hot evening they're dry before bedtime.

I return to my bunkbed to set up for the evening, only to find I've lost it. I'd selected a bottom bunk; put my boots under it, my jacket on the bed-end, and my pack alongside the pillow. Now someone else's sleeping bag is spread out on my bunk, claiming it. Stunned, I stand staring at the alien sleeping bag on my bed.

The accepted method of laying claim to a bed, is to spread your sleeping bag on top of it. In my rush to get to the shops before closing time, I'd not spread my sleeping bag on the bed.

Damn! I thought my boots, jacket and backpack would have been sufficient to stake my territory. Obviously not. How stupid of me. I won't make that mistake again.

I look around the dormitory. All the other bottom bunks have been taken.

Damn! Am I getting complacent? Or am I getting careless? This morning I nearly ran out of food, now I've lost my bunk. What's happening to me? Now I have to take the top bunk and as usual there are no ladders. I'll have to climb.

I whip out my sleeping bag and spread it out over the top bunk before I lose that one too.

Damn! How on earth can I get up onto the top bunk? Oh well, if I tread on the lower bunk-thief in the night, it will be his own darn fault for pinching my bed!

The picture my mind conjures up of treading on the lower bunk occupant amuses me. I smile to myself, feeling some small consolation at the thought.

'I need to get some small snack for an evening meal tonight,' Katrina informs me. 'Do you need to get anything at the shops, Linda?'

'I've had a large lunch today but I may get hungry later, I should get something small. We could go to the supermarket before it shuts.'

We set off together, find a *Supermercado* and buy salad ingredients for dinner. I top up on nuts and buy other protein snacks while I have the chance. An absence of kitchen facilities at the refuge means dinner will have to be a picnic in the park. Esther and Carlos join Katrina and me at the picnic table. We share red wine, picnic provisions and laughter as I relate my story to them about the bunk-thief.

CHAPTER 24

Con Men and Searing Heat

Bus to Leon—Walk to Villadangos

KATRINA IS UP, PACKED AND gone well before 6.00 am. The rustling in the early hours as she packed her things earned grumbling complaints later from others in the refuge.

The Americans, Cathy and Peg, join me for breakfast at the picnic table outside.

'We're going to take the bus to Leon today, too. Peg's feet are not getting any better, her pack is too heavy for her, and we also need to make up some time.'

'I'm booked on the 5.00 pm bus. Which one will you be taking?' I ask Cathy. We compare notes on bus times and travel needs. Cathy and Peg intend to buy their bus tickets after breakfast.

The refuge must be vacated by 8.00 am, so I have a full day to explore Burgos. It's Sunday, everything's closed on Sundays. I hope with shops shut, there won't be many people in the city.

I'll be able to wander around and enjoy the architecture without crowds of tourists.

'*Hola.*' Esther and Carlos wave to me as I'm about to leave the refuge.

'*Hola.*' I'm delighted to see them. 'I am going to be a tourist today. Then I'll catch the 5.00 pm bus to Leon.'

'We leave tonight also,' Esther tells me with a pained look: 'Back to work tomorrow.'

'Oh, I'm so sad you're leaving.'

'Yes. It is sad. But …' Esther shrugs her shoulders, as if to say, 'that is life.'

'Oh.' I'm disappointed I won't see my friends again. 'That is very sad.'

'Why don't you store your backpack in the bus station? There are lockers there you can hire for the day.'

'Really? I didn't know that. It'd be marvelous not to have to carry this around all day.'

'Yes, it's very easy, and very cheap.'

'Is it safe?'

'Yes, of course. Ask at the station. They'll show you the lockers. We're going to be tourists today too. We'll store our packs at the bus station until it's time for our bus. Why don't we have lunch together?'

'That'd be lovely. Thank you.'

'Same restaurant as yesterday? By the bus station?'

'Yes. Perfect. What time … 12 o'clock?'

'Yes. 12 o'clock. See you then.'

'See you then. Bye.'

I head off immediately to the bus station to deposit my load, leaving Esther and Carlos at the refuge still eating their breakfast.

What a bonus, having lovely friends, and being advised of the possibility of storing my pack. I stride off happily humming. Once the pack and poles are secure in a locker I head into the city centre to explore. The cathedral is first on my list of must-see places. It's been declared a world heritage site by UNESCO and is enormous. Its magnificent gothic arches and spectacular stained-glass fill me with awe.

Burgos has to be one of my favorite cities. I wander out of the cathedral to find the way to the castle, the next must-see on my list. The castle stands watch over the city from the top of the hill. I hike up the steep ascent. The castle is closed, but the view from the castle is an extraordinary panorama of the city below. The effort of walking around the perimeter of the castle combined with the weariness of the last few days, washes over me in a sudden and unexpected wave. I find a patch of lawn under a shady tree, lay down and put my hat over my face.

Ah! The privileges of being a pilgrim!

A few hours later, I wake with a start, recalling my luncheon appointment with Carlos and Esther. I check my watch and I have plenty of time to get back to the bus station area to meet them.

The television in the restaurant is blaring and an enraptured audience is gathered beneath it when I walk in. Spain is playing Greece in the Basketball World Cup. Carlos, an avid basketball fan, is loving every second of the game. It's entertaining watching Carlos' excitement as we dine.

When the meal and the game finishes, I write my email address on a piece of paper and hand it to Esther.

'Here's my email address. Let's keep in touch?'

'Please, if you need any help on the Camino, if you have any problems, please call us. Bilbao is not far. We can come and get you.' Esther writes her phone number on a piece of paper and hands it to me.

'Thank you, Esther. If you ever come to Perth, please let me know. You can stay with us.'

We say sad goodbyes and part company. I hurry back to a bar near the cathedral for a 2.30 pm farewell get-together with Manuella, a German girl I shared a room with in Ventosa. Manuella is also going home today ready for work tomorrow.

Everyone's leaving. A sense of loneliness engulfs me as I make my way to the bar to meet Manuella. Once again I feel cut off from my family and far from home.

I haven't heard from Serena for a few days. I hope she's alright. I'll email Larry tonight and ask him if everyone is ok. I'll email Celeste too. It's been a few days since I heard from her as well. I wonder how she's going. She's probably been busy with her business. I don't hear much from Amy, that probably means she's happy and settled. But I haven't heard much from anyone for a few days, I hope everything's alright? Don't be silly. If something's wrong, you'd have heard. You've heard nothing so everything's fine. They're just busy.

'*Hola.*' I greet Manuella. She's sitting at the bar waiting for me.

'*Hola*, Linda. How's the Camino been?'

'Excellent, thanks.' I climb up onto a bar stool next to her. 'And for you?'

'I'm ready to go home today. It's been good, but I'm ready now to go back to Germany.'

I smile knowingly at her comment, understanding exactly how she's feeling.

'It's hard to be away from family.' Yearning thoughts of Larry, my girls and Eddy, tug at my heart.

I miss them so much. I want to hold my daughters in my arms and tell them how much I miss them. I'm still thinking of family and home when I become aware that Manuella has paused in her chatter and is looking at me inquisitively, apparently waiting for an answer.

'Sorry. What did you say?'

I said, 'Are you going on to Santiago?'

'Yes. Yes, I'm going to Santiago, at least that's the plan. I'm missing my family, though. But I've posted my things to Santiago so I have to go.'

'You don't have to walk all the way. You could finish now, take a train to Santiago. Then come back another year to finish it off, if you want to go home now.'

'Yes, I could. I think I'll walk though. I'll see how I feel.'

'Now is the opportunity to change your mind; from Burgos you can get transport.'

'No. I'll go to Leon tonight.' My mind is made up. 'I'll keep walking … for now.'

I finish my drink and wish Manuella a safe journey back to Germany. Then wearily wind my way down to the river bank. Engulfed again by fatigue, I stroll along the river bank until I find a shady tree. I curl up under it and surrender to the deep weariness.

Is this fatigue purely physical? I've been on the go everyday now for eighteen days. Or is it emotional? I'm missing Larry, Serena, Celeste, Amy and Eddy, terribly. I do feel very lonely today. Is my fatigue loneliness? Should I go home now? I don't have to keep going.

My thoughts trail off as sleep takes over. Later, at the bus station, Cathy and Peg are already on the bus when I climb on board. Still heavy with sleep I nod to them, find a seat, and doze off again.

Cathy taps me on the shoulder as the bus pulls into the terminal in Leon.

'Linda,' she whispers, waking me gently. 'We're here. This is Leon.' Cathy and Peg make their way out of the bus.

'Thanks.' I feel so heavy, it's hard to stand and my head is leaden.

I climb down out of the bus, hoist my pack and with a foggy brain, trudge out of the terminal in the direction I think town will be. As I cross onto the city's outer perimeter from the terminal, I'm accosted by a tall, ginger-haired German youth.

'Please help me. I'm a pilgrim. My pack's been stolen. I need some money to phone home and get my credit cards stopped. I'm a doctor. I need something to get a bed for the night and a meal. I just need twenty euros. Please help me?'

He's probably a con man. I glance around the square at the faces of the Spaniards sitting watching, looking for a clue from them as to whether he's a fraud or not. In Indonesia, I've seen locals drag a pick-pocket off a bus and beat him up for preying on a tourist. I look around the square again at the faces of the locals sitting there as the German speaks, making eye contact with several of them looking for a sign from them that this man is a con artist. No response, the spectators all sit stone-faced watching.

I think he is trying to con me, but the locals are not giving me any signals to confirm that.

As the German continues his plea I survey our audience again. There's still no indication from any of them that this man's a fraud.

He must be con-man. I start to walk away, shaking my head at him.

'Even six euros would help,' he continues. 'I need to make a phone call to cancel my credit cards. Please can you help?' He stands in front of me blocking my way. I step around him and walk on. He gets in front of me again and walks backward in front of me as I walk.

What if he really is a pilgrim in need of help? It's only six euro he wants. What would I do if I'd lost everything? He might be a pilgrim. But, my gut tells me he is a con-man. Okay, you might be a pilgrim in need—I'll give you the benefit of the doubt.

I give him six euros and walk away.

At the outer edge of the square, I turn and look back. He's smugly swaggering over to a group of nearby Spanish youth. He says something to them and laughs. They smile back at his success at conning yet another pilgrim.

Humpf! You'll get your just deserts someday.

As I walk away, I'm annoyed at the locals in the square who sit doing nothing to warn his victims. A simple shake of a head from a bystander would have been enough to confirm he was a fake. *They are as guilty as he is. They are accomplices in his crime of conning pilgrims. I resent being an actor in a play for their entertainment.*

Casting my annoyance to the wind I stride towards the city centre. I want to find a tourist office; I need a map of the city to find my way to the refuge.

Cathy and Peg are alighting from a taxi as I walk into the refuge. Cathy rushes towards me as I approach.

'You know what? I've just been taken for five euros back at the bus terminal!' she gasps to me.

'I was taken for six.' I grin back.

'By the young German guy pretending to be a pilgrim?' she asks.

'Mm hmm.' I nod.

'Oh, I don't feel so bad now,' Cathy retorts—we both burst out laughing.

Leon city is the capital of the province of Leon in the community of Castile and Leon. The city sits along the banks of the Bernesga River and is the last major city on the Camino before the trail climbs west into the Cantabrian Mountains that separate the province from Galicia.

The Leon refuge is in a splendid monastery and inside the monastery is a huge inner square. In the square pilgrims are sitting and relaxing, there are clothes hanging to dry and a collection of bikes (apparently belonging to cycling pilgrims) is stored there. The dormitory, most unusually, is divided into male and female dorms; a rare treat. It means a night undisturbed by the roaring of a room full of snoring. It also means I won't have to share the shower room with men. The women already in the dorm are as equally delighted as I am and there's much excited chatter about the privilege of privacy.

Showers in most refuges are so tiny that I cannot change clothes inside the shower cubicle without getting my dry clothes wet. In the first days of this journey modesty made me change inside cramped cubicles. I hung my clothes inside the shower cubicle with the result that my clothes always got wet. European women on the other hand undressed outside the cubicle in the changing area. Pilgrim men politely lower their eyes when they enter a shower area. It took several days of wearing soggy clothes before I too shed my inhibitions and followed the example of the Europeans.

As I drop into my first deep sleep for many nights, I wonder briefly what it sounds like in the men's dormitory tonight.

The cool crispness of early morning calls, as I farewell Peg and Cathy. With pack and poles I stroll off happily into the pre-dawn light, taking a shortcut across the city to reach the point where the Camino heads out of the old part of the city.

A rather greasy-looking café has a sign out front saying *Desayunos-Huevos y bacon* , breakfast–eggs and bacon. I'm hungry and in need of breakfast, but the greasy café doesn't appeal.

A bar will have tapas and be more appetising. I keep walking. A kilometre further and it seems I've missed my only chance of a proper breakfast.

Damn, Linda, you're a fool. You should have learnt that Camino lesson by now: "When an opportunity arises, take it. Don't wait for something better, it may never come."

Hunger pains gnaw at my empty belly as light-headedness stalks my brain.

There must be somewhere else to eat up ahead. I'm still within the town—surely there'll be another café. I reach the outer-edge of town before I see a bar.

It's just as greasy as the first café but this one will have to do.

I make my way down the side street to the bar and find the only food on offer is olives, a potato dish swimming in mayonnaise, and octopus with green capsicum. None really appeal for breakfast, but today octopus and green capsicum will have to do.

It's surprisingly tasty and fills my empty tummy. I wash it down with mint tea, nod goodbye to the curious locals standing watching from the bar and set out on the road again.

The morning is hot–*very hot*. I'm disappointed to find the Camino follows the highway. *I'll have to watch out for cars and trucks. I can't enjoy the scenery now.*

Hours pass and my stamina wilts beneath the unrelenting sun. The pain from my injured foot, along with the searing heat, wears me down.

This stretch of the Camino is just too boring, too hot and too dangerous, with all the trucks that are roaring past.

I check in to the refuge at Villadangos, spread my sleeping bag on a bunkbed and go to shower. Under the soothing shower I notice huge angry red raised blotches all over my arms, legs, bottom and back. Uncomfortable, but not yet itchy, the rashes look nasty. *Hmm, must be a heat rash.*

I lay on the bunk, legs in the air and massage my wounds. The once ugly blackened toe has almost healed. *At last my toe's on the mend.* I drop off to sleep.

A couple of hours later, hunger pains wake me as I remember I haven't eaten since the octopus at breakfast time. Now it's siesta time and nothing will be open till 6.00 pm. I rummage through my pack and find my cache of nuts; a few mouthfuls will have to tide me over. At siesta's end, I wander into the tiny village in search of a supermarket or corner store, planning to buy salad vegetables for my evening meal. A teeny supermarket demands inspection, but it has nothing that even remotely appeals for dinner.

A roadside signboard indicates a "restaurant" at what appears to be a hotel nearby. I stroll over and check it out. Dinner 8.00 pm–the sign out front states.

That's too late. I need to eat now. Further down the street I poke my head into a bar to see what tapas are on offer. *An old men's drinking bar!*

I go inside to investigate but there's no food apart from sweets and potato crisps. *Yuk!* Hunger pains growl again. *What do I do? I need something to tide me over. The supermarket's my only option.*

I go back to the microscopic supermarket and buy a couple of pieces of fruit to keep me going. Wandering back to the *albergue* I notice a sign for another restaurant down a side street. It's part of a bodega, the sign says, a place where wine is made. It opens at 7.00 pm. *That will do!*

The underground bodega's ornate and gently curving vaulted ceiling speaks of ancient times when wine was once stored in this cool cellar. Now the tables and chairs that welcome guests have an aura of old-time hospitality. Tunnels, arches and thick internal walls protect the cellar from the blistering heat outside. My keen interest in the building animates the owner who takes me on a tour.

'This is where grapes were pushed through from above.' The owner points to vertical tunnels in the ceiling from the land surface.

'It's astonishingly cool down here.'

'Yes, of course. It was for the wine.' The owner smiles with pleasure at my amazement. She shows me to a table and presents the menu.

'Why don't you try the typical menu from our region?' She points to an item on the menu.

I study the menu and with no clue to what the typical menu consists of, accept her suggestion. I've read in a guide book that the "typical traditional" specialty of Leon was Calf Lung. From my very limited knowledge of Spanish I'm reasonably sure that calf lung is not on the menu tonight. *I hope I've read the menu correctly.* The first course arrives.

Garlic with green beans. Not green beans with garlic. It is definitely garlic with green beans. Good thing I'm sleeping alone.

The main course arrives, it's fried eggs, fried chips and fried chorizo sausage.

What a disappointment. Eggs, chips and sausage! I'm not fond of chips or fried eggs or sausages, or any fried food really. Oh well, at least it's an authentic local dish.

I pick up a knife and attempt to cut the sausage. It's remarkably difficult to cut and even more difficult to chew. It's a bit like trying to gnaw on a highly-seasoned old leather boot. I fight my way through as much of the old boot as I can but it's a struggle to get the last mouthful down.

I wonder if it was made from calf lung after all? Too late now, it's halfway down.

Oh, I'm sure it's not calf lung. I try to will the last lump of leather down my gullet.

The basket of bread accompanying the meal is a welcome diversion. A myriad of thoughts race through my mind on the range of possibilities of what animal the piece of leather could have been from. I'm not entirely sure the meal is going to stay down.

I hope the bread helps to keep it down.

I tend to avoid bread back home; wheat makes me bloated and gives me flatulence.

'Bon Camino.' The owner farewells me as I leave the restaurant.

As I amble out into the light hot night, a little fart escapes. *Oops! I really do have to give up wheat. But Spanish bread is so nice. After Santiago de Compostella, then I'll give up wheat.*

I wonder how many pilgrims will be in the refuge when I get back?

The refuge in Villadangos consists of triple-decker bunks with six bunks to a cubicle. To my delight, I have an entire cubicle to myself. It's another hot sticky night and the rash is spreading further over my body and it's difficult not to scratch. Tossing and turning it's a while before I fall into a troubled sleep.

CHAPTER 25

Camino "Walking Sisters"

Astorga to San Catalina de Somoza (Province of Leon)

BY MORNING THE RASH HAS spread across fifty percent of my body and is increasingly uncomfortable. I study the angry blotches and consider my options. The next two days' trek to Astorga will once again be on flat baking shadeless terrain.

I'm sure this must be a heat rash. It's not worth roasting myself and making the rash worse for two days of boring flat countryside.

I pack my bag and poles and catch a bus for Astorga. Clambering onboard the bus, I park myself on the first available seat. Hefting my backpack onto my lap, I wedge my trekking poles between myself and the poor slightly built chap sitting next to me.

'Sorry,' I meekly offer as I cramp him up against the window.

I hope he doesn't want to get off too soon. My backpack and I firmly block his exit. I notice a scallop shell on his waist bag. *He's a Camino pilgrim.*

'Where are you from?' he asks in halting English.

'Australia.' I smile. *From his accent he's Northern European.*

'Australia! Very far!'

'Yes. Very far. Where are you from?' I enunciate slowly.

'Austria.' He smiles. 'Australia and Austria.'

'Yes. Very similar. But very far.'

'Are you going to Astorga?' he enquires.

'Yes, where are you going?'

'Astorga.'

Good, I don't have to move my load before then. I can relax a little.

'My name is Linda.' I try to offer my hand but nearly lose my pack and trekking poles before deciding against it.

'I am Franz. I have a bad leg. Cannot walk far.'

I nod understanding.

'I have bad feet. It is hard to walk much. Now I have a rash too. So I take the bus,' I tell him.

He nods.

'I have a wife and three children,' Franz tells me, a little too quickly.

Don't worry your virtue is safe with me.

'I'm also married and have children. I'm in contact with my family every day,' I reassure him, smiling to myself.

'I speak to my family every day too.'

Having sorted out spousal and familial obligations and commitments we're both comfortable to become travel companions for today at least. Less than an hour later the bus pulls in to Astorga.

How demotivating! It would have taken two days to walk what the bus did in an hour. Get over it, Linda! You're a pilgrim now!

We climb out of the bus and hitch on our packs.

'I'm going to find the Tourist Office. I want a map of the city,' I tell Franz.

'I also want a map. I will join you. Do you speak Spanish?' he asks.

'Only a little. Enough for now.'

'Me too.'

The tourist office is not yet open. We find a café, have breakfast and chat until opening time. During that time it becomes clear that Franz' Spanish is far more limited than mine. *It's a comfort thing for him to join me at the tourist office; I can ask for maps for both of us.*

Astorga, the capital of Maragateria county in the province of Leon, is steeped in history. It's a medieval walled town, and sits on the crossroads of the Pilgrims Road to Santiago de Compostella and the Via de la Plata–the Silver Road. In Roman times the Via de la Plata was used to transport metal to trading ports in the south.

San Javier refuge is one of the loveliest refuges on the Camino. It's run by German volunteers and has a delightful central courtyard.

'You can sit here.' A volunteer points to the courtyard. 'Over there you can wash your clothes, and hang them to dry here. At this fountain, you can sit and put your feet in the pond to cool off. We have a kitchen, a bar, and internet.'

It even has pegs. Talk about luxury on the Camino. I shower, wash my clothes and go to explore the city.

Antoni Gaudi designed the Bishops Palace in Astorga, it looks like a fairy-tale castle sitting alongside the cathedral.

Of all the Gaudi buildings I've seen so far, this one is my favourite. Walt Disney must have got his inspiration for Fantasia Land castle from that building, I wrongly guess.

The ancient city walls magnificently frame the picture-perfect view of the cathedral and the Gaudi Palace. Roman ruins are being excavated in the city, including Roman baths, I set off to see them, but I don't find them.

It's market day in the Plaza Mayor. Weaving my way between the market stalls, I'm amazed at the huge range of products the stall holders bring to the local community. One stall sells nothing but socks. *People here have a greater choice of socks at this market stall than we get in a department store in Perth.*

Another stall sells as large a range of bras and pants as I'd find in a boutique lingerie shop in Perth. The next stall sells every kind and size of denim jacket imaginable. Another sells embroidered shawls; another cotton lace tablecloths. The square is packed full of stalls and then at 2.00 pm they all vanish–it's siesta time.

Good idea. I head back to the refuge to get out of the heat of the day, have lunch and retreat to the comfort of my bunk for siesta. My tourist guide says that the gastronomic specialty of Astorga is a dish called Comida Maragata, which is a type of stew made with seven meats, chickpeas and cabbages.

I'll have to try that tonight. But first I need a foot massage.

The volunteer at reception said a massage lady would be coming to the refuge at 7.00 pm. Still unaware that I've broken a bone in my foot I'm keen for a massage to try to ease the pain. I sit in the designated waiting area, reading a book, waiting for the masseuse to arrive. A queue forms behind me. *I'm glad I got here early.* A Swiss chap sits next to me.

'Sore feet too?' he asks.

'Yes.' I nod, smile and point to the rest of the queue. 'I guess we are all in the same sorry state.'

Hannah, the masseuse, is German, and uses a combination of Reiki, acupressure, reflexology and massage. She finds every sore spot on my feet and legs and works hard on every problem area. The agony and ecstasy is over far too soon and it's time to find somewhere for dinner. As I make my way down the old narrow cobbled laneway, a horse and coach come clattering along. I step aside and let it pass before I realise it's in spirit, a ghost coach. I take a deep breath of the hot night air; it calms my mind as I stroll off in search of a meal.

'Now, Marcus, where do I go for dinner?'

'Go to Restaurant Gaudi.'

'That sounds expensive.'

'Go to Restaurant Gaudi.'

'OK, if you say so. Lead me to it.'

Marcus leads me on a winding route. When I look up I'm standing outside a large building with a sign out front that reads "Restaurant Gaudi". On the footpath is a blackboard sign *"Specialty Comida Maragata"*. *Aah, the typical dish of the region.*

The restaurant looks very posh. I hesitate. I'm in pilgrim mentality of frugality.

I should trust Marcus and do as he says. Whenever I over-ride his advice it turns out to be a mistake. Marcus is always right.

I go in, find a plush leather seat and sit down. A waitress approaches.

'Peregrino?' She asks if I'm a pilgrim.

'*Si,*' I confirm.

'De Albergue San Javier?' From San Javier Albergue.

'*Si,*' I confirm again. *Why is she asking if I'm staying at San Javier refuge?*

'*Bueno.*' Good, is all she says before she walks away. *Now where has she gone? Why didn't she take my order? Oh well, go with the flow. This posh restaurant is such a change from some of the dodgy looking places I've been in. These leather seats smell wonderful.*

The waitress re-appears with a first course of lasagna with salad.

I haven't placed an order yet. It must be a set pilgrim menu.

I ask the waitress about the Comida Maragata, the typical dish advertised on the sign out front. I understand that it's not available, but I don't understand enough Spanish to comprehend why it's not available, considering it's on the sign out front.

It's too difficult to argue. I'll settle for the pilgrims' menu.

I find out later that the owner of Restaurant Gaudi owns the *Albergue* San Javier. He offers a special pilgrims' menu and rate, for pilgrims who stay at the *Albergue* San Javier and eat at the Restaurant Gaudi.

The lasagna is delicious and is followed by beef of some sort in two cm diameter round chunks served with a tasty sauce and accompanied by grilled capsicum and chips. A bottle of red wine and a bread roll come with it. Normally a half glass of wine is my limit but this wine is superb. Half a bottle of wine later, and feeling exceptionally mellow and slightly tipsy, I send a text message to Larry.

'I'm sitting in a posh restaurant wearing thongs, getting tipsy on red wine, in a city I think you'd enjoy, watching a large bouncing bosom on a passing Spanish matron.'

A reply comes back immediately.

'I've never seen a tipsy Linda, nor a bouncing bosom, so my mind is rather boggled. I'm in a restaurant in England waiting for my meal to arrive.'

After my final course of fresh fruit I ramble off, happy and contented, back down the alley ways to my bed in the *albergue*. Another hot sleepless night follows. The lady in the bunk above tosses and turns restlessly, shaking the whole bunk. I fear it may collapse on top of me–but it doesn't.

The next morning, Franz excitedly informs me his Spiritual Master has told him that he and I are to be "Camino walking sisters". We'll walk together.

'Ask your Spiritual Master!' he implores. I'm more than a little surprised that Franz is so sure I have a Spiritual Master, as I haven't told him. Plus I doubt that Marcus would suggest I walk with anyone. Before I left home,

Marcus told me that I must walk the Camino alone to get the full spiritual benefit I need from the journey.

Using my guide book, I choose a refuge only ten to eleven kilometres away at San Catalina de Somoza, for my destination tonight.

I have breakfast with Franz before going to pack my things. While brushing my teeth I ask Marcus if I'm meant to walk with Franz.

'Franz will help you over the mountains. He's Austrian, he understands mountains and you'll benefit from his companionship. Franz will help you get over the mountains.'

Oh! I'm surprised, puzzled and slightly disappointed. I now apparently have a "walking sister". I had been certain that I was supposed to do this alone.

I finish packing and go downstairs to find Franz to tell him he's right, we are to be "walking sisters". Franz has already left.

First he tells me we'll be "walking sisters" then he leaves on his own. What on earth is all this about? I head off down the Camino pathway, puzzling over the morning's strange events.

It is absolutely perfect. Exactly what I want; to walk alone. But now I have a "walking sister" to meet up with in the evenings. Or perhaps at lunch stops. It will be some company in between walking. A smile creeps across my face at the thought of Franz being a "sister".

'Thank you, Marcus.' I'm still grinning at the notion of having a male "sister" as I head out across the countryside.

I've been terrified of crossing mountains. The blizzard in the Pyrenees made me paranoid. Bussing it over the mountains was an option but now I think it'll be okay. I'll face my fear—I'll walk over the mountains, face any problems that arise. I'm still afraid of getting caught in a storm on a mountain, but now the Universe has sent me a "walking sister" to help me. Thank you, Universe.

I've been walking for three weeks now. I'm a lot fitter and I can feel new muscle on my hips. I'm walking more strongly but my feet are still painful, so eleven kilometers will be enough for today.

It's 10.30 am when I walk into San Catalina de Somoza, my feet hurt, but I feel it's much too early to stop. I'm about to continue on, but check with Marcus first.

'No, stop! This is the place you planned to stop. There's no rush. Have two easy days before you cross the mountain.'

I don't argue. I find a table outside the bar, heave my boots off, and order a soda water. Relaxing under the shade of an umbrella I sip my drink and wait for Franz to catch up. I passed him before dawn just forty minutes out of Astorga. By 11.30 am he still hasn't arrived so I go in to the restaurant at the *albergue* and order a slice of potato tortilla for an early snack.

'Marcus, it's early. I'd like to go on. Must I stay here?'

'Stay here,' is all he says.

I know it's always best not to argue, he's always right. I check in to the *albergue,* shower, wash my clothes, hang them out to dry and curl up on my bunk for a nap. Franz arrives at around 1.30 pm.

He really must suffer with his leg. It took him six hours to walk what took me three, and I thought I was walking slowly.

We go into the restaurant for lunch. It advertises Cocida Maragata, the special regional dish I wanted to try yesterday, so that's what I order. Franz isn't game. He orders salad.

The Cocida Maragata comes as a large platter containing every imaginable animal body part as well as a few unimaginable ones. I thought it was going to be a sort of a stew. This platter of body parts piled high is off-putting. I munch on a pig's ear, chew a piece of intestine and nibble on other unrecognisable leathery body parts. I can't conquer the dish of flesh and signal to the waiter to take it away.

To my *horror,* the waiter re-appears with another enormous platter. This one is piled with boiled cabbage, chick peas and potatoes. Not wanting to offend, I try a few mouthfuls. It's tasty, but the platter of body parts has put me off; my appetite's gone. Franz' salad is enormous. He can only eat half of it and offers me some. I nibble a piece of tomato and decide I've had overload.

The waiter looks offended when I call him to take away my platter of cabbage. He returns with a bowl of soup and places it in front of me.

'No, *gracias*. No!' I shake my head and push the soup away. *'Gracias.'*

He takes it away and brings me a platter of fruit. I'm speechless. Franz tries not to smile at the look on my face. I pay my bill and leave with Franz close behind.

'I need a siesta now,' I tell Franz as I go inside to lie down.

'I am going to phone my family,' he says.

'Okay. See you later.'

The epic meal was such a struggle that I unknowingly walk out of the restaurant leaving my hat and camera behind on a chair. A half an hour later, Franz appears with the hat and camera in his hand. A Spanish cycling pilgrim had found and returned them to the restaurant owner. He gave them to Franz for return to me.

'Oh dear. All of my Camino photos are on that camera. Thank goodness for the honesty of pilgrims,' I say to my smiling walking sister.

What on earth is happening to me? I pack my things away.

'Linda, Franz has chronic pain. Give him some healing.' It's Marcus' voice.

I don't normally give healing sessions to anyone other than family and close friends. It will seem rather odd offering to give someone I hardly know a healing, but Franz is my "walking sister", I remind myself, and walk outside to find him. He's sitting in the sun in the courtyard looking troubled.

'Are you alright?' I ask.

'It's my leg. Sometimes it's not good.'

'Would you like me to give you spiritual healing?'

He looks puzzled and unsure.

'Right here. Now?' I point to the courtyard to reassure him, in case he's thinking I'm planning on taking him somewhere private and doing evil things with his body. He looks a little relieved.

'Yes. That would be good.'

'Get comfortable and relax,' I instruct. *He'll probably be uncomfortable if I focus on his leg, best not touch him, keep my distance.*

I hold my hands away from his body, one in front of his chest and one behind his back. I relax, slow my brain-waves down to a meditative state, then lower still into a Theta state. I go up through the Theta channels, up to the *Godzone*, and request healing energy be sent back down through the channels to where his body needs it most. I close my eyes and visualise healing energy flowing into his body.

The Spanish cycling pilgrim, who'd handed in my hat and camera, comes into the courtyard with his brother. Sitting enjoying the sun, they watch curiously as the healing session is under way. Twenty minutes later I finish the session and the two brothers come to join us.

'What were you doing?' one asks.

'He has a bad leg. I was giving him some healing.'

They look at Franz as he stretches his leg.

'It's much better,' he informs them, stretching one leg first, then the other. Looking startled, he adds: 'It's good.'

'I've got a sore knee,' the older cyclist looked hopeful, 'but I suppose you'll be tired now.'

I'm very tired and simply nod.

'Where are you from?' I ask them.

'Cadiz, in Andalusia. It's the oldest city in Europe. Have you been to Cadiz?'

'No,' I admit.

'It has lovely white beaches all along the coastline. The best beaches in Spain. Cadiz is from Phoenician times. Sorry, this is my brother, Antonio. He doesn't speak any English. He's a technical architect. He's very curious about what you were doing.'

Antonio kept interjecting in Spanish asking questions for his brother to interpret. We chat throughout the afternoon until I excuse myself to take a stroll around the village.

CHAPTER 26

Crossing The Mountain

Rabanal del Camino to Village of Al Acebo

THE NEXT MORNING ON MY bunk I divide the remaining kilometres of my journey by the number of days up to the date I need to be in Santiago de Compostella. *I only need to do ten to fifteen kilometres a day. That makes my target for today Rabanal del Camino.*

Although it's the earliest I've ever set out, Franz and I are still the last to leave the *albergue* as we step outside into the blackness of early morning.

'I don't like to walk in the dark,' I comment to Franz.

'It's okay,' is all he says.

With a shrug I follow him into the darkness. There are two pilgrims just in front of us so we follow behind them. *I hope they can see the way-markers.* In twenty minutes the sky begins to lighten a little and I see we are in the countryside on a track running beside the road.

'Tomorrow we cross the mountain,' Franz tells me.

'Yes. I'm afraid of the mountain. I'm afraid of getting caught in a storm on the mountain.'

'The mountain is no problem,' Franz says. 'If it's fine I'll walk and if it rains I'll take a bus. It's no problem going over the mountain.' His words of calm confidence resonate in my head.

'You think you can walk over the mountain?' I ask him.

'I'll walk slowly. If it gets too hard, I'll take a bus.' He shrugs his shoulders before continuing. 'You walk at your own pace, go ahead when I slow down. Don't wait for me. I'll stop many times.'

'Okay. I'm going to Rabanal del Camino tonight.'
'Yes. I'll see you at Rabanal del Camino.'
'Bon Camino.' I stride ahead and leave my "walking sister" behind.
'Bon Camino,' he calls after me.
Within forty minutes I've left him out of sight.

Violet mists of Erica flowers carpet the ground before San Catalina, washing the mountain slopes like a painter's canvas. The Camino snakes upward, through the purple brushwork, climbing higher and higher. Deep blue ragged mountains frame the rolling mauve hills. The Cantabrians slumber silently ahead, their watery colours and calm stillness spread before me in a vista that soothes my soul. Their magnificent splendor nourishes my spirit as I deeply draw in their grandeur and strength.

An hour passes. I'm totally alone now; not a creature in sight. *No* farms, *no* buildings; only *silent, undulating, lilac hills*. I'm in wonderland. I fill my lungs with *fresh* mountain air, lift my face to the sky and scream loudly into the waiting silence. The release of power sends a rush of energy surging through me. Giggling with pleasure, I lift my head and scream again into the empty blue sky. It's 10.00 am when I reach Rabanal del Camino.

I'm getting faster. I could continue on.
'No, Linda. Stop here,' Marcus advises.

I buy a soda water and wander around the village. The town's small church with its Roman remains once belonged to the Knights Templars from Ponferrada. Evidence of the Knights Templars can be seen all along the Camino; they were the protectors of pilgrims in days of old, fighting off bandits to create a safe passage for pilgrims on their way to Santiago de Compostella to pay homage to St James.

I choose *albergue* de Pilar refuge to spend the night, select a bunk and lay my sleeping bag out on top of it. I shower, wash my clothes and as I hang them out to dry a Swiss woman begins to chat.

'It is not too far to go now.'
'No, we're nearly there.'
'My husband is flying to Santiago to meet me as I enter the city,' the woman tells me. 'Then we'll take a week's holiday together.'

'My husband is coming to meet me too. We're going to take a week's holiday in Castellon, we have a villa booked,' I tell her.

'It is good,' the woman responds. 'My husband will arrive in Santiago on the twenty-sixth. I plan to arrive on the twenty-seventh so he can welcome me as I walk into the city.'

'That's nice. I plan to arrive in Santiago a couple of days before my husband, so I can get a haircut, wax and facial before he arrives. I'll get tidied up for him first,' I tell her.

'Oh, I plan to do that afterwards,' she says. 'It's more important for me that he greets me as I finish my Camino. I'll get a haircut and facial later. He won't mind. He'll go sightseeing in the city or something, while I get tidied up. My need to be welcomed as I enter Santiago and finish my trek is greater!'

A knot forms in my gut as I finish hanging my clothes on the line. I ignore it and go to the bar of the restaurant in the *albergue* for lunch.

'Mixed salad please.'

When the salad arrives, it's huge; a salad bowl full of lettuce, tomato, onion, olives and tuna. A group of seven very noisy French pilgrims arrive and check in. I go into the empty refuge and lay on my bunk to write my diary. The French group come in to the dorm and set up their beds in the bunks right above and beside me.

Why have they set up above and around me? There's plenty of room. There are forty beds for crying out loud. Why didn't they go to the other end of the albergue.

When the group go to the bar for lunch I move my things to a bed at the far end of the *albergue*.

It should be quieter here. The last thing I need is a bunch of noisy strangers reminding me of my aloneness and distance from home.

The dark hole of yearning for my loved ones is growing deeper.

I'm not far from Santiago. I'm tired and spent but not about to quit now. I wonder if I've any news from home?

I go in search of an internet and get my family news fix, then it's time for siesta.

Life is good.

A chill wind blowing through the window wakes me some hours later. The sky is ominously dark. Grey clouds tumble angrily over the hills heralding rumbling thunder. Lightning angrily hurls spears of startling electric power into the ground around the village.

With only a windproof jacket, waterproof trousers and a plastic poncho for protection, I have an uneasy feeling I'm inadequately prepared.

I'll reassess my travel plans in the morning when can I see what the weather is like.

I quickly gather my washing from the drying area and arrange with reception for it to be put through a dryer.

I chat with some fellow pilgrims, everyone seems to have only just begun their pilgrimage. They're mostly French cycling pilgrims, travelling in groups of six or eight. As they sit tending their newly acquired blisters and dressing their freshly injured feet I overhear pairs of them whispering about me.

'She's come from St Jean,' one says to his friend.

My spine lengthens and my chest puffs out with pride. A few minutes later I hear another say with some awe in his voice: 'The Australian began her walk back in France from St Jean Pied de Port.'

I feel like an old timer, a veteran, as I listen to them discuss the kilometres I've traveled.

I wonder where all the other walkers from St Jean Pied de Port or Roncesvalles have gone. Have they already finished the walk? Or have they quit and gone home? I'm outnumbered by short distance cyclists. I've lost Franz too. I don't think he made it as far as Rabanal del Camino.

I go into the village to buy food supplies for tomorrow and see Gabriel and Mario.

'*Ciao.*' I wave as I approach them.

'Linda.' They grin. 'Your feet have brought you this far?'

'Yes, my feet made it … so far.' I laugh at their joke.

'Where are you staying, Linda?'

'The *albergue* over there.' I point to the building behind me. 'Where are you both staying?'

'That one over there.' They point to another building nearby.

'Oh, I didn't know that was an *albergue*.'

'Yes. It's cheaper and quieter than that one,' Gabriel informs me.

'My guidebook doesn't mention another *albergue* in the village. Oh well… *Ciao*.' I wave goodbye to the Italians and go in search of supplies.

'Bye.'

Tomorrow I shall go over the mountain. There is nowhere to get food or water on the next stretch, so I must be well prepared. I'm frightened of the mountain. The storm this afternoon is not helping my fear.

My innards knot and nausea churns as I fret about crossing the mountain in the storm—which continues to grow, *dark* and *ominous*.

During the night, the sound of a Swiss woman vomiting in the toilet wakes me. I get up and knock on her locked toilet door.

'Are you okay, is there anything I can do?'

'No, thank you, I'm alright.' She throws up again.

Back in bed, listening to her throwing up, I wonder if she has food poisoning, or whether she's frightened of crossing the mountain too. I know she is also traveling alone.

The next morning, cold fear tightens my chest, and with my head aching with stress, I set off. At the outskirts of the village where two roads merge into one, Gabriel and Mario are heading out too. I speed up so that they're only slightly ahead of me. I don't want to start this day's walk on the mountain alone, but don't want to impose myself on them either. I keep them in sight, but also keep some comfortable space between us. Gabriel stops to tie a boot lace and I pass them, then slow my pace slightly so as not to get too far ahead. They soon catch up and pass. I maintain just enough speed to keep them in sight, until one of them stops to take photos, have a drink or take a … whatever, then I'm forced into the lead. We leapfrog taking turns to lead or follow for most of the morning.

After a couple of hours, enveloped in my thoughts, I've lost sight of the two men. I don't know if they're in front or behind me. I continue alone and focus on Franz' words from the previous day.

'If it's fine, I'll walk and if it rains I'll take a bus. It's no problem going over the mountain.'

I repeat Franz' words over and over as I climb higher up the mountain. Lonely, afraid and needing comfort, the emptiness from missing my family becomes palpable.

I wonder what Larry's doing now? He'll be working. Is he still in England? It's hard to keep track of his travels without my computer. I miss him so much. I wonder what Serena is doing? It will be late afternoon back home now, I wonder if she's home? Probably not. I enjoy the occasional phone calls from Serena; it's lovely being able to stay in touch, when I'm so far away. Eddy and Amy would be at work now. Celeste—Celeste has had a rough time but she always stays positive, always puts on a cheery face.

Overwhelming feelings of combined love and loneliness rise up. A tear streaks a path over my cheek.

I worry about Shelley too. I do wish she'd find a partner to take care of her. People say our family is strange; they don't understand how we can all be friends with ex-husbands and ex-wives. But they are as much a part of our family as anyone. They're parents of our children. Why should people become enemies just because they grow apart? Perhaps we're odd? But I don't understand why people feel ex partners should be hated.

I stop for a moment to wipe the tears away, take a sip of water and adjust my backpack. As I do, I turn and look behind.

Wow! What a view. I didn't realise I'd already climbed so high. It is so peaceful and so beautiful.

Sweeping rolling hills define the lonely countryside that melts into blue haziness in the distance. There's not a living thing in sight.

Is that a farm building in the distance? I'm not sure. It's so lonely up here.

I put my drinking tube away, tighten my boot lace, adjust my pack, turn back to the path up the mountain and slip back into my thoughts as I walk.

I wish Larry was here to put his arms around me. I brush away another tear.

Piles of stone rubble that had once been buildings line the Camino. It's eerie walking through the ruins of what had once been a village, but is now a silent empty ghost town. A solitary café sits cheekily amongst the rubble; a pile of stones that's been restored.

Curious, I go inside to investigate and order a cup of mint tea. Old photos and ancient notices on the wall proclaim the rubble pile to be the abandoned village of Foncebadón. In days of old the village served the pilgrim trade. The Camino passes through several ghost villages like this one, ruins reflecting a former glory, many rubble piles now have a café rebuilt amongst the stones that once again serves the pilgrim trade.

Pondering the history of the village, I sip my tea as another pilgrim ambles in and asks if he can join me. I nod and smile.

'Amazing, isn't it?' he asks.

'Pardon?' I'm startled out of my reverie as he nods towards the rubble outside.

'These villages are being reborn,' he answers.

'What happened to them? Why were they abandoned?'

'Franco.'

'Franco?'

'Yes. Villages rose up hundreds of years ago to give food and beds to pilgrims traveling to Santiago. When Franco came to power pilgrimages ended. Now religious freedom is allowed and pilgrims are back. People are again opening cafes like this one.'

'Great opportunities.'

'I suppose so, if you can handle the isolation and long hours.'

'It's like observing history in action,' I comment. 'Villages died and now they're being re-born in front of our eyes. It's fascinating to see how the cycle of commerce makes and re-makes history.'

The ruins of Foncebadón are quite high and the views are spectacular. It was once an important stop on the Camino and appears in records as early as the 10th century. A hermit, Gaucelmo, who died in about 1123, built a hospital and hostelry here for pilgrims crossing the punishing Foncebadón pass.

It's a lonely stretch from Foncebadón to Cruz de Ferro, which at 1504 metres is near the highest point of the mountain range. The Cruz de Ferro, or Iron Cross, was put there by a hermit in the 12th century. The cross sits on top of a tall wooden post that is planted on a large pile of stones. The cairn of stones was built to mark the pass, the way over the mountains, before Roman times.

Tradition has it that pilgrims bring a stone from home, in which they've imparted their troubles and sorrows. They place the stone at the base of the cross, giving up their troubles to God for God to deal with. The pile of stones over the centuries has grown into a hillock; I guess lots of problems have been left for God to handle. A large congregation of pilgrims is gathered at the cross when I arrive.

I didn't know about the stone tradition before I left home, so not wanting to be left out, I find a stone on the track leading up to the cross, shove it full of all the worries I can think of, and pop it in my pocket ready to offer up when I reach the cairn.

I climb to the top of the cairn, extract my worry stone from my pocket and offer it up to God, asking for the worries I've implanted in it to be taken away. Ceremoniously, I place my offering at the foot of the cross to join the millions of other worries already left.

My problems disposed of, I straighten up and look around. From that vantage point, I see many pilgrims sprinkled around the area, including Gabriel and Mario on one side of the hillock and Franz on the other. Mario waves to me and I wave back. Franz is sitting among a group of pilgrims, soaking up the spiritual energy. His arms spread wide, his eyes closed, he has a look of bliss on his face.

'If I can reach Cruz de Ferro, I'll be happy.' He told me a few days ago. 'If I can make it to Cruz de Ferro, maybe I can make it to Santiago. But for me that's not so important. My goal is Cruz de Ferro.'

It was repeating Franz' words over and over that calmed my fears and helped me climb this far. His words helped me deal with my fear of getting caught in a storm. He helped me this far, but I'm not over the mountain yet.

I've not seen this many pilgrims in one place before, other than inside a refuge. I pick my way carefully down from the top of the cairn and around the other side to speak to Franz.

'Congratulations! You made it.'

He grins and nods. 'This is good, very good.'

I can see he wants to enjoy his moment alone, so I turn and take one last long look at the Iron Cross on the mountain top.

I made it too. I made it to the top of the mountain.

My face raised heavenward, the warm blue skies bathe me in welcome, the sun kisses my cheeks in congratulations and wraps arms of warmth around me. I stand a moment longer and soak in the bliss of achievement.

I am standing on top of the world. A conqueror. I've conquered my fear of climbing the mountain, of being caught in another storm on a mountain top.

My heart expands with joy.

Only a few days ago, I felt this was an impossible feat. Today the Universe has blessed me with perfect weather.

I raise my arms in supplication to the power around me and absorb the energy.

Thank you. Thank you. Thank you.

There are pilgrims relaxing under trees, perching on boulders, laying on the grass and sitting at picnic tables.

It's a glorious day. But, will the weather hold until I can get off this mountain?

I wave farewell to Gabriel and Mario at the picnic area before once again joining the Camino. I'm eager to get the mountain behind me while the weather is kind. From the Cruz de Ferro the Camino picks its way along steep mountain ridges overlooking deep valleys.

Larry would love this. He loves mountain peaks. The weather was like this on the morning of day one, sunny and beautiful, then the storm came in. It can turn angry in an instant.

I hurry on.

There's still a long way to go.

The track becomes narrow and stony as it meanders along the ridge of the mountain range.

A goat trail. Yes, Larry would definitely love this place. He loves goat trails.

On the other side of the peak, around a bend in the trail, I come upon a lonely isolated *refugio* amid piles of stone rubble.

Another abandoned village.

The *refugio* is Manjarin. It's a haven from the blizzards that strike so often on this mountain top. It's run by a passionate man called Tomás, who went on a hunger strike when the Spanish power authority sought to discontinue the electricity supply to this unprofitable location. Tomás, through his utter devotion to his cause and belief in the need to care for pilgrims, won in the end, with the Spanish authorities continuing to supply power to the remote refuge.

The vast vistas and isolation of the mountain top is humbling and the spiritual energy surrounding Manjarin and this piece of mountainside overwhelm me. Tears of emotion spill down my cheeks as the energy here seduces me to linger. Just outside the abandoned village an ancient water trough hewn from stone perches on a smoothly rounded, vivid-green, grassy bank, at a bend in the track. The water trough, framed by the breathtaking panorama, beckons me.

Such a magical place! I'll sit here, have lunch and soak in the energy.

A gap in the sturdy wooden fence railing is just big enough to squeeze through. The primeval trough's mossy surround is a perfect spot to sit and gaze across the vastness of the valleys and ranges. Dropping my pack and poles to the ground, I pull my lunch bag out and settle down on the grassy knoll to enjoy my meal.

Gosh, I wish the family could see this place. The whole Camino has been worth it so far–just for this view.

Munching happily on a delectable Spanish tomato I'm absorbed in the tranquility of the alpine scenery. My spirit is beginning to soar when suddenly a cow's head seems to materialise out of the ground before me.

'Oh!' I gasp, startled.

The wide-eyed cow halts. It too looks startled. An extremely steep, invisible rise, just below where I'm sitting, completely concealed the cow's approach.

I recover my composure. 'Sorry, cow. I didn't mean to startle you.'

It gently nods its head as if accepting my apology and plods a circuit around me to suck water from the trough. A moment later another cow's head looms in front of me.

'Come on, I won't hurt you!' I tell it, still rather taken aback.

It too ambles up over the hidden rise and around my other side to drink from the water trough. There's a cow on either side of me as I sit happily chewing my food. The presence of the two cows, though unexpected, is enjoyable. In this rustic setting, I feel *in tune* with nature; a *reconnection* to the earth, to my roots, to my ancestors, to the origins of civilisation.

This is where our spirits need to be, connected to nature, not sitting in offices tapping away at computers. That's not what our spirits yearn for. We've moved too far away from nature. City living leaves us ungrounded, out of touch. The natural environment holds so much power, we've lost that connection. It's no wonder there's so much crime and illness in the cities. We need to reconnect to nature, to restore our spirits and recharge our bodies.

A pilgrim approaches on the pathway and stops abruptly when he sees me. He exclaims in French, something that sounds like "magnificent cows".

They are magnificent; their huge eyes and long eyelashes are beautiful. Such docile creatures. I gaze lovingly at the beasts.

Another pilgrim arrives. She too stops and surveys the scene, then pulls her camera out of her pack and begins taking photos of me sitting among the cows on the edge of the world. More pilgrims appear and join the watching pair before taking their own photos.

A third cow appears over the rise as more pilgrims gather. A crowd has accumulated; most have their cameras out and are taking photos.

Strewth! My lunch break has become a spectacle. So much for my quiet panoramic mountain lunch stop, it's time to move on. I'll finish my lunch at the summit instead.

I gather my gear together, shove my unfinished lunch into my pack, squeeze back through the gap in the fence and leave the crowd behind as I continue along the mountain ridge and up the next rise. Although the sun is shining brightly, the altitude is too high for it to be excessively hot. As I climb higher, the flora is more sparse and coarse and the ground rockier. A large flat rock near the summit provides a place where I can finish my lunch. Although less comfortable than the mossy trough mound, it showcases an awe-inspiring one hundred and eighty degree panoramic vista of the valleys, mountains and ridges. I sit quietly meditating on my good fortune as I finish my meal.

Hola! Bon Camino! I nod greetings to pilgrims as they trickle past. *The descent down the mountain will be challenging. This is a good place to rest a while.* Sitting in my scenic mountain top throne I soak up the magnificence of the kingdom below.

Then it's time to go. While making careful foot placements on my way down from the summit, my spiritual entourage make their presence known again.

'Hello, Mum, Rod, Hans. Hello, Marcus.' I smile my greeting to them.

Mum speaks.

'I'm so sorry, Linda. I wish I'd known how much Hans had meant to you.'

'That's okay, Mum. I don't think I even knew how much Hans meant to me in the beginning.'

'I'm sorry too, Linda,' joins in Rod. 'I didn't know how much he meant to you.'

'Well, I guess I never really told you, or Hans. I think I've always been bad at letting people know how much they mean to me. I let you all down. I'm sorry, very sorry about that. I think I do better nowadays than I did back then. I think I've learnt to tell people how much they mean to me? Haven't I? I don't want to let anyone else down. Is there anyone now I am letting down?'

'You could clear the pathway with Amy,' Mum responds.

'What do you mean?'

'Well, when she moved out you thought she wanted some distance, some space between you, once she was in a relationship, and you gave her that without talking it through with her. You just made an assumption. Not talking things through can lead to misunderstandings and hurt feelings. It's always advisable to discuss things. That way it keeps the air clear. Why don't you discuss it with her now? Reach a new level of understanding?'

'Now?'

'Yes. Why not?'

'Oh! Okay.'

I send a text message to Amy, explaining to her that when she moved out I thought she'd wanted some space, so I gave it to her. I expressed that I missed her and needed to be certain I'd read the situation correctly. Lastly I said, *I love you very much.*

The thought that I might still be letting people down, that I may have let Amy down too, sits cold and stone-like in my gut. It drags me down from the euphoria I'd felt at Cruz de Ferro. My phone rings, it's Larry. He hears the sadness in my voice.

'What's wrong?'

The pain in my heart is too sharp to be able to discuss the comment from Mum or my resulting text to Amy.

'I'm just tired,' I tell him, unable to discuss my feelings. He seems to accept that. I feel emotionally drained.

The precipitous downhill trudge torments my tired trembling knees. Slowly I pick every foot placement, determined not to injure myself on the rocky and isolated track.

The temperature rises under the midday sun, sucking the moisture from my body; sweat trickles down the back of my legs. The sight of the village of Al Acebo in the distance sends relief flooding through my quivering muscles. Al Acebo is my destination for today.

I'm dehydrated and miserable as I check in to Meson Al Acebo. I spread my sleeping bag on a bunk, shower, wash my clothes, hang them out to dry, go to the bar and order a soda water. My water pack did not quench my thirst today, now the soda water is somewhat soothing. I seek the cool of the refuge and the comfort of my bunk and flop despondently on my bed.

CHAPTER 27

Honour Your Own Needs

Ponferrada

SOMEONE IS SHAKING ME. My eyes spring open from a deep sleep.

'Linda! Linda!' It's Cathy standing over me, grinning and shaking my shoulder. 'We've got a *private* room upstairs with an extra mattress. You can have it if you want.'

Foggy with sleep, I sit up, trying to take in what my American friend is saying.

'Pardon?'

'We've got a *private* room upstairs,' Cathy repeats. 'There's an extra mattress on the floor, for you, if you want. At least we can have a room to ourselves. It will be much quieter.'

'*Wow. Yes, please.* Thanks. How did you manage that?'

'We just asked and there was one left. Top of the stairs on the right. Bring your things and come on up.'

'I'll be right there.'

I shove my things into my pack, bundle up my sleeping bag and race up the stairs to their room.

'There. There's the spare mattress.' Cathy points to the mattress on the floor.

'Fantastic! Thanks so much.' I test the mattress; it's firm and comfortable.

I spread my sleeping bag across the bed and unpack my things again. As I do, I look up and see Cathy smirking at me.

'Habit.' I grin, knowing that Cathy's amused that I'm spreading my sleeping bag to secure my bed. 'Can't be too careful,' I add. 'Never know who might pinch your bed around here.'

The two American women roar with laughter. Once settled, we go together in search of a shop to buy breakfast supplies for morning. On the way to the shops a reply SMS comes from Amy. She writes, she *had* wanted some space when she moved out, but was now looking forward to spending time together when her baby arrives.

That night, rolling thunder, sharp lightning and rain, reflect my mood. I consider mum's message and the afternoon's events and realise I still haven't embraced how to discuss issues with my loved ones. If I had, I would've told Larry why I was down when he asked, instead of just saying I was tired. Regret hangs like a shroud over me but I resolve to change from hereon.

Time to sleep and switch off my low mood. I roll onto my back to listen to the storm howling and cracking outside. *Thank goodness the mountain peak is behind me. Tomorrow will be more of the crippling descent,* I remind myself as I drift into sleep.

Cathy, Peg and I are awake before dawn, packing our gear. Peg has an enormous amount to pack.

That's too much for her tiny frame.

'Peg, why don't you post some things to yourself, care of the post office at Santiago de Compostella, to lighten your load? That's what I did and it's much easier to walk with a lighter pack.'

'I need it all,' she says.

'I've tried to tell her,' Cathy adds with a shrug. 'She won't listen.'

I shrug my shoulders and drop the subject. We exchange email addresses and promise to write to each other. I say farewell to Cathy and Peg, gather up my pack and poles and make my way down the stairs in the dark. The crispness of the pre-dawn darkness swallows me up as I leave the refuge.

Steep, rocky, and treacherous, the descent that morning into the Bierzo valley tests my trembling thigh muscles. They shake and quiver as slowly I pick my way down the mountainside. Loose rocks underfoot send me stumbling and sliding. Anxiety balls in my gut each time I lose my footing. I'm afraid my knee will give way and leave me injured and stranded. I slow my pace even more and choose each foothold deliberately. Swinging a "salsa" with my hips, I carefully pick my way down the mountain.

The Bierzo valley is hemmed in between Castilla y Leon and Galicia. It was formerly a Roman mining area. The Romans planted grapevines in this area but blight wiped out the vines a hundred years ago. Now the area is once again making a comeback as a wine region.

Although it's still very early when I reach Molinaseca I find a little café just past a medieval stone bridge is already open. Famished, I go inside, sit down and order scrambled eggs with bacon for breakfast. Fried eggs and bacon arrive. I study the fried eggs.

Hmm, must be my Spanish language skills lacking again. Oh well.

The eggs are tasty and fill my empty belly, and I'm grateful for that. I move on and at the outskirts of Ponferrada a sign indicates a Roman fountain is nearby.

A Roman fountain. Wow! I wonder what a Roman fountain looks like.

I detour off the Camino to explore this curiosity. The fountain's ancient steps lead down into a subterranean cavern so large I can stand upright inside the cool moist grotto.

This was built and functioning two thousand years ago. I'm awestruck and struggle to comprehend the skill and engineering of the remarkable Romans. *Two thousand years later, the fountain still works!*

The water is cool and inviting and I'm tempted to take a drink, but a workman nearby says something in Spanish, then shakes his head. I gather he's indicating to me not to drink the water. Disappointed, I nod and obey.

If engineers built a fountain today, would it still be working in two thousand years? Highly unlikely. We seem to have lost the skills and the will to construct strong durable lasting little edifices. The fountain is two metres below ground. Was it always two metres down? Or is this two thousand years of dust and dirt that has accumulated above it? If it is accumulation, where did all that dust come from? I'm not going to get any answers here.

I make my way back up the steps, out of the fountain and back to the Camino. The long hot dusty slog into Ponferrada has my feet and legs aching. I'm soaked with perspiration. On the city perimeter, a Spanish man points me in the direction of the *albergue,* and indicates to me that the

Camino takes a very round-about route through the town before it reaches the a*lbergue*. He suggests a more direct route.

Is my tiredness that obvious?

It's midday when I arrive. A number of pilgrims are already waiting outside, including Mario and Gabriel, and the girl who vomited all night two nights back. The girl tells me a number of pilgrims are ill and vomiting.

I wonder if it's a gastro virus, or a bad water source they could've shared. The last thing I want is a virus. I offer the girl my sympathy, wish her well and move away a little too hastily. It's obvious she's displeased by my swift departure. Weariness and sickness confronts me with the growing number of pilgrims, the arduous day reflected in their faces.

I secure a bed, perform my ablutions, and dash into the city to buy provisions for breakfast and lunch tomorrow.

Everything will be shut soon for the weekend so I must scarper.

The raised red rashes continue their angry itching march across my body. During the day a long-sleeved shirt and long trousers keeps both sun and insects off my body. In the evening, I want fresh air on my legs to cool the burning rash. I hunt out a camping shop in the city and buy a quick-dry t-shirt and a pair of shorts. *My evening wear is certainly not glamorous, but I hope it does the trick.*

I need a waterproof jacket for the next mountain crossing, but the camping shop doesn't have one. Strolling absent-mindedly back towards the refuge I'm confronted with a sight so stunning I freeze in my stride.

A fairytale castle ruin. Castillo de Los Templarios, the Castle of the Knights Templar, stands begging to be explored. In days-of-old, the castle was the Spanish headquarters of the Knights Templar. It's being restored and draws me inside, where spirits bustle, preparing for a battle.

Weariness overcomes me. *I'll stay another day in Ponferrada to rest. I need to buy a waterproof jacket when the shops open Monday morning. In the meantime I'll have to find a hostel for tomorrow night.*

Back in the refuge as I tiredly tuck myself in to my bunk I recognise Cathy's voice outside my room.

My American friends made it to this albergue. I'm pleased to hear Cathy's voice and smile before turning over and drifting into an exhausted sleep.

In the morning, seeking out the 10th century Moorish church, Santo Tomas De Las Allos, I find my city map to be unhelpful for tourists. Three times I stop locals and ask directions before I find the church. The key-holder for the church lives at a nearby house. She's a friendly obliging lady and unlocks the church to let me in. Graceful arches adorning the interior of the church emanate a feeling of knowingness, of a history rich and spellbinding. Sitting in a pew, I struggle to comprehend the church's antiquity.

It's over one thousand years old! Will it stand for another one thousand years? What would life be like here in a thousand years' time, will it be as we know it. The way we are destroying our environment, I doubt humanity will survive, though the church might.

The helpful keeper of the key asks if I'm a *peregrino*, a pilgrim.

'Si.'

Using body language with Spanish, she indicates she'll stamp my *credential,* my pilgrim's passport. I happily hand it to her. *A stamp from this church would be a treasure indeed.* Each church or village has its own unique rubber stamp for stamping a pilgrim's passport, it's to prove how far a pilgrim has walked, in order to get the Compostella–*the certificate*–at the end of the walk.

My collection is becoming impressive. It's going to be a real treasure by the time I finish the Camino.

Back at the *hostel* I empty my pack, assessing what else I can send ahead to the post office in Santiago de Compostella. *Hmm, not a lot: a handful of receipts, a couple of postcards for my memory book, a mechanical pencil in need of refills, two fridge magnets and a deck of Camino Santiago spiritual healing cards. But, the weight does all add up and besides, I did want to get some trekking sandals on Monday. I need to lose some pack weight to compensate for the weight of the sandals.*

'Marcus, will it be safe to post the first book of my diary to Santiago? Will I retrieve it at Santiago? I don't want to risk losing my diary.'

'Go ahead and post it, Linda. It'll be fine.'

A steamroller of tiredness crushes over me. My eyelids are so heavy I can barely keep them open. The leaden coat of fatigue imprisons me on the bed and forces my eyes closed. I sleep for three hours before I have the strength to get up and finish sorting and packing for the morning.

Being in a hostel means I can take a bath. It's a doll-size bath in a shoebox bathroom. I have to undress in the bedroom, then sit in the bath with my knees up around my ears. Even so, after weeks of showers and washing with shampoo, it's bliss to attempt to wallow in a bath and wash with soap.

Oh the simple pleasures in life! The hot water soothing my sore spent body is ecstasy. My mobile phone buzzes: a text message has come through.

Oh no ... to read it or to wallow? It will probably be from Larry. I can't enjoy the wallow wondering what the text message says. I unfold myself out of the bath, retrieve the phone, put it on the toilet seat and fold myself back into the bath. I want to enjoy both the text message from my man, and the bath.

Larry's text reads, 'I will arrive in Madrid from the USA on the afternoon of the twenty-seventh at 3.30 pm. It's a six hour drive from Madrid to Santiago de Compostella, provided I don't get lost on the way. I'll be jet-lagged, so may need to stop overnight and continue the following day to meet up with you. Once we meet it will be a fifteen hour drive to the villa in Castellon. I suggest you take the bus or train to Madrid and meet me there instead as it will be much easier for me that way.'

Disappointment wells inside me, but I can't really understand why the message upsets me so much.

I won't respond tonight, I'll sleep on it and reply in the morning.

Oh, I smell so clean, I dry myself down. *Did I smell so unclean before?*

I've not been aware of any other pilgrim's body odour, nor my own. Boots can get rather a strong smell though.

Perhaps pilgrims develop a unique Camino fragrance? Right now, without my boots, I feel clean through to the pores of my skin. In this heat that won't last long. Besides, I'll be back on the Camino trail tomorrow, back being a link in the never-ending chain of Camino pilgrims. I'm looking forward to being part of something, connected. I need to reconnect with the Camino again.

I go to a nearby restaurant for dinner and as I sit eating my evening meal I hear an Aussie accent at the other end of the bar.

'Hello, I heard you say that you'll be starting your Camino tomorrow. My name's Linda. Where are you from?'

'Hello, I'm Beth, from Perth. Where are you from?'

'Perth.'

Beth plans to sleep outside under the stars each night, but has no sleeping bag. She's brought a pair of denim jeans, a pair of regular sneakers and a thirty cm square of quick-dry material for a towel. That's her total preparation for her Camino trek; no research and she doesn't even know that people started back in France or Roncesvalles. She hasn't learnt any Spanish nor brought a phrase book to help order meals or find her way around, has no idea what a refuge is and knows nothing about obtaining a *credential*.

She has a huge learning curve ahead of her.

'I think you should go and buy a sleeping bag,' I advise.

'Oh, do you think I'll need one?'

'I think so. Get a sleeping sheet too, sometimes it's hot, sometimes it's very cold, depending on the altitude. The sleeping sheet will keep the mosquitoes off if it's hot and the sleeping bag will keep you warm if it's cold.'

'Oh, so you really think I'll need a sleeping bag?'

'Yes!'

How on earth does she plan to sleep under the stars without one? She'll freeze on the mountains.

It's a hot noisy night in the city as I make my way back to the *hostel*. I slip between the crisp clean sheets and think through the evening.

I wonder if my kinsperson is sleeping on a field?

Just after midnight, the sound of explosions wakes me. Bright lights flash at the window and the sky is illuminated with colour. I venture into the courtyard; fireworks bedazzle the castle, painting it in reds, yellows and green. I climb on the stone wall to watch. Another guest joins me.

'What is this?' I ask the other spectator.

'It's a local festival. Tonight is the last night.'

Later I wake in the early hours sick with anxiety. I'm distressed over Larry's text message from last night.

'Marcus, why am I feeling so upset about his suggestion? It seems a rational solution to his problem?'

Marcus holds a mirror to my soul. He replays the vision of the conversation I had a few days ago with the Swiss woman. It shows me clearly why I'm hurting so much. *I really want someone at my finish line, welcoming me to the end of my journey, someone to say, 'Well done!' I want recognition of my achievement and a loved one to share it with. But I've never been able or felt worthy to ask for my needs to be met.*

Now my gut churns with a deep uneasy feeling. *I've made a habit of burying my own needs so deeply that it's often hard to see what my needs really are.*

I've ignored my soul's deeper need to be welcomed as a hero at the end of my long pilgrimage, because I thought Larry would not want to be there. Instead, I planned on getting myself tidied up, and that again is because I don't think Larry would want to wait around while I visit a hairdresser or a beautician on our holiday time.

Realistically, he wouldn't even notice whether I had a haircut, waxed legs, facial, or not. He just wouldn't see it. On the other hand, I haven't even asked him to meet me at the end of my journey, or wait at a beautician—I've just assumed he'd be annoyed by it.

I feel low because I'm considering taking public transport to Madrid–because it'll be *easier for him.*

'Linda, the spells of depression, stress, low self-esteem and low self-confidence you've experienced over the years and are feeling now, are because you don't honour your own needs. Instead, you consistently put other people's needs first and *deny your own*. Acknowledge your own needs. They're as valid as anyone else's. If you don't honour your own needs, nobody else will. You must nurture your soul by telling others what your needs are and ask that they be met. They won't know what you need if you don't tell them. To bury your needs and suffer the pain in silence serves no purpose. It only destroys your own evaluation of your worth in this world. Your spirit deserves better than that. Your spirit should soar, but you crush it by your own deeds and beliefs. You must learn to honour yourself.'

Then, like viewing movie clips of my life, Marcus replays scenes from numerous times over the years when I'd agreed to something because it made it easier for the other person, even though it wasn't really what I wanted.

He's right. I don't voice my needs. I bury them, particularly if someone wants me to do something that makes life easier for them, but is contrary to my own needs.

A deep pain stabs my heart as I recognise how I betray myself through my own choices of consistently putting others' needs before my own.

I wound my soul every time I ignore my own needs. How can I find the line between looking after my own inner needs in a healthy way and putting myself first without being selfish? How can I take care of my own needs and still effectively help others. Will I be able to do that?

I can't even stand up for myself. What a fool I am.

I sit and weep at the confrontation of this new reality.

I've been stupid. So stupid. Stupid and weak. Why am I always so weak? Why can't I stand up for what I want?

I can see that I have to start nurturing my spirit and honouring my own needs. But first I need to figure out what my needs are. It won't be easy to break the habits of a lifetime, to muster the courage to ask for my own needs to be met.

It'll be harder still to even know what my needs are. I've buried them for so long, it'll take a lot of digging to uncover them. I WILL leave that bad habit behind me here on the Camino. I need to allow my needs to surface, and then ask that they be met.

As daylight lightens my window, I make myself a new promise. With a new resolve I wipe away the last of the tears.

'What would you like to do now?' I ask my inner self.

'Soak in the bath again.'

The bath is sheer bliss.

CHAPTER 28

Conquering the Final Range

Cacabelos to Hospital de la Condensa
THE NEXT MORNING I DAWDLE at check out, shops don't open until 10.00 am at the earliest, and I want to buy fruit for breakfast.

I'll listen to my body too and only eat when I'm hungry. Fruit and salad will be my sustenance for the next few days.

I find a sports store and buy the lightest-weight waterproof jacket I can find.

Everything has to be ultra-light-weight if it's going to travel with me now. Something else from my backpack will have to go to compensate for this extra four hundred and eighty grams of jacket.

'Marcus, is it safe to post the second book of my diary now?'
'Send it.'

Great. The post office is my next stop. I post off a few things to Santiago to lighten my load again.

My pack still feels heavy! It's that one and a half litres of water I put in my hydro pack. Tomorrow, I'll only put one litre. The extra weight is slowing me down and paining my hips.

As the day wears on I walk trance-like, deep in thought about Marcus' words. It's mid- afternoon when I reach the municipal refuge at Cacabelos. It has two beds to a room, great showers, and a sunny courtyard. There's no kitchen in the refuge, but on the way I passed plenty of bars and restaurants. It's siesta time, but gnawing hunger pains send me foolishly searching for an open bar in the hope of an early meal. Of course it's a waste of time.

'Kitchen is closed till 7.30 pm,' was the repeated response.
No point! Give up! Go back to the refuge until 7.30 pm.

Tonight, in the restaurant, I intend to have only a salad, but the waitress convinces me that I would be remiss not to follow the salad with roast chicken and wash it down with a half carafe of red wine. She is of course, quite right.

After dinner, back at the refuge, I ask my roommate if she's Spanish.

'No, I am Catalonian from Barcelona,' she replies. 'You?'

'I'm Australian,' I tell her. 'From Perth, Western Australia.'

With an indignant shrug of her shoulders, my roommate reluctantly concedes, 'Oh ... *Si*

... Spanish ... I'm Spanish then.'

She makes it obvious she does not like to classify herself as "Spanish". She's Catalonian! This is not the first time a Spaniard has introduced themselves as being Basque, from La Rioja, Catalonian or Navarra—in preference to admitting they're "Spanish".

I would feel very odd indeed if I introduced myself to a foreigner as being Western Australian rather than Australian. Is this a new world versus old world difference in attitude, I wonder? The only time people here seem happy to call themselves Spanish is on the international sporting arena.

My topographical map illustrates that the fifty kilometre climb from Villa Franca to O'Cebreiro, a tiny hamlet atop the mountain range that separates Leon from Galicia, will be steep and difficult. I choose Villa Franca as the starting point tomorrow, for the beginning of the demanding ascent of the Cantabrian mountains. It'll be a short journey today to Villa Franca but it'll give me time to explore the legendary town.

Villa Franca has long been an important point in a pilgrim's journey. It's here that pilgrims too ill or injured to continue on to Santiago de Compostella can enter through the *Puerta del Pardon* (the Door of Forgiveness) of the Romanesque Church of Santiago. Passing through the Door of Forgiveness, they are granted the same benefits as if they'd completed their pilgrimage to Santiago de Compostella. A market town, Villa Franca, has a castle and a number of architecturally interesting churches.

I spy a lovely pair of earrings in a jeweler's window and have to buy them. Inside the jewelry shop, I ask the lady if there's a beautician in town who can wax my legs. *I feel scruffy and in need of a little bit of self-nurturing.* She leads me down a side street to the beautician's unmarked door and rings the bell.

I would never have found this on my own.

With the aid of my Spanish phrasebook, I ask the *Estetica*, the beautician, if she'll wax my legs. The *Estetica* indicates it would be "much later" before she can do it.

'At what time?' I ask her.

'Much later.'

'At what time?' I repeat, not knowing enough Spanish to phrase it any other way. The *Estetica* doesn't seem to want to give me a time. I persist and finally she concedes 'at 2.00 pm.'

I struggle to comprehend what has just taken place.

Perhaps one doesn't make appointments at places like beauticians, perhaps they are supposed to just turn up and wait.

I go to the market for some fruit, tomatoes, and half a roast chicken.

There goes my fruit and vegetable diet.

Walking through the door of the Church of Santiago I feel a profound upsurge of emotion—I feel totally enveloped in love. Overpowered by the sensation, tears flow and I have to sit down. *It's the same experience of being engulfed by love that I felt at Manjarin.*

'Marcus, what is this feeling that encircles me causing such emotion, and tears to flow?'

'It is your soul connecting to its home, to its source of love, the Universal energy. The energy is nurturing your soul,' he replies.

'It feels beautiful. How can I access this energy when I'm not here?'

'Just remember it. Bring it to mind and remember the feeling. Experience it mentally and your mind will open the way for your soul to be renewed.'

'That's all ... just remember it?'

'Remember and relive. Your mind holds the key. Feel, experience and visualise the Universal energy—allow your soul to access it.'

I head back to the rooms of the *Estetica* as my appointment time with the beautician approaches. Three people sit watching the beautician cut a customer's hair; I join the audience. She finishes cutting and then escorts her client into another room. On re-entering it appears the client has undergone a lip wax.

The beautician then endeavours to convince two women who have been waiting, to return tomorrow. As far as I can follow, the beautician explains to them that I came that morning and she told me to come back now.

Hmm, it certainly doesn't appear to be appointment based. Must be a turn up and wait system.

Eventually, one of the ladies reluctantly agrees to come back tomorrow, but the other stands her ground. The beautician answers the phone, jokes with waiting clients, keeping them entertained, while continuing with her current client.

She's an excellent retailer; entertaining waiting customers while performing highly skilled tasks.

The beautician cut a man's hair next.

Hmm, she's a beautician, a lady's hairdresser and a barber, all rolled into one.

Then it's my turn. I am ushered into the other room for the leg waxing. She speaks no English and my Spanish vocabulary, now adequate enough for general pilgrim life, does not extend to leg waxing requirements. With gestures and chuckles, the beautician and I reach an understanding and my legs are swiftly denuded.

Grey clouds roll across the sky as I hurry back to the refuge. Splashes of rain begin to fall as I break into a run to retrieve my washing from the clothes line. Being the only English speaking person in a refuge full of large noisy groups of French and Spanish, I feel isolated and lonely. I regret not being able to speak fluently in either language and stroll into town for an early meal. When I return to the *albergue* the pilgrims, many of whom have just commenced the walk, are in high party mood in their respective language groups. I go to bed feeling very much an outsider.

Thunder drums across the sky and a chill descends over the town as I fall into a deep sleep. Summer has passed, autumn is upon us.

In the morning I'm the last to rise. Despite the partying last night, the French and Spanish pilgrims are up very early. As I dress, I notice muscles on my hips where previously I've never had muscle.

No wonder my hips have been aching–they have been busy creating muscle.

Blackness blankets Villa Franca as I join the chain of pilgrims heading out on to the Camino. A chill wind bites my ears and numbs my nose and lips. I stop to pull on my waterproof trousers and waterproof jacket. It's not raining but I need the protection of my waterproofs against the nipping cold.

The ascent of this final mountain range to O Cebreiro, located where the Os Ancares and O Courel mountain ranges converge, will begin today. The ranges comprise a succession of valleys and peaks that joins León and Galicia. It's going to be a big day. The coolness of the morning makes walking easier as I swing my toned hips to the rhythm of the universe.

Keep it slow, it's a tough day ahead. I remind myself, *slow and rhythmical.*

I swing my trekking poles in a steady rhythm as I stride out. Wild mints, salad burnet, fennel and yarrow weave a carpet of herbs along the roadside between Villafranca del Bierzo and Vega del Valcarce. Blackberry, heavy with fruit, mingle with rambling roses laden with rosehips. Ivy and Clematis with flowers gone to seed, struggle with each other, as they scramble up trees. A shallow river rushes over rocks and boulders alongside the road as I slowly climb this final mountain range of the Camino. I stop frequently to nibble plump juicy blackberries.

Mmmmm, delicious.

Entering Vega del Valcarce, I pause outside one refuge and ponder whether to wait till it opens or go on into town to the municipal refuge. A local village woman stops; I presume she asks if I need assistance.

'This *albergue* or the Municipal refuge,' I ask in Spanish, using body language to indicate I'm weighing up the decision between the two.

'Municipal refuge,' the lady nods and points further down the road.

'Where are you from?' she asks in Spanish.

'Australia.'

She seems surprised.

'Do you speak Spanish?' she asks.

'Only a little.' I indicate a very small amount with my fingers and smile apologetically at the lady.

'Do you speak French?' the lady asks.

'Only a little.'

'Bon,' she replies and then explains in French that she'll walk with me to the municipal refuge. She'd like to walk the pilgrimage to Santiago, she tells me, but it's not possible as her feet are bad. She's very impressed that I've walked from France. She calls out to other villagers as we pass, telling them she's walking to the municipal refuge with a pilgrim from Australia who has walked from France.

I enjoy the woman's friendly conversation, despite a lot of it being beyond my limited comprehension. I answer the lady in a mixture of French and Spanish and we both get the general gist of what is said. It's enough. The woman stops at one point to read a notice pinned on a board and when she catches up tells me the notice refers to a "shoot". The woman says she's not interested in "shooting"–that's for men. She'd prefer animals were left to live, she emphasises with a roll of her shoulders, before waving goodbye as she turns down a small pathway.

At the end of the day's journey, the refuge is a welcome sight. On my walk into the village to find a meal sometime later, I am joined by an Australian pilgrim, Max, a school principal from Brisbane. Max walked today with a French Canadian, Jacqueline, and invites me to join him and Jacqueline for lunch. Over lunch I learn that Max's father left Poland in 1939 when he was fourteen.

'We have relative peace, stability, security and wealth, compared to our parents and previous generations. We need to remember we live in privileged times, yet we often think it's our right. It's not, and we could lose it far more quickly than it was gained. We need to remember the past and learn from it.'

Max and Jacqueline agree and after lunch we walk the length of the tiny village. Forest-covered mountains surround the village and a castle ruin sits crown-like perched on top a nearby mountain. Tracks used for hundreds of years wind their way up hillsides. Cranes towering above rooftops and the noise of construction, heralds a re-birth. In this once dying village, restoration and renovation follow the inflow of funds from increasing pilgrim numbers.

Weary pilgrims, wearing sandals, walk the streets hunting for shops to buy provisions for their evening meal and tomorrow's breakfast. Old village men bend over, quietly hoeing the rich earth of their vegetable gardens. Somewhere dogs bark incessantly.

Vegetable gardens in this part of Spain are enviable.

Apple, pear and fig trees laden with fruit and gardens full of tall bean plants, tomato bushes, zucchinis, massive pumpkins, firm red capsicums and two-metre-high Brussel sprout-like plants, are all around.

Each ancient village I've passed through seems to be inhabited by very old people. The young, I'm told, have gone to seek work in the cities. In many villages, the crops from the fruit trees fall to the ground, the bounty more than the old can pick or eat. Quietly they tend their vegetables and watch the fruit from the trees rot on the ground. Their centuries-old houses sit in silent witness to the changing fortunes of the village.

Pilgrims breathe new life into villages so houses and churches can now be restored. One-by-one, shops, bars and refuges are being resurrected from the rubble. Little by little, work is created and once again villages take a new breath of life.

The next morning, blackness, cold and drizzling rain greet me as I step out into the morning air. I feel strangely light and elated as I begin the morning ascent of this final mountain range. It seems as if a transformation deep within my soul that's been taking place over the past few weeks is beginning to manifest. I feel different; an inner strength, a confidence, a sense of peace that was not there before. It's as though I've removed some imprisoning layers to release the person trapped inside.

The morning is so dark that for the first time since I started walking the Camino I need my head torch. Winter is approaching and the nights have begun to lengthen. There's been days up till now, when although I've felt nervous walking in the dark and feared I may miss the way-markers, I could still see to walk. This morning though, the blackness is so intense I need the torch just to see the path. I pick my way slowly. As I enter the next village of Ruitelan, I come upon a group of four pilgrims just setting out for the morning.

'*Hola,*' I greet them as I pass.

'*Bonjour,*' they respond.

Ah, French people.

A little further on at a fork in the road there are no way-markers immediately visible. I pause and consult my guide book, checking the correct route to take. I'd just determined the correct road when the first of the French group arrives. He was about to take the other fork in the road.

'*Ici,*' I call to him. 'The Camino is this way.' I point to the marker that I'd only just noticed.

'*Ah merci!*' He thanks me and signals the correct route to his friends. He stops and waits for them to catch up as I walk on ahead.

Morning light creeps slowly across the sky, lightening the now changing countryside. Autumn has washed the landscape with new tones. Splashes of gold and rust are beginning to blush the mountain landscape. As a cold wind sweeps newly fallen leaves across the fields, the French group catch up with me.

'Dominique.' The lady in the group points to herself.

'Linda.' I smile and point to my own chest.

'Francais.' Dominique again points to herself.

'Australian.' I point at my own chest again.

'Australia, oh it is far.'

'*Oui,*' I agree.

'My English is very little,' she says.

'My French is also very little,' I assure her.

From that point on Dominique speaks in her limited school-girl English and I respond in my limited school-girl French. We bond. Dominique introduces me to her companions: Anton, Gerard and Henri. Dominique and I chat for some time as we walk along. We travel together as a group for the remainder of the morning until we reach O'Cebreiro. In the cold mist and chilling rain I feel secure climbing the mountain with these warm and friendly people. My fear vanishes in their company.

The hamlet of O'Cebreiro, at an altitude of 1,337 metres, is the highest summit of the Camino in Galicia. Declared a National Historical Heritage Site, it has a strong Xacobean tradition, where the Order of St John of Jerusalem settled to serve and protect pilgrims. It has a 9th century church and also hosts the Parochial Church of San Xoán, constructed in the 15th century. It is one of the few hamlets that preserves its pre-romanesque "pallozas" (traditional thatched houses). My plan is to spend the night at O'Cebreiro.

I make such good time up the mountain that I reach O'Cebreiro ahead of schedule. Max and Jacqueline are in a café when my group reaches the hamlet. The mountain top is shrouded in low damp cloud that obscures the view from the peak and creates a cold and eerie atmosphere. I feel chilled and damp through my clothes.

It's too early, too cold, too wet and too dismal a place to stay. I'll move on. I don't like this village. It's creepy in this mist, but first I need something to warm me up.

I find a warm bar and order my favorite mint tea. The waitress picks up a teabag for my tea, then stands dangling it in the air as she chats to two other people sitting at the bar. I stand shivering, waiting for the waitress while she carries on a very long personal conversation with the two locals. I wait and wait. Then, numb with cold and frustrated by her rudeness, I gather up my things ready to walk out to another café. The waitress quickly puts the dangling teabag into a cup, adds boiling water and with a look of sour disdain, slides the cup across the bar towards me. I take the cup and turn to find a place to sit.

A man, obviously a pilgrim, sitting nearby, nods at his table, indicating for me to join him. I sit with him; nodding my thanks. He's tall wiry and rugged looking - a European in his forties I estimate, with a mop of brown wavy hair. I can't guess his nationality and assume from his silence and body language that he doesn't speak English. I sit silently and sup my tea for a few minutes until curiosity overcomes me.

'Espanol?' I ask him.

He shakes his head. He's not Spanish.

'Francais?' I ask.

Again he shakes his head, he's not French either.

'Deutsch?' It's my last attempt.

No, he's not German either. I give up and continue to sip my hot tea in silence. He points to me and raises his eyebrows in a gesture of enquiry, which I assume is asking my nationality. Definitely a man of few words!

'Australian,' I respond, with a shrug of my shoulders.

'Oh, good. We speak English, then.' His reply is unexpected.

'Oh.' I'm startled. *I thought we were not going to be able to speak.*

'You?' I ask.

'Czech.'

'Ah.' *That's a nationality I hadn't considered.*

'You going to Santiago?' he asks.

'Yes.' *I can be a woman of few words too.*

'Where did you start?'

'St Jean Pied de Port.'

His eyes widen in surprise and the conversation ends. I pull out my mobile phone, find I have reception, and send a text message letting Larry and the girls know I've reached the summit of the dreaded final mountain range. I finish my tea, bid the Czech *'Bon Camino,'* gather my things and walk out of the café into the misty shroud cloaking O'Cebreiro.

The weather could get a lot worse on this mountain-top. I'll be happier to get off the mountain now, and move on to Hospital de la Condensa.

As I leave the bar the low grey cloud enveloping the village reminds me of old English horror movies I saw as a child. I shudder. Zipping my jacket up to my chin I step into the bleak eeriness. I can see only a few feet in front of me and feel nervously uncomfortable striding out into the thick grey blanketing mist.

As I search the streets looking for Camino-markers to show which path to take out of the village, I run into the Czech who's doing the same thing. We don't speak until I notice a marker.

'This way,' I call to him, pointing to the marker.

'No. It's pointing this way.' He points in another direction.

'No. I think it's this way.' *I'm not going to be led astray.*

'No.' He's just as adamant. 'It's this way.'

I shrug my shoulders at him and stride off in the direction I believe is correct. A few minutes later he's by my side. I nod acknowledgement to him and keep walking. The track is indistinct and visibility is low.

'Do you mind if I walk with you till we've crossed the mountain?' he asks.

'No, I don't mind.'

'You have a phone, if we get lost, you can phone for help. For that reason I'd like to walk with you.'

'That's fine.'

We walk together, mostly in silence, for a few kilometres, picking our way through the dank gloom. The summit of the mountain is covered with a thick ancient almost-supernatural forest. Ancient twisted gnarled trees covered in lichen are both spectacularly beautiful and frighteningly ghostly-guardians of the mountain summit, as the Camino weaves its way through the forest. We pick our way between the lichen covered sentinels and I shiver in this eerie forest. This mystical forest I'm sure once held fire breathing dragons in the thick grey-white mist.

Once through the forest and over the crest of the mountain the track widens out. As we descend through the cloud the sun's warming rays emerge leaving the ghostly shroud and ancient forest behind.

Out of danger of getting lost, the Czech bids me *'Bon Camino'* and strides on ahead. At his much faster walking pace he's soon out of sight. Having passed over the crest of the ranges and into the sun, I feel another weight lift from my shoulders; I've safely achieved the final and most feared mountain crossing. Today, although it's been a difficult, wet and uncomfortable climb, it's been problem-free. For that I'm profoundly grateful. The three ranges have provided three unique experiences.

The warming sunshine on the other side of the mountain illuminates spectacular farmland on the sprawling countryside below. The trepidation I'd felt in the other-worldly mist lifts and with that release of tension, the realisation that I've conquered the final range, floods over me.

'I did it,' I say out loud to the trees, lifting my face to their canopy.

My heart feels bursting with joy. I want to share this moment and this awe-inspiring vista. I send a text to Serena. I know she'll understand my joy at this achievement. She rings straight back.

'Wow! You did it Mum. Well done.'

'You should've seen the forest I just came through Serena. It was on the top of the mountain in the mist. The trees were ancient, really spooky. It was amazing. Quite surreal.'

'*Wow, Mum*, you made it to the top of the mountain!'

'Yes, the view is *breathtaking*. I have to make it down the other side now, but at least the weather has held out—no storms.'

'Well done, Mum.' I hear the genuine pride and awareness in Serena's voice, of what the feat means to me.

I feel deceptively at peace as Serena tells me the news about her friends and then wishes me safe travels.

I've conquered the three ranges and faced my fears, I've emotionally completed my mission.

'Linda, you still have the descent from the mountain,' Marcus reminds me.

Finishing the Camino is no longer so important as I've achieved all I needed to. I could happily catch a bus home now. My knee clicks as I pick my way down the steep slope.

I don't need to risk injuring my knee, or myself, on the descent from this mountain. I'll catch a bus tomorrow, from Hospital de la Condensa to Sarria, from which it is only one hundred kilometres to Santiago. I can walk the last hundred to Santiago, get my Compostella, and go home. Yes, that's what I'll do!

From Linares the rain sets in again, heavier than before. I'm grateful to reach the tiny farming pueblo of Hospital de la Condensa. The walk up the village's single cobbled street is a classic rural walk, with a herd of cows using the street—probably twice a day—to do their round trip from the barn to their field and back. Their path has left the street several inches thick with cow dung. With the heavy rain, the dung street has become a sloshy, deep-green river, through which I've no choice but to wade.

Must remember to wash my boots before I fly to Australia, I note to myself, as I look at the dark green slime coating up to the top of the boot laces.

Deep in thought and manure, I reach the other end of the village and have not seen the refuge. I have to turn around and splash my way back through dung river again.

This is not great!

Retracing my steps through the odorous green muck back to the entrance to the village I still can't find the refuge–and there's nobody around to ask.

Damn! Turn around. Back down the street again. Damn!

Plodding back through the thick stream of sloppy smelly cow shit, I notice a gap between two buildings and walk closer to check it out. It is a narrow alley; the only alley running off the main street.

The refuge must be up there.

I slip and slide up the slimy, shit-covered cobblestone alleyway. At the top I notice a sign that might possibly indicate a refuge. I make my way over to it and find the building closed. There's still not a soul around. Back down the alleyway I slide, trying very hard not to fall over.

The last thing I want is to end up covered head-to-toe in sloppy green cow poo.

I'm sore, tired, cold and becoming increasingly more irritable, having to wade through filth. My legs are covered in green muck as it begins to rain.

Do I walk on to the next refuge? My feet are sore and I'm worn out. I've had enough today. I don't have the energy to walk on.

Outside the building, I'm deliberating what to do, when a woman dashes out of a nearby building ready to disappear into another doorway.

'Excuse me,' I call to her in Spanish. 'Where is the refuge?'

She points to the building I've just left.

'It's closed?' I respond, shrugging with an open-palmed, querying gesture.

'*Uno momentito.*' The woman indicates for me to wait a moment at the building. Back up the alleyway of cobbles, polished smooth from a thousand years of feet and hooves, I slip and slide once more in the centuries of muck. My clothes are soaked and filthy with manure. I stand shivering, waiting in the rain for what seems an eternity. The woman reappears with a key and opens up the refuge.

What a relief to be out of the weather.

I sign the register, impatient to get under a hot shower to warm my icy bones. I choose a bunk, lay my sleeping bag on it and get under the shower. The hot water thaws my chilled body and coaxes away tensions as I begin to unwind.

Two Italian women arrive soon after.

'Only three of us,' one comments. 'It's very good to have the refuge to ourselves.'

'Yes. I hope not too many people come tonight.'

I doubt we'll have it to ourselves for long.

The space and peace doesn't last long. The refuge fills quickly. *It's too wet to wash my clothes; they'll never dry by morning.* Famished, I decide to go straight into the pueblo for a meal. As I walk out of the refuge, a couple of pilgrims are being offered the floor of the reception room to spread their sleeping bags tonight; there are no more bunks available. They glumly accept.

So glad I got here early.

Earlier, while trudging up and down dung street, I passed the one and only cafe in the village. That's where I head. On my way back down the track to the main street of the pueblo, I once more retrace my tracks, but this time in a pair of sandals. The manure oozes up between my toes. Trying hard to ignore the green slime, I shudder and keep walking.

When I return to the refuge, more newly-arrived pilgrims are being turned away from the now overflowing refuge. None look pleased at the prospect of continuing on in the rain.

I wash my sandals and filthy feet and climb wearily onto my bunk. It's so crowded and noisy I'm unsure if I'll get to sleep, but at least I'm dry and warm. The two Italian women are sitting on their bunks reading. One looks up and gives me a nod and a look that indicates her displeasure with the crowd and the noise. I smile back and nod my concurrence as I slide into my sleeping bag.

In bunks on the other side of the room a young couple remind me of a pair of African love-birds. They spend the entire night grooming each other, oblivious to everyone else and totally absorbed in each other's company.

A young Spanish man, so fat he hasn't seen his willy in years, has taken the bunk above me. I'm concerned the bunk above might not be strong enough to hold his weight and fear I could be crushed to death if his bunk gives way. One of the Italian women gives me a look of worry, with a nod at the Spaniard, showing she shares my concern. I visualise throwing myself off the bunk onto the floor at the first cracking sound of the bunk collapsing. I wonder if I'll have enough warning and study the floor beside my bed to see if there's enough landing room if I need to fling myself.

Hmm. I need a bit more room if the bunk above gives way.

I climb out of my sleeping bag and clear away all obstructions on the floor, just in case I need to hurl myself off my bunk., then slide back into my sleeping bag and zip it up. I think through the possible scenario of the bunk collapsing and decide to unzip the sleeping bag, in readiness for a quick escape. I lay tense and poised ready to throw myself onto the floor.

The Spaniard returns from the showers with a small towel wrapped around his copious loins. I turn on my side and wriggle to the very edge of my bunk, poised ready to throw myself onto the floor.

The Spaniard comes around to the side of the bunk I'm facing. As he stretches up over his bunk his towel falls to the ground, exposing his naked willy inches from my nose.

Ugh!

I pull my sleeping bag over my head, focus my mind on green hills far away, and pray that the bunk above holds his weight. It creaks and groans as he climbs onto it. I tightly squeeze my eyes shut and prepare to fling myself onto the floor.

Please God, make the bunk strong enough to hold him. Please God keep me safe tonight.

Running those thoughts over and over in my mind, I eventually drift into a stress-filled sleep, vigilant all night for sounds of a cracking bunk. I don't sleep well, vaguely aware that it rains all night.

When morning breaks, it's cold, bleak and raining, but I'm still alive. The bunk held.

Thank you, God.

CHAPTER 29

The Final 100kms

Sarria to Barbadelos

A PAIN SHOOTS THROUGH MY kneecap as I climb out of bed and clicks all the way to the bathroom.

Will it hold out on the slippery mountain descent? I doubt it.

Then I remember my resolve the previous day. *I'll catch a bus into Sarria.* It's dark and wet as I make my way outside. *There's no bus shelter, but yesterday I witnessed a bus stop just outside the refuge.* I wait at that place in the rain, aching with cold, for twenty minutes until the bus arrives. As I board the bus a twinge of guilt nudges me.

I should be walking.

Click. My knee reminds me as I climb the last step onto the bus, why I'm not walking this morning. A sharp shooting pain follows the click and my guilt dissipates. *It's a pleasure to be inside the bus and out of the chilling wind.*

The steep descent would have destroyed my knee, I reassure myself.

The bus pulls into Sarria at 8.30 am. I buy something for breakfast, and munching happily, find the trail, and stroll out of town for the final one hundred kilometres of the Camino. As grey clouds rush overhead, I stop and pull my raincoat out of my pack and put it on. The grey clouds pass and the sun comes out. I take the coat off. It warms up a little more, so I take my wind-stopper jacket off. Clouds and rain blow in so I put the rain coat back on again. I spend the entire day playing tag with the weather's caprices.

Galicia is beautiful, even if the weather is fickle. Tiny hamlets lay snug on counterpanes of verdant hues. Smoke wisps from invisible chimneys.

Cow bells chime from distant dales. White and grey clouds fashion kaleidoscope designs in the azure sky. The Camino from Sarria meanders through a woodland of ancient oak, with their twisted trunks creating gnarled faces of old men.

Passing through the forest, the path leads into fields of tall corn with ripening cobs and potatoes ready for harvest. It roams through tiny hamlets with neatly laid out and lovingly tended family vegetable plots. Old slate-covered farm buildings in various stages of decay or renovation are scattered along the trail. Herds of cows amble along the winding path, making disinterested but pleasant walking companions.

The day fills me with ecstasy: I've achieved my goals, conquered my fears, dealt with my demons, learnt some lessons, and am on the last stretch to home.

Life is wonderful, I'm blissfully unaware of what lies ahead.

I'm approaching another perfect little village that I saw from a rise half an hour before. I can see ahead where the Camino joins the road and know I'll soon be in the village of Barbadelos.

I can get another stamp in my credencial there.

My heart is singing. As I approach the point where the track joins the road I notice a motorhome parked right alongside the Camino. A steel band *clamps* around my chest and *squeezes* my lungs so hard that I can hear my heart pounding.

Calm down. You left Louis five weeks back, it won't be him. No, of course it won't. You're being paranoid, Linda.

I take a deep breath, focus on the steel band around my lungs and will my taut muscles to relax and the panic to subside. A few metres further and I see a man sitting in a folding chair inches from the track. He's watching approaching pilgrims. *Waiting.*

It's Louis.

Light-headedness swirls. On the edge of blackness, my stomach churns. *Crikey! What do I do now?*

I'm a hundred and fifty metres away. There's nowhere else to go but straight ahead. I think back to the time many years ago, when Ethan, in one of his *out-of-control* episodes, held a loaded rifle to my head. Each episode was heralded with that same black look that I'd seen on Louis' face. In one of Ethan's rages he'd held me hostage in my house for several hours. Hysterical and fearing for my life I'd tried repeatedly to escape. After one escape where I'd managed to get out of the house and run down the road, Ethan caught me, dragged me back to the house and threw me onto a bed. He held a loaded rifle to the back of my head and released the safety catch. At the touch of the steel of the rifle barrel on my head and the sound of the safety catch being released, my hysteria subsided. I lay there … waiting … thinking *It's all over now*. I waited for him to pull the trigger.

That moment taught me an important life lesson in self-preservation. Whatever happens, stay calm, don't panic. That day years ago calmness saved my life.

Now here in Spain I have another madman to deal with.

Keep calm. Don't panic. Don't inflame him. Stay cool.

Oh, God help me! I implore. *Smile, Linda. Act like you're pleased to see him, like it's normal for him to be sitting there, waiting. I could pull the rainhood down lower to hide my face. It's too late.*

He's been waiting for me. He saw me coming long before I knew it was him.

Oh, God help me!

I'd forgotten all about Louis and the threat of meeting up with him again. I give my best attempt at a cheery wave as I approach.

'Hello, Louis.' I smile.

I'm only metres away from him and my pace is fast. I dare not slow, nor speed up, in case it inflames him. He stands and strides towards me with that horrifying black look.

He's going to attack me. Other pilgrims are not too far behind, but he's oblivious to anyone else around. Is he going to attack me?

With my gut liquefying and my knees trembling, I pray they'll hold me.

'Linda, come and have a cup of coffee. Take your pack off.' It's an order, not an invitation.

'Nice to see you, Louis,' I lie.

I smile at him and he stops striding towards me. I struggle to control my shaking body.

He's going to kill me, he's insane. Keep talking and act friendly. Talk him down, it's your only chance.

'It's been a long time, Louis. How've you been?' I maintain a forced smile.

His murderous gaze, his tone and body language reflect his insanity. He stands clenching and unclenching his fists. I want to run but force myself to stand and face him. He points to the chair, indicating for me to sit, then he fetches another. I place my pack and trekking poles carefully on the ground next to the chair, poised ready so I can grab them and run. I try to think calmly as I lower myself unsteadily into the chair.

He wrenches the second chair open, and tosses it alongside. Louis stands towering over me, clenching and unclenching his fists. I'm petrified, but smile at him, trying to make it look genuine. I tilt my head to one side and look up at him–smiling.

His body language changes in an instant. He drops his chin to his chest, looks to the ground, and hangs his arms limply at his sides. He looks dejected and sorry for himself.

The immediate threat has passed. *He wants me to feel sorry for him, to take pity on him.* I ignore his ploy.

'Have you been well, Louis?'

He stands in silence, head bowed looking at the ground.

He's trying to look like a sad little boy but it's a ploy and it's not going to work. I'm not out of danger yet. He could fly into a rage at any second.

'Let's see, it was Viana …' I continue, but he cuts in.

'When you left me!' he accuses. 'You left me in Viana! Three weeks ago.' He spits the words out like a betrayed lover, his tone full of hurt.

Keep calm and act natural. Ignore his comments. His tone is very odd. He's definitely a nutter.

My gut churns.

'That's right. It must be three weeks ago.' I smile as pleasantly as I can.

He raises the brewed coffee pot in a gesture of offer.

'I'd rather have a glass of water please, Louis.' *I don't want this to be more than a very brief meeting. Coffee is much too social.*

'You must have stayed an extra night somewhere,' he snarls accusingly. 'I expected you to have finished the Camino by now!'

Agree with him. Don't inflame his mood.

'Yes, that's right. I did stay an extra day.' I smile gaily at him. *I hope he doesn't notice my trembling. I don't want him to think he has fear as an advantage over me.*

'Have you spoken to your husband since Viana?' he asks sulkily.

'Yes, every day,' I lie.

'What does he say ... about us?'

Us? There never was an "us". Chilled by his madness and whatever he imagines exists between "us" I choose my words carefully, wary lest I spark off a lunatic reaction.

'He's in Birmingham today, shifting his father's things.' I try to sound bright and choose to ignore the "about us" figment of his unhinged mind.

'Birmingham! I didn't know he was in England.' His eyes widen in surprise.

'He wasn't three weeks ago but he is now. I'm finishing the Camino early and we are going to meet up. We're going to Madrid.' It's almost the truth.

'I offered to take you to Madrid ... if you recall,' he interjects with a cynical sneer. 'I offered you lots of things, but it seems it wasn't to your liking.'

I ignore his comments.

'Thanks for the water, Louis. I must push on before those rain clouds reach here.' I point towards the gathering darkness in the east. 'Take care.'

I stand, hoist my pack and gather my trekking poles, trying not to appear rushed.

Louis once more drops his chin to his chest and looks to the ground.

'Bye.' I feign cheerfulness as I turn to go. He doesn't speak.

With knees shaking and gut churning, I'm so frightened I feel about to throw up.

Fear empowers. Bluff your way with a smile and a wave, don't let him see you're afraid.

I wave and stride off, shamming confidence and all the while fearing a bullet in my back or a blow to my head.

Have I seen the last of him? I hope so.

My confidence has just taken another beating.

CHAPTER 30

My Spiritual Journey

Portomarin to Palas del Rei
WILL LOUIS LAY IN WAIT for me somewhere else along the track? While still fearful Louis may be lurking somewhere, I now walk with a strong sense of having conquered another demon. Walking briskly through the afternoon I reach Portomarin at 5.00 pm, the inherent terror that was in my bones throughout the day has passed. I feel in control, yet somehow detached, from life. I feel as though I'm present in mind but not one hundred percent present in body. *Is this a coping mechanism?*

Evening falls and I find myself studying people around me. The Camino has been a cosmopolitan coming together of people from all cultures of diverse habits who would not otherwise have met. On the Camino we've become a family of adventurers born into this unique kinship through the shared experience of hardship and suffering feet. Dull little moths fluttering around bright shining lights, budgerigars chattering happily in social clusters, and tonight … I dine with a python traveling the Camino of life with a sociable puppy. The snake and the dog are an unlikely American pair. The snake is a tall thin cold and unfriendly woman. Every time her happy puppy partner speaks she hisses her displeasure at him. He chats happily to everyone and is one of the friendliest people I've come across on the Camino. This afternoon, the puppy and I walked and chatted together part of the way while the python always walked fifty metres ahead. At first, I didn't even know they were together. Tonight, he invited me to join them for dinner but after twenty minutes at their table I couldn't stand the snake's hissing at his every word a moment longer. The python seemed to be waiting to devour her happy dutiful puppy whole. I make an excuse and leave.

The Camino is life in microcosm. As I walk away I ponder the relationships I've seen. *How would they classify me: my marriage, my relationships? It's easy to put others into boxes. What was my box? What is my box now?*

I have a distinct feeling the Camino has changed my box. I feel I'm a different person; I'm not the same person who set out walking from St Jean Pied de Port.

I've almost fulfilled my promise, almost finished the Camino. Soon I'll be able to close the door on all those years of struggle to get my life back. Soon it will be over.

Sitting in the restaurant pondering my life I see Italo, the staring Italian. It seems months since I last saw him in Logroño.

'Linda! *Bella,* Linda. So far! Your feet–so bad!' He sounds stunned to see I've made it this far.

'*Si.*' I smile back, genuinely pleased to see him. He comes and sits with me and we chat in 'Camino-talk' a mish-mash of English and Italian and charades to get the meaning across.

The next morning, rising and preparing for the day in the early morning darkness is made more difficult by a lack of light switches in the refuge. The sound of rustling and dark shapes moving around indicates people are dressing, packing their backpacks, bandaging their feet and washing by feel-in-the-dark. Most refrain from using their torches, only occasionally a torchlight glimmers briefly. A sensor light over the stairs comes on for one second at a time. Grumbling pilgrims stumble out of the refuge, most have gone before 7.00 am. At 7.30, as I'm about to leave, the lights come on automatically, but only in the kitchen.

Italo says something to me in Italian and slaps me good naturedly on the arm as he leaves. A European lady standing next to me chuckles at the exchange. I shrug my shoulders and with a smirk say to her, 'I've no idea what he said.' She throws back her head and roars with laughter.

'He said, "I'll wait for you at the next stop." You didn't know what he said?'

'No, I don't speak Italian.'

She screeches with laughter as I shrug and step out of the refuge into a grey morning. It's cold and drizzling as head bowed I plod up the long incline leading away from Portomarin. The path climbs through thick comforting oak forest, then into a sinister whistling pine forest before the landscape returns to oak again. The track emerges from forest into tall golden corn fields and farmland. By noon, sunshine and blue sky have pushed the rain clouds away; even so, it seems to take forever to reach Palas del Rei. It's 2.00 pm when I arrive–and I'm *famished*. I have lunch and then fear it could be too late to continue and still get a bed tonight.

This stretch is so crowded with pilgrims who are just walking this last one hundred kilometres, that I might not get a bed if I arrive after 4.00 pm. I'll stay here tonight and head off again in the morning.

Palas del Rei, although a small town, has several places to eat. It's Saturday and the town is bustling: the central square is crowded with bands, music and people dancing. I have no trouble finding a *Meson*, a restaurant, with a menu to my liking, and sit enjoying the meal and lively atmosphere. Fireworks crack and whiz at 1.30 pm and then again at 7.00 pm in full daylight both times. *They must be purely for the loud explosive noise.*

That night, a dream torments me; a man relentlessly pursues me, trying to force me into his car. He appears at every bend in the road, refusing to leave me alone. He pulls out a knife, threatens me and pushes me toward his car. I try to fight him off but in the struggle his throat is cut with his knife and blood spurts everywhere, covering me. His throat is gaping open, but still he pursues me. I sit up in the bunk, gasping, sweating with fear, my whole body trembling and my heart pounding.

What an awful dream!

'Marcus, what did my dream mean? Was it about Louis? What does it mean?'

Marcus shows me the dream again before he explains.

'You've been on a *spiritual journey* the last five weeks. Even if you are not aware of what's happening, you're redesigning and rebuilding your spiritual, physical and emotional houses. What is pursuing you is your own fear: your fear of change, of growing out of your old "house", discarding it, and creating a new one. Your own fear is threatening to cut your throat if you speak out. You're afraid if you voice your own needs and begin to build your own new "house" that you will be "cutting your own throat", that you'll lose your husband, your family's love, and your friends. This is a fear that you must face if you are to grow. Face and accept what you fear most and it will lose its power over you. You'll then be able to step forward, speak out and move on towards self-fulfillment and the achievement of your goals.'

That's a lot to think about. I didn't know I'd been running away from my own fears. I thought I was dealing with them!

It's dark, cold and raining when I leave the *albergue*, the way-markers are difficult to find. A number of pilgrims search the tracks to find the Camino. I walk for another hour, still thinking through Marcus' words as the sun rises through the steady rain. Showers persist all through an acutely pensive day before I place a mental peg in the ground.

'I will face my fears, Marcus.'

It's a resolve that runs deeply. Even as I say it, I feel a further easing of an invisible weight that I'd not been aware I was carrying.

Sixty kilometres from Santiago de Compostella. The final stretch of countryside is steeply undulating and arduous. The terrain puts enormous strain on my beleaguered broken foot, but I'm otherwise considerably fitter and stronger. I cover twenty-seven kilometres as, with music playing loudly somewhere in the distance, I stagger into the village of Ribaldosa at mid-afternoon. The *albergue* looks welcoming and it's a relief to get my boots and wet clothes off and take a warm shower. The rain stops and the sun comes out.

Franz is in the *albergue* and so is the Czech from the mountain. A lot of pilgrims are scattered on the lawn enjoying a rest in the sunshine. I put my sodden things in the sun to dry and lay on the grass to let some warmth soak into my body. Emotion hangs in the air, hearts are heavy with knowledge of a special experience soon to end. Franz joins me.

'Hello, walking sister.' I smile to him as he sits down. 'You made it this far.'

'Yes, it is good,' he answers. 'We're almost there.'

As we stretch out on the grass, the warmth of melancholy and late afternoon autumn sunshine lulls us into silence. The distant music continues all afternoon. I doze off and I think Franz must have done the same. The sun moving lower in the afternoon sky takes its warmth with it and the sudden cool stirs me. It's time for dinner. Franz and I stroll off in search of a meal. A couple of pilgrims returning to the refuge tell us a fiesta had been on all day in a park nearby.

'Cutlets are being grilled on a barbecue,' they tell us.

We head in the direction of the music to find food. The Czech from the mountain and two Australian teenage girls from Adelaide are lolling when we return. Everyone is resting up before the final leg of the tramp to Santiago.

CHAPTER 31

Lessons Learnt on the Camino

Arzua to 'Santiago de Compostella'

THE DAYS GROW SHORTER NOW as winter approaches. Waiting for the sun's rays to lighten the window before I rise is no longer an option. Even so, the discomfort at the notion of walking in the darkness holds me willing prisoner in the warmth of my bed, longer than in earlier days. When I rise, only a few pilgrims linger, most have gone. The kitchen, like at the last refuge, is barren, not even a kettle to make a cup of tea.

Arzua is only three and a half kilometres away, I'll get breakfast there.

The damp cold fog outside is a relief; at least it's not raining. A heady aroma hangs in the air; it's Eucalyptus from the surrounding forest. The familiar fragrance sends pangs of longing coursing through my mind. *I miss my family. It's been six weeks since I began this trek; it'll be good to get home with loved ones again soon.*

Striding rhythmically, trance-like, through green and undulating hills, breathing deeply and in tune with the universe, I conquer the hills with ease.

'Linda, there's something else you need to do.' Marcus interrupts.

'What is it, Marcus?'

'You are still holding on to emotions and regrets that would be best let go.'

Head down watching the path, I listen mindfully as I walk, somewhat disappointed that I've yet another lesson that Marcus feels I'm yet to learn. I wait for him to continue. He replays for me visions of incidents that I've long locked away; incidents I deeply regret. A sharp inhalation accompanies the pain of recall.

'Only by letting go of negative emotions can the opportunity to experience and give more love be created,' he counsels. 'Holding onto the regret of past mistakes prevents the chance to move on. It blocks the ability to fully give and receive love. Holding onto the pain of the regret is a way of punishing yourself. It's time to forgive yourself. What's been done cannot be undone.'

I weep.

'Visualise those regrets; gather them together. See them? Now blow them into a large round balloon.' He waits a few moments. 'Are they inside the balloon?'

I construct the mental image as he instructs, then nod, blinded by tears.

'Look at the balloon. Observe it. Now cast it towards the sky. Watch it float away. Let it go. It's of no use now.'

Tears become a deluge, I stumble on the pathway as the ball of heavy agonies drifts upwards.

'Now, look at what eventuated from the decisions you made back then; decisions you viewed at the time as bad decisions. Look at what flowed from them.'

Marcus illustrates the positive events that followed those choices; the people and the love that came into my life.

'Look at the positive outcomes. There's nothing to be gained by dwelling on the negative. From every occurrence you perceive as a regrettable mistake, there's always a way to look at the outcomes in a positive light. It's time to redirect the energy you put into punishing yourself and turn it into love for those who're in your life now.'

A riptide of grief and joy, pain and love, devastation and elation, course through me. Images, feelings, agonies, joys and fears, in a tsunami of confusion–crash on the shores of my mind. It washes all that had been before away, destroying the tenacious hold of the buried past. Smiling images of Serena, Amy, Celeste and Larry follow with a second cleansing wave of love. It's too much. I sob uncontrollably as the agony of remorse is washed away and I stumble, barely able to see the path in front of me through the tears. A dizzy faintness swirls as a tightness lifts from my chest. Through the giddying lightness I see what my life's journey from this point forward must be.

'I'll focus on the love that I have in my life,' I tell Marcus. 'I see now that good exists in everything. I just need to look for it.'

'It's time for a new beginning,' Marcus advises as he steps back and allows my three Spirit guides to step forward and surround me. Wrapping me in blinding whiteness, they infuse me with a sense of profound peace. It's plain I have to focus on the lessons I've learnt and build a new framework for my life, but first I need to go over all the lessons I've learnt on the Camino.

Now let's see, what were all the lessons, hmm …?

1. Don't give up–When you find yourself in a difficult situation and it feels like you can't go on, don't give up; search out the core of your inner-strength and take hold of it, don't let it go, use it to help you focus on your goal and keep going.
2. Be happy–Problems and hardships are a part of life, change what you can change and accept what you can't, then focus on the positive aspects and be happy.
3. Think Positive–Think positive thoughts and speak positive words. You attract to you what you give your energy to. If you think negative thoughts you attract negativity to yourself. Think positive thoughts and you attract positivity.
4. Focus on light and healing to shut out pain–Concentrate on the light and ask for harmony and healing to flow through your body and force the pain away from the centre of your focus.
5. Respect your body–Flow with the rhythm of the universe. The mind must listen to the body while the body listens to the mind; the two must work together in harmony.
6. Give up the need for approval–Just be. Learn to love the person you are this day, this moment, this second. Don't wait until you've changed something. Don't worry about whether other people like you or dislike you, whether they approve of you or disapprove. Just be you. Accept yourself as you are and love the person inside.

7. Stay in the present moment–Always live fully in the moment, totally focused on the present moment. Cherish every second and never ever waste it; only by being totally aware and focused on this present moment can you fully appreciate and enjoy life. Don't let this moment slip past you, it may be all you have.
8. Value family and friends–To live life to the full you need to value friends and family. Money and material possessions do not enrich the spirit; only love and joy nurture the spirit. Family and friendships are the foundations of love and joy, take time to enjoy the company of family and friends.
9. Let go of fear and embrace love–Love is the richness of life. Let go of past hurts and the fear of being hurt and open your heart. Give to others the essence of your soul. Expect love and you will receive love. Expect hurt and pain and you will receive hurt and pain. Let go of fear and open your heart to give love and you will receive it.
10. Go for your dreams–It is better to have a dream and strive to achieve it and fail, than to have a dream and never try to reach it, because of the fear of failure, that is a tragedy. To fail is to lose nothing. To never try is to lose everything.
11. Stay calm to control fear–Fear muddles the mind and prevents you thinking of a solution. By staying calm you stay in control and keep the power to yourself. Fear gives power away.
12. Laugh out loud–Program your subconscious mind to be happy with what you have and to enjoy every day. Happy people draw friends like magnets, unhappy people drive them away. Throw back your head and laugh at what life brings your way and you will draw others to you.
13. Speak your mind clearly–People are not mind-readers and may misunderstand your intentions if you are not specific with them. Don't make assumptions, that is dangerous. Spell out your thoughts and your intentions and the reasoning behind it. Speak with love and clarity at all times.
14. Honour yourself–Acknowledge your own needs. If you don't honour your own needs, nobody else will. You must nurture your

soul by expressing to others, with care and understanding, what your needs are. They won't know if you don't tell them. Your *spirit deserves to soar*, not be crushed by your own deeds and beliefs. Learn to *honour* yourself.

15. Allow time for silence—Your mind is the key to connect to the Source – allow time for stillness to allow the mind to connect. Your soul connects to its home, to its source of love, the Universal energy, and that energy nurtures your soul.
16. Choose the life you want to live—Focus on what you want from life, don't focus your thoughts on your problems and fears. What you focus on is what you attract into your life. Focus on what you want to bring into your life, focus on the love around you and on your goals. Your thoughts are energy, which act like a magnet, attracting what you give your energy to. Choose the life you want and focus your thoughts on that.
17. Forgive those who do you harm—It only harms yourself to bury hurts. Talk about the hurts, forgive and move on.
18. Don't hold on to regrets—Regret serves no useful purpose. Let it go. Instead look for the good that has come out of every situation.

Reflecting on the lessons I've learnt, I know now that deep inside my soul the voice of the person I've suppressed for so long is ready to be heard. As I walk into the central plaza of the cathedral of Santiago de Compostella I have a feeling of anti-climax, a feeling that there should be someone there to celebrate my achievement with me, but I'm alone. I climb the cathedral steps and look back at the people milling around in the plaza, many are pilgrims I recognise from the past weeks. I wonder if they felt a sense of anti-climax as they climbed the cathedral steps or if they felt elation at having completed their pilgrimage. As I pass through the doors of the cathedral I'm overwhelmed by a sense that that this is not the end of the journey; it's the beginning of a new one. It's time now to board my jumbo jet.

EPILOGUE

Larry struggled with the changes in me for the first eight months after I returned home; me being so different made him fearful I would leave him. Changes in me meant there also needed to be changes in our relationship, and ultimately concessions from him. Not only was I voicing my needs, I demanded that he voice his needs too. It was difficult for us to find the common ground on which we could both begin to reconstruct our marriage.

We realised that if our marriage was to survive and succeed then we had to discuss the changes that needed to be made and decide how we could accommodate those changes in our work, family, and personal lives. It took months of often painful and emotionally draining discussions, but with each discussion we took one step closer to finding a mutually acceptable resolution.

Today we have a very different relationship from what we had before the Camino; we've grown closer, while at the same time giving each other more space to be the people we've become, and we are still working on our relationship.

Celeste, Amy and Serena accepted the changes much more easily. Our relationships morphed and changed with a fluidity that comes from love and acceptance and a willingness to see those close to you grow into the best they can be. They've each blossomed into the beautiful spirits they truly are.

Nine months after I returned home, my acupuncturist said he'd noticed a very deep healing that had remained in place for the past nine months and he asked what I'd done to achieve such a deep healing on so many levels. **"*I walked the Camino,*"** I told him.